Praise for *The Eternal Bond*

"As always, Dr. Roseman has produced a book that is emotionally rich and practical. Her ability to see where the gaps are in healing and to display out-of-the-box approaches set her work apart. Her book reaches deeply into a woman's heart and provides a greater appreciation for the mother-daughter bond whether our mothers have passed or are still with us."

—JUDITH THOMPSON, ND, Dean of Herbal Medicine, American College of Healthcare Sciences (ACHS)

"Dr. Roseman is a gifted writer that magically transforms a painful life phenomenon—mother loss—into a natural, developmental life process not to be feared but to be embraced in the metaphysical realm. The book provides research-based and anecdotal narratives that will touch your heart and assist you in nurturing the land of mother grief....She invites us to believe in the unbelievable, to see the universe with our eyes closed, to feel eternity even in pain, and to follow those who walked through pain and isolation from mother loss before us—and made it."

—MERCEDES B. TER MAAT, PHD, LPC, ATR-BC, HLM, professor, Department of Counseling, College of Psychology

"Allow this book to be the companion who holds your hand, soothes your heart, and shows you the way. Janet Roseman, PhD, has created for you in this book a very special healing pathway for those who have lost very special women, who were also their very special mothers. Dr. Roseman has successfully blended together a guide to assist you in the natural process of death, the reality of the spirit realms, and the process within our physical lives."

—TINA M. ZION, internationally acclaimed spiritual teacher and award-winning author

"Here daughters write about the presence of their mothers even after death. These brief testimonies provide a mythic dimension to our ordinary lives.... We come to understand that the veil between the living and the dead may at times disappear."
—**ANN FILEMYR, PHD**, former president of Southwestern College, founder and director of the PhD in Visionary Practice and Regenerative Leadership

"A rare and beautiful book that speaks directly to the heart of what it means to lose a mother. With deep reverence and honesty, Janet Lynn Roseman, PhD, creates space for the spiritual, emotional, and even mystical aspects of grief that are so often overlooked. This book validates experiences many daughters hesitate to share, from subtle signs to powerful moments of connection, and invites readers to view grief not as something to fix, but as a sacred continuation of love. It is a profound contribution to the conversation around loss and healing."
—**CHRISTINE ANASTOS, MS, BS**, founder and CEO of Connect & Thrive, Inc.

"Dr. Roseman combines her personal experience with grief and loss alongside moving stories from other daughters who have walked a similar path. The way she explores the deep, lasting connection between mothers and daughters, even after death, felt so relatable. I found comfort in her reflections on signs from the other side.... The book also offers spiritual insights and healing practices that felt like a gentle guide for navigating grief."
—**KELLY DAUGHERTY, MSW, FT**, founder of the Center for Informed Grief, LLC

"Dr. Roseman walks us through not only the practical business of living with grief, but also offers the reader an opportunity to listen to and identify with other women who navigate the unique bond and loss between mothers and daughters. Through sharing her personal experience, she lovingly weaves both science and spirituality into a story of understanding and hope."
—**THERESA WYATT PREBILSKY,** spiritual director and author

"Dr. Roseman shares her own incredible journey of grief and triumph over grief after the death of her beloved mother. She validates the multicultural phenomenon of after-death experiences that accompany the death of a loved one. She describes dreams, visions, and visitations by the dead in a practical, realistic, and supportive manner that explores human spirituality."
—**ALISON BESTED, MD, FRCPC, ABOIM,** director of Hyperbaric Medicine and associate professor of the Department of Internal Medicine at Dr. Kiran C. Patel College of Osteopathic Medicine

"The voices and stories in *The Eternal Bond* pierce through the veil of loss, revealing that when the physical relationship ends, a vast, Divine love begins. With honesty, reverence, and raw beauty, these daughters affirm that the Mother-Daughter connection does not die—it transforms. It becomes a silvery, luminous thread that stretches toward the Divine: ever-present, ever-healing, ever-guiding. Dr. Roseman has offered us all a sacred invitation—to recognize the holiness of your mother while she lives, and to celebrate her eternal presence when she has passed."
—**AMELIA VOGLER, MS, SEM,** specialist in Energy Medicine

*the
eternal
BOND*

the eternal BOND

Daughters Honor Their
Mothers on the Other Side

JANET LYNN ROSEMAN PhD
Foreword by Christina Puchalski MD

WOODBURY, MINNESOTA

The Eternal Bond: Daughters Honor Their Mothers on the Other Side Copyright © 2025 by Janet Lynn Roseman, PhD. All rights reserved. No part of this book may be used or reproduced in any manner whatsoever, including internet usage, without written permission from Llewellyn Worldwide Ltd., except in the case of brief quotations embodied in critical articles and reviews. No part of this book may be used or reproduced in any manner for the purpose of training artificial intelligence technologies or systems.

First Edition
First Printing, 2025

Book design by Christine Ha
Cover design by Shira Atakpu

Llewellyn Publications is a registered trademark of Llewellyn Worldwide Ltd.

Library of Congress Cataloging-in-Publication Data
Names: Roseman, Janet Lynn author
Title: The eternal bond : daughters honor their mothers on the other side / Janet Lynn Roseman, PhD.
Description: First edition. | Woodbury, MN : Llewellyn Publications, a division of Llewellyn Worldwide Ltd, 2025. | Includes bibliographical references. | Summary: "Exploring physical, emotional, and spiritual components, this book fills a void in grief publications and sheds light on the sacred bond between mothers and their adult daughters"– Provided by publisher.
Identifiers: LCCN 2025027480 (print) | LCCN 2025027481 (ebook) | ISBN 9780738779874 paperback | ISBN 9780738780061 ebook
Subjects: LCSH: Loss (Psychology)–Religious aspects–Christianity | Grief–Religious aspects–Christianity | Suffering–Religious Aspects–Christianity
Classification: LCC BV4905.3 .R674 2025 (print) | LCC BV4905.3 (ebook)
LC record available at https://lccn.loc.gov/2025027480
LC ebook record available at https://lccn.loc.gov/2025027481

Llewellyn Worldwide Ltd. does not participate in, endorse, or have any authority or responsibility concerning private business transactions between our authors and the public.

All mail addressed to the author is forwarded but the publisher cannot, unless specifically instructed by the author, give out an address or phone number.

Any internet references contained in this work are current at publication time, but the publisher cannot guarantee that a specific location will continue to be maintained. Please refer to the publisher's website for links to authors' websites and other sources.

Llewellyn Publications
A Division of Llewellyn Worldwide Ltd.
2143 Wooddale Drive
Woodbury, MN 55125-2989
www.llewellyn.com

Printed in the United States of America

GPSR Representation:
UPI-2M PLUS d.o.o., Medulićeva 20, 10000 Zagreb, Croatia,
matt.parsons@upi2mbooks.hr

Other Books by Janet Lynn Roseman, PhD

Dance Masters: Interviews with Legends of Dance

Dance Was Her Religion: The Spiritual Choreography of Isadora Duncan, Ruth St. Denis and Martha Graham

If Joan of Arc Had Cancer: Finding Courage, Faith, and Healing from History's Most Inspirational Woman Warrior

The Way of the Woman Writer

Disclaimer

The contents of this book include suggestions for holistic healing and ideas for spiritual, physical, and emotional sustenance. Some of these practices the author personally used and found helpful. Before you engage in any holistic therapy practices mentioned, which include the use of herbs, vitamins, energy medicine, and other elements, please seek advice from trusted health care practitioners. These ideas are not a substitute for medical advice from experts in the field. The author has worked in integrative medicine fields for many years and has made suggestions based on her research, personal experiences, and academic work.

Dedication

This book is dedicated to my mother, Theodora, "Toby," my companion, mother, best friend, and teacher. I also honor the spirits of the mothers who are written about in this book. My vision is that my mother and those beautiful women are celebrating together with the knowledge that they are deeply loved by their daughters.

Contents

Exercises xxi
Foreword xxiii
Preface xxv
Introduction 1

Part One: The Mother Loss Journey: *Empowering Women Through Mystical Moments, Research, and Mother Mary*

    Chapter One: Mother Loss and Some Miracles: *My Personal Experiences with Grief* 9

    Chapter Two: What Does the Research Say? 31

    Chapter Three: The Honor of Grief 53

    Chapter Four: Unlikely Companions: *Grief and the Other Side* 75

    Chapter Five: Sacred Connections: *Dream Healing* 97

    Chapter Six: The Ultimate Mother: *Mother Mary* 109

Part Two: Healing Narratives

    Narrative Medicine   127

    Valerie Remembers Frances   129

    Monica Remembers Ann   135

    Lisa Remembers Jyoti   139

    Ann Remembers Ann   145

    Debbie Remembers Rosemarie   151

    Kristen Remembers Lisa   157

    Christine Remembers Loretta   161

    Lavoie Family Daughters Remember Shirley

        Pam Remembers Shirley   171

        Barb Remembers Shirley   175

        Jean Remembers Shirley   177

        Mary Remembers Shirley   179

        Michel Remembers Shirley   181

        Angie Remembers Shirley   184

    Frances Remembers Adele   185

    Erin Remembers Eloise   193

    Toni Remembers Patricia   199

    Jeanne Remembers Sharon   205

    Stephanie Remembers Doris   215

    Suzanne Remembers Rene   227

Laurie Remembers Julie   233

   Michele Remembers Janet   239

   Michelle Remembers Maria   245

   Amy Remembers Judy   249

Part Three: Grief Wisdom: *Prescriptives for Healing Mind, Body, and Spirit*

   Grief Prescriptions   259

   Spiritual Prescriptions   293

Afterword   303
"Thinking of Those Gone On"   311
Acknowledgments   313
Empowerment Resources   315
Recommended Reading List   323
Bibliography   327

Exercises

Mother Connection   90

Creating a Dream Stick   107

Questions   262

Remembering   263

Finding Messages   263

Letting Her In   264

Trust   265

Narrative Medicine   266

Support   268

Finding Ritual   269

Commitment Miracle   270

Body Dialogue   270

Somatic Checks   271

Sound Healing   273

Spiritual Wounding   274

Nourishment   275

Throat Chakra Questions   276

Throat Chakra Healing   277

Mandalas   278

Hydrotherapy   279

Meditation with Mother Earth   280

Working with Healers   282

Grief Partnering   283

Connection with the Ancestors   284

Monitoring Your Emotions   285

Connection with Your Guides   287

Meditation with Your Personal Grief Symbols   288

Gemstones for Healing   289

Discovering Your 120 Minutes   290

Balancing Activities   291

Spiritual Comforts   296

Spiritual Dialogue   296

Spiritual Connection   297

Spiritual Allies   298

Spiritual Energies   299

Spiritual Support Affirmation   300

Honoring Your Healing Journey   301

Candle Magic   301

Foreword

Grief, in some ways, is the most neglected spiritual distress in clinical settings and in society. "I am sorry for your loss," while sincere, does not even begin to scratch the surface of a pain so deep. Yet bereavement is a spiritual distress diagnosis, one that all clinicians should address by providing care as well as offering to refer patients to health care chaplains or grief support groups.

Unlike other clinical diagnoses, however, grief is not necessary pathology. The greatest gift a clinician can give a patient who is experiencing grief is compassionate presence, a sacred act of deep listening and accompaniment. Dr. Roseman's *The Eternal Bond: Daughters Honor Their Mothers on the Other Side* is a powerful book. It offers tools, stories, and research not only for daughters but also for anyone experiencing grief. In addition, *The Eternal Bond* can serve as an excellent resource for health care professionals as well as a text for medical, nursing, and other clinical professional training.

—Christina Puchalski, MD, ODCS, FACP, FAAHPM
*Executive Director,
The George Washington University School of Medicine
Professor of Medicine and Health Sciences*

Preface

Before you read this book, I would like to share a letter that was sent to me after my mother's death in 2007 from my wonderful friend Jane Grossenbacher. Jane was a famous photographer I met years ago when I was a journalist in San Francisco working for fashion magazines. We collaborated quite often, and she took pictures of the celebrities I interviewed for publication. Jane deeply understood grief because her mother had died when she was a young woman. Mourning my mother was difficult, and I was desperate to hear a comforting word from someone who would understand. And she did.

    Tragically, she was facing her own death from ovarian cancer when we spoke, and I did not know this would be our last conversation. She had a particular talent for making me laugh and was a magnificent woman—smart, kind, beautiful, and talented. We talked, laughed, and cried for over an hour. When I hung up the phone, I felt better. I was grateful that she had taken the time to listen to my aching heart in the midst of her own pain. A few weeks later, I received a letter from her, a final cherished present. She died four months after our exquisite conversation.

Her words of wisdom not only helped me over a decade ago, but they continue to assist me when I have difficult days. I hope her words can help you.

* * *

Hello Janet,

Hello my dear. I have been thinking all week on what to write to you. To lose a Mother is a hole in the heart. Grief lessens but nothing is ever the same again. The pleasures of memory are a balm and the dreams where she's entered are beautiful, I know that. For me, the intensity of my attachment has found other places to thrive. Sisterhood—the exquisite company of women is so nurturing and art—well it conquers, saves souls, and constantly reminds you of our quest to be human beings. Whether it is your work or the journey of others—there is much substance there.

Big deep black depression has never been a long nightmare for me, so I am at a loss on what one can do. I really don't know what solutions work. When I have had the short black periods, I endeavored to take them on like sitting down with a stubbed toe and feeling the pain and discomfort instead of walking or hoping the pain just goes away. I know a stubbed toe is a teeny, tiny matter but halting all distractions and feeling the pain and riding it is what I mean.

What can you do? Talk to a professional—so many to choose from, take a pill, and invent something that cures you. Janet, I am so sorry about your Mother and the perplexing sadness that you feel at this time. I am looking at or waving or squinting at my own upcoming death and I still, will never, get it. But I am cozy and have made peace with the mystery. Yes, all my favorite people in history are dead, some flailing, some good sports, and some just disappeared to us and themselves. You are going to look in the mirror and see her. Repeat her stories, anecdotes, recipes.

Wear some of her jewelry. Be your magnificent self and she will tag along in your bones or in an expression or when and where you smile. Make a ritual and lay down her burdens, acknowledge her sufferings and make them disappear. You will imagine the best way to go to the next avenue, in the same world.

With love,
Jane

Introduction

Why a book for adult daughters who have lost their mothers? Because it is needed.

Death is the eternal mystery, a mystery that fills our souls with both awe and terror. The consequences of the death of one's mother are not like those of any other ordeal in life. Daughters are often faced with resurrecting a new life without a road map, catapulted upon the ruins that remain while enduring indescribable emotional pain. Based on my experience of my mother's death, and the shared narratives with other daughters I have spoken with through the years, this journey is both courageous and terrifying. *The Eternal Bond: Daughters Honor Their Mothers on the Other Side* can provide guidance to you—because I know you are seeking comfort and advice to navigate this difficult road. You *will* regain your balance, but you will not be the same person. I have never surrendered my love for my mother or my yearning for her, and you do not have to either. It is a myth that during grief you need to "let go" of her. There is great solace that can be gained by bringing your mother into your life, and the contents of this book offer concrete suggestions for how to do this. After an extensive, painful process of rediscovering who I could and would be without her physically present, I was able to create a life that is rich and satisfying, and this new life *includes* her because her spirit is always with me, and she continues to live inside of me.

My heart goes out to the many daughters who have been deprived of spending time in the hospital with their mothers at the end of their lives. If you did not have the opportunity to be present or even visit your mother because of the restrictions imposed during the coronavirus pandemic, you understand how this prohibition wreaked havoc on your grief. I understand that these limitations were prudent; however, they robbed countless women of the chance to share their mother's last moments. I hope this book can offer inspiration, grief empowerment, hope, and most importantly practical tools for you to traverse your uncharted yet sacred path.

After my mother passed away, I was brokenhearted. Soon after, I had a conversation with a daughter whose mother had passed away several years earlier. Although at the time I did not believe a word she said, I now realize that what she told me was true. "Janet, although the gap in your heart will never completely heal, you will survive and flourish—but it will take time." The time factor is notable because it took me years to feel whole again without her physically present. Everyone's grief is deeply personal, and no one can tell you how long it will take for you to not feel ripped with pain and anguish. Grief is not one-size-fits-all, nor is this book a glib offering filled with cutesy advice.

Grief is often a taboo topic, and many women in mourning are not only distraught but feel alone and disconnected. You may feel the same way. I assure you that you will regain your stability. Constructing a life with meaning, a life that is psychologically sound, is empowering, especially when daughters feel abandoned and hopeless after their mother's death. This book was written to honor your unique experiences of mother loss and, most importantly, to validate the unwavering connection you have with your mother—a connection that crosses the spiritual realms and continues after death. The mother-daughter bond is mysterious and varies for each woman, regardless of gender identification. This eternal bond is boundless, infinite, and everlasting because it is the energy of love, and love cannot be destroyed or lost. Although her physical presence is removed, the bond between you can never be taken away. When I speak to skeptics, I often cite Dr. Albert Einstein's theory that "energy cannot be created or destroyed; it can only be changed from one form to another."[1] Love is the best example of these energies.

I wrote this book to offer advice, comfort, and inspiration to daughters who are seeking grief wisdom. In the first chapter, I discuss my grief journey in detail and some of the miracles that occurred during this time. The second chapter of the book discusses the results of a research study that I created and conducted to find out what other daughters *actually did* to accelerate their healing from mother loss. I wanted to know specifics I could practice that would be beneficial for myself and other women like me. This chapter also includes research studies that discuss mother loss for adult daughters, most of whom were caregivers.

The third chapter discusses the honor of grief and why grieving is a sacred act. It includes my interview with a scientist who is an expert on the recuperative powers of crying, myths of the "hysterical woman," grief rituals, and why I believe Dr. Kübler-Ross's stages of grief are harmful to the griever. In the fourth chapter, I share some of my beliefs about the powers of grief and how it can open up possibilities for daughters to make connections with the other

---

1. *Atomic Physics*, United World Films for the J. Arthur Rank Organization, 1948, US National Archives, September 25, 2015, https://www.youtube.com/watch?v=KUvPgArrwE8.

side. This chapter offers suggestions that integrate metaphysical and spiritual communications, bereavement visions, and Indigenous practices. Also included is advice that you may find helpful before consulting psychics.

Chapter 5 contains anthropological information about the history of ancient dream temples devoted to Asclepius, considered the god of healing. His daughters were as gifted as he was in the healing arts, and their contributions are cited. Learning how to use your dreams for guidance to help you discover your inner resilience and strength is discussed, along with ideas for designing effective dream healing practices. Chapter 6 includes some of my private revelations with Mother Mary. I share how she offered support and love to me when I was most in need. A compilation of interviews with women whom I met at various sacred shrines are examined because Mother Mary's influence speaks to many women, whether she is recognized as Mother Mary, the Mother, or the ultimate goddess.

Part 2 of this book consists of meaningful narratives written by daughters that offer timeless and effective advice. In the essays, the daughters describe and embrace their spiritual connections with their mothers, and they include descriptions of dreams, visions, signs, and inner knowing in their accounts. This confirmation of the sacred dimension authenticates that we are not alone, and we are not crazy. These stories certainly supported me because they were written by kindred spirits.

According to a Pew Research Center survey in 2023, over half of participants who had lost loved ones indicated that they had experienced connections in direct visits or dreams.[2] These experiences can be comforting, as I have found, but they may be upsetting

---

2. Tevington and Corichi, "Many Americans Report Interacting with Dead Relatives in Dreams or Other Ways."

for you. If you are unable to function, anxiety ridden, or have any thoughts of harming yourself during your grief process, please seek out a trusted therapist, friend, or family physician whom you can talk with. You do not have to suffer alone.

Therapists, physicians, and academics can learn from the daughters who share their wisdom through these narratives. Their revelations of loss can assist the understanding of mother loss and offer much needed insights. Clinicians and educators can reduce the suffering of their patients and students by listening to these spiritual stories with an open mind and heart. This is particularly important so daughters do not feel judged, disparaged, or isolated, especially when they have the courage to discuss otherworldly occurrences. This book supports their voices because they know—as I do—that these encounters are true. Our shared experiences confirm the heart connection between mothers and daughters that can never be severed because those bonds are eternal.

Part 3 of the book contains tools and spiritual "prescriptives" that can help heal mind, body, and spirit. I also included grief advice for you to share with friends and family who may want to help you heal but do not know how. I hope that these prescriptions can offer healing wisdom to help you grieve and find sustenance, particularly if you had a challenging relationship with your mother. Part 3 is followed by empowerment resources to assist you and a list of some recommended books.

There is no magic prescription that can remove the emotional pain of loss, but it is my sincere hope that this book can guide you. This is a book about love between mother and daughter and is unlike other love stories that can be broken by divorce, infidelity, or serious illness. These stories are eternal and can offer therapeutic prescriptions that daughters truly long for—to continue their connection with her. The guidance in this book was written by women like me, women who truly know what mother loss is.

I hope you find peace and empowerment while reading this book and that your journey can be eased—even for moments. I am not the first daughter to lose a mother, nor will I be the last; however, *The Eternal Bond* could have given me support and consolation when I was most in need on a very lonely journey. This is the book that I could not find. It was written for Toby.

Part One
The Mother Loss Journey
Empowering Women Through Mystical Moments, Research, and Mother Mary

Chapter One
Mother Loss and Some Miracles
My Personal Experiences with Grief

In this chapter, I share highlights of my grief journey and explain how my mother's presence continues to accompany me after her death. I write about my visions and how the privilege of being her health advocate and caretaker profoundly influenced my life. She was the key to my inner resurrection and the messenger of unlikely miracles.

From Rhode Island to San Francisco to South Florida and Some Stops In Between

I grew up with an older brother in Rhode Island, a place that I still adore and try to visit as often as I can. After attending college in upstate New York and graduate school in Cambridge, Massachusetts, I received my MS in expressive therapies and planned on working as a therapist or professor. When my former roommate in college contacted me and invited me to live with her in the Bay Area, I leaped at the opportunity. I lived there for more than twenty years, working in a variety of fields including journalism and academia and particularly enjoyed my work as a dance critic. It was exciting to attend prestigious dance concerts in some of the most beautiful venues in the world, and I loved that I could invite my friends to attend with me. When my mother came to visit, she insisted on coming with me to several performances even when she was not feeling top-notch. It would take a few years before I knew why.

I considered pursuing my doctorate degree for a long time, but it wasn't until the late 1990s that I enrolled in a program at the Union Institute and graduated in 2001 with a PhD in philosophy with a specialization in spirituality. In fact, it was my mother who urged me to seek this degree even though at the time I was beginning my role as her caregiver. I thought that with this degree, I would remain in the Bay Area and teach courses in spirituality. But my life changed significantly when she was diagnosed with a rare cancer. A few months after I received my PhD, I immediately packed up my life on the West Coast to move back to Rhode Island (and later to South Florida) to accompany her on her cancer journey. I was her main caregiver and health advocate for almost a decade, and during this time, I learned a great deal about medicine and myself.

She Changed My Life

My mother's life, her death, and everything in between changed my life and my career. I studied many integrative medicine modalities to help her recover from the wounding and pain she experienced from countless surgeries. I became a Reiki master and a hypnotherapist, and I also studied with a wonderful shamanic healer. During the time she was suffering, I was willing to learn anything that I thought would help her. I only wanted her to live. I believe the energy treatments she received prolonged her life. During one of the surgeries, I convinced her surgeon in Boston to let me accompany her in the recovery room to give her Reiki treatments, and he reluctantly agreed. A nurse told me that before

I arrived, my mother lost her breath. She thought my mother had died, but then she resumed breathing. When my mother was conscious, I asked her if she remembered what happened, and she told me that she knew she had died, but only for a moment. She said she understood that she had to come back. I would like to believe she returned for me because I was not ready to let her go and she knew that.

Light Therapy Path

Before I left San Francisco, I had the unique opportunity to find a therapeutic modality that gave my mother a great deal of relief, especially during her numerous surgeries and recoveries. I was desperate to find some modality that would help her. Even my discovery of light therapy seemed planned by other forces, and I didn't have a clue about its efficacy. I came across this medical modality one afternoon when I was in a bookstore in San Francisco, seeking some type of therapy that could help relieve my mother's pain. I was on a ladder trying to reach up to the top shelf to look at a metaphysical book that had caught my attention. Another book—a book on light therapies—literally hit my head. When I opened it up, the page turned to a chapter on colorpuncture, a noninvasive form of acupuncture using colored light applications on the body that was practiced in Europe. I knew intuitively that this was the modality that would benefit my mother.

What was remarkable was that there are only two people in the United States who offer these trainings. I had the good fortune to study with both Rosemary Bourne and Manohar Croke, experts in colorpuncture theory, training, and applications.[3] I called

---

3. Please see the "Empowerment Resources" section for more information about Bourne and Croke.

Rosemary, an acupuncturist whose office was fifteen minutes away, and told her I wanted to study with her. After an initial session that impressed me, I spent time with her to learn as much as I could before leaving the West Coast. Through the years, I trained in colorpuncture from both women. My work has continued with a focus on pain control with oncology patients. I was fortunate to have the opportunity to create a pain relief study with patients who suffered from fibromyalgia and chronic fatigue at the Institute for Neuro-Immune Medicine in Fort Lauderdale and published my positive findings. My mother would be so proud! I would never have chosen this path if it was not for my commitment to helping my mother. Funny how our course in life takes detours, and even though we may struggle with these diversions, they often bring us our true direction and clarify who we really are.

When my mother was ill, I honestly believed if I studied enough, I would discover some method to keep her alive. Since I was a kid, I knew I possessed healing gifts and was always getting in trouble for saying things that I just *knew*, even though they were not always welcomed. Now my talent had purpose—to help her. My mother sent me a validation of my abilities when she wrote that she was "counting on my spiritual gifts" to help her through her many surgeries. When I recall all the surgeries and procedures she endured in often unkind medical environments, I take solace in knowing that the Reiki healing and colorpuncture sessions helped to relieve her pain, because when you can decrease acute suffering even in small measures, especially for someone you love, that is a miracle. I am also mindful that these gifts are not from me but are offered through me from a higher healing dimension. I cannot take credit, for I was and continue to be the conduit for this healing modality.

Spirituality and Medicine Path

My mother was treated at various clinics, hospitals, and physician offices in New England and Florida. I was quite disturbed by the lack of compassionate care that my mother received and had a sick feeling in my stomach when one of the patient advocates in a world-renowned hospital told me that my mother was not safe in her hospital room. She urged us to hire a night nurse so my mother was not alone when my father and I left her room in the evening. So we did. This was acutely disturbing, as you can imagine. I was disheartened, and the lack of empathy was often palpable.

I decided I would try to connect with physicians in the New England area who were conducting research in compassionate care and found Dr. Gowri Anandarajah, an expert in spirituality and medicine at the Warren Alpert Medical School at Brown University in Rhode Island. We met, and she became an inspiration for me and a magnificent role model. I will always be grateful to her for her kindness and assistance in creating an academic appointment for me in the Family Medicine Department. This opportunity helped me later in my career when I was hired at Dr. Kiran C. Patel College of Osteopathic Medicine in Fort Lauderdale, where I remain. I also met Dr. Christina Puchalski, the founding director of the George Washington University Institute for Spirituality and Health (GWish) in Washington, DC. We met when I was a scholar at the Kluge Center at the Library of Congress when I received a fellowship in spirituality and medicine. She was very supportive of me and welcomed my interests in spirituality and medicine and compassionate care. Dr. Puchalski also was gracious enough to invite me to write a chapter for her book *A Time for Listening and Caring: Spirituality and the Care of the Chronically Ill and Dying*.[4]

---

4. I wrote the chapter "Reflections in Dance and Music Therapy in Palliative Care."

I believe I was led to this spiritual path of teaching medical students in compassionate care because of my mother. I would never have chosen to teach spirituality and medicine courses or courses in death and dying in medical schools if it was not for her. My mother is the reason for my work. I speak her name in my courses and share with the medical students some of our experiences in the hope that the medical culture can be elevated and they can understand the power of humanistic care. My mother deserved better care, more compassionate care. I don't want to let her down.

My Mother's Passing

The years I spent in health care offices and hospitals as my mother's caretaker and health ally were very difficult. I had to learn quickly about her unique cancer and researched any possibility I could find for solutions that would help. It was often ugly. I still have images of her body cut from top to bottom haphazardly from one of her surgeries, among other grisly memories. We had always been close, and watching her courage during this time always amazed me. If I was the patient, I don't think I would have gotten through it.

After I returned from my stint at the Kluge Center in Washington, I was offered a fellowship at the Harwood Museum of Art in Taos, New Mexico. I struggled with the decision to accept it because I was torn. I knew that it would further my research on dancer Martha Graham and her profound connection to the state. I knew my mother was very ill, but I held out hope she would be well enough to visit me and that by some miracle the possibility of this visit would change her serious health status. I told myself and my parents that I could always hop on a plane if needed since the fellowship was short term. My mother encouraged me to seize the opportunity, although I deeply regret leaving her. Years later I still have moments when I beat myself up for my decision. Upon reflection, I realize that I was in denial and in desperate need of respite after years of hospital and doctor visits; however, this knowledge does not change my feelings of remorse.

While I was in Taos, she left me her last message. She told me she was very tired but she would "wait for me." I thought she meant she would wait for my phone call, but she was waiting in hospice. My father didn't want me to know how serious her condition was and waited until she was admitted to hospice to tell me. I understand that he was trying to protect me, and it took years for me to stop resenting him for the time with her I could have had if he was honest. I felt cheated, and sometimes, I still do. When I finally got the call from him, I immediately packed up my things. I drove through a snowstorm from Taos to the Albuquerque airport. I was an emotional wreck, and I called the hospital every hour on the hour. Frankly, it's a miracle I didn't crash because I was so distracted.

I made it to the airport and boarded the plane, exhausted and silent. The flight stopped in Dallas, and I remember buying a coffee while I was waiting to board the final leg of the flight. A strange woman approached me and hugged me and didn't say a word. I thought that was so peculiar. I am rather shy, and it surprised me that I appreciated the embrace. Once I boarded the flight from Dallas to Florida, I sat in my seat with thoughts of my mom lying helpless in a hospital bed yet again. This time I knew she would never go home. The anxiety and despair I felt was horrifying.

Sitting next to me on the plane was a woman quietly reading a book, and we never said a word to each other. When I stood up to leave, she turned to me and told me, "You are going to help your mother now. It will be the most difficult thing you ever do, but you have the courage you need. She is waiting for you." That is all she said, and I didn't respond.

It was late evening in Florida when I arrived, and my brother picked me up at the airport and drove directly to the hospital. I was both physically and emotionally exhausted and only wanted to see her as soon as I could. The energy was cold and clinical in the hospice unit. After accompanying her in countless hospitals, I was used to it. She was unable to speak, drugged heavily, and almost lifeless while the ventilator monitored her every breath, but I talked to her and let her know I was there. I told her how much I missed her and loved her. I was certain she would hear me even though the nurses assured me that she could not. I asked my mom, as I had done countless times before, if she wanted a light treatment. She was a huge fan, and it had helped decrease her pain in the past. I told her that if she wanted treatment all she needed to do was raise her hand up. Her left arm quickly rose from her bed with strength that she did not appear to be capable of. When I think of that moment, a painful memory, I try to focus on the fact that although she was in a coma, she heard me. Her oncologist later told me that he didn't believe me, that she couldn't have heard me. But he was wrong. I know *she heard me.*

I told her I would not leave her, and I didn't want her to leave me. I moved the chair close to her bed and prayed for her to live. Exhausted by the flight and my emotions, I dozed off only to wake up in the middle of the night. I told her telepathically that it was okay if she wanted to leave and that I would always love her, and her love was all that mattered to me. This was and is our eternal bond. She died a few minutes later. I consider those moments beautiful and tragic, and I was fortunate that I was with her.

I climbed onto her bed with my arms wrapped around her minutes after she died and was stunned when the color returned to her ashen face. She was always a beautiful woman; however, in death, she was positively radiant. I watched her face transform from pain to freedom, a sign that she wasn't suffering anymore. This was a sacred moment. I lost track of time, and later my father had to pry me away from her because I was clutching her body tightly on the bed. I didn't want to let her go. Although I have repeated that scene over and over in my mind, years later, it is still an agonizing memory.

Communications with Light

After they took my mother to the funeral home, I was in a daze, and my father, brother, and I returned to my dad's condominium. It was eleven in the morning, and the sun was shining outside. I was still in shock and wanted to take a shower when she gave me a sign that I will never forget. While I stood in one of the bedrooms, in plain sight before me was a spiral of white light that rotated and gracefully danced around me for several minutes. I knew she was telling me through this gentle image that she was all right.

Her communication continued. I stayed with my dad not only because I had given up my apartment for the fellowship in Taos, but frankly, I was not in any shape to be on my own. Knowing that my father was near helped me to feel somewhat secure. Although he would never admit that he was psychic, I recently discovered that my ancestral roots included a medicine woman. I hope to learn more about her since she is a mystery in the family tree. We both witnessed the continuous blinking of the fire alarm in his bedroom for months even though the battery was removed. He agreed that it was a signal from my mother. After a lengthy stay, and when I felt ready, I moved to an apartment not too far from his house. My light visions began, and when I discussed them with my dad, he never disparaged my experiences and thought they were interesting.

Visions

My visions consisted of huge colored orbs with hues so bright they were almost blinding. I wasn't scared. In fact, I yearned for those moments and hoped they would continue, and they did for about a year. Light orbs are not uncommon in photographs; however, it is unusual to see a light orb with the naked eye. There are several theories about light orbs and their significance, including the belief they are paranormal energies, souls of the deceased, or even angels. I thought how miraculous it was that I would see "light" since I had been working as a healer using light therapy with oncology patients and my mother. Light was my medium, and my mother understood that. I am reluctant to share other visionary experiences because they are so personal, but I assure you there are other dimensions of life. These dimensions are real, and when you experience them, even for moments, they are immensely therapeutic. In moments when I doubt there is another side to existence, I remind myself of the many revelations I have had the good grace to experience.

Starting Point: Grief Journey

It is not unusual to experience a lack of security in the world and to feel starkly alone without your mother, but at the time, I didn't know that. After my mother died, it was a horrific time, and less than two years later, my father passed away in the same hospital. The last night before he died, we had dinner together, and I remember he kissed me and thanked me for everything I had done. He was not a demonstrative man, and I was taken aback. I was so happy to hear his words that night and receive his affection.

During the year and a half after my mother's passing, we had the opportunity to cultivate a strong bond, something I had yearned for my entire life. Although that period was difficult, we had the chance to really *see* each other during our most vulnerable time. He was struggling with his own anguish and didn't know how to handle my deep grief. I cried all the time. I know he didn't understand fully the depths of my pain, but he tried. He even took the initiative to find a therapist for me to speak with, something I find quite extraordinary since I know he disliked therapy in general.

I would like to offer a word of advice about therapists. They can provide a protected space to share your stories, fears, and terrors about what life is like without your mother, but be very choosey about who you work with. I interviewed several therapists, and I was truly amazed at how little insight they had into mother loss. After several sessions with a few different people who were not a match, I was fortunate to find a therapist at the oncology center where my mother has been treated. Barbara Pearl saved me and helped me through an incredibly dark time. She was never dismissive when I told her about my numerous metaphysical experiences and listened with kindness and presence. I will always be grateful to her for her sage wisdom and friendship.

My father recognized how emotionally broken I was and encouraged me to write since he knew that when I was working on a writing project, I felt safe. I am still amazed that I was able to write, much less think creatively, and I wrote the book *If Joan of Arc Had Cancer: Finding Courage, Faith, and Healing from History's Most Inspirational Woman Warrior* during the next year while following him around like a puppy. I was imprisoned by my grief, but his home offered sanctuary.

Although we were both similar personalities, headstrong and stubborn, we became the closest we had ever been, regardless of any disagreement that we had. The foundation of our relationship was mutual respect. I remember a conversation with him where I told him that I loved him, but I loved "her" differently and hoped he was not insulted. He responded with compassion and told me that he truly understood. He was ill with a diagnosis of chronic lymphatic leukemia. I hated going to the oncologist's office, but I made sure I accompanied him so he wasn't alone. Now my job was as his health advocate. After each appointment, we would go to a local deli and have lunch. I remember spending many of those lunches in tears, unable to talk or eat. This was the same place where I shared lunches with my mother as our after-oncology appointment ritual. Witnessing both of their deaths, although sacred and traumatic, has taught me a great deal and shaped my personal and professional life. But it came at a high price.

Books Were My Solace—Kinda

I found some solace in books, my realm of safety, and I read many books on grief, desperately seeking something, anything that could help me. Untethered, I needed a secure place to land. Everything that I read with few exceptions seemed dismissive and juvenile and offered cookie-cutter advice that did not speak to me at all. I did not relate to the stages of grief that most books espoused, and I was so frustrated. I was experiencing spiritual encounters, and I wanted to know more about them and what their significance was. I devoured books on death and dying, spirituality, and the afterlife and visited the library in a local seminary in search of something that would help me. Some of the information I found was informative, but it was not enough. I needed something more. I wanted validation that my experiences were truthful and powerful. I wanted to know how to bring her into my life again to regain my balance. I asked myself, What was I supposed to do now without her? Where was she? Who was she with? And most importantly, how could I contact her?

Psychics, Healers, and Daughters

I spoke with psychics, healers, and grief counselors, and I was often told that my mother was on her own journey, ready to be reborn, or she was reevaluating her life. What was most disturbing to me was to hear from several psychics that she was totally detached from her former life. That was not what I wanted to hear. How could she forget me so quickly, I thought. Some of the people I consulted shared pearls of wisdom and assured me that my mother could hear me. She knew I was having a difficult time. That was reassuring.

Desperate to regain my connection with my mother, I decided that I would ask other daughters about their experiences of loss and learn from them. This was so helpful to me and also gave me hope that I would indeed survive my mother's passing. On my quest, I spoke with women whose mothers had passed away, and what surprised me was their enthusiasm to share their stories. It was quite remarkable. Whenever I mentioned that my mother had recently died, strangers would open up to me and disclose intimate moments of their relationships with their mothers. All these daughters (and there were many) wanted to share their stories once they knew I would not judge them. It is worth noting that they would speak with authority recounting their dream connections, visions, and other signs from their mothers but would often begin with "Janet, please don't think I am crazy." Their fear of being ridiculed if they told their therapists, physicians, and even close friends was extensive. However, we knew that these metaphysical phenomena were real. Although I have certainly had doubts, as an intuitive healer, I want you to understand that these otherworldly connections exist.

I asked fellow daughters many questions. Did they dream of their mothers? Did they ever experience visions? How did they rebuild their lives? They were full of love and shed their tears unabashedly and even offered hugs. After I spoke with them, I felt stronger, courageous, and, most of all, calmer. I was not alone after all.

The Kindness of Strangers

During one of my shopping outings at the local mall in Boca Raton, Florida, I found myself in a dressing room of a store where I used to shop with my mother. Reduced to tears, I sat on the chair sobbing because *she* was not with me. One of the saleswomen heard me and asked if I was okay. Of course I was not. When I told her my mom had died recently, she hugged me and told me that she had also lost her mother and shared her story with me. Listening to a kind and compassionate voice helped me a great deal. I realized that she truly knew what it was like to lose her.

Another meaningful and truly enigmatic experience occurred when I was food shopping. I noticed a woman who resembled my mother, and courageously I approached her and told her that she looked like my mom who had recently died. She did not say a word but embraced me and smiled. It was oddly comforting. In the same store months later, a man I did not know came up to me and said, "I want you to know that your mother is with you, and she will never leave you." Then he walked away. I never saw him again.

Other Signs

I used to take walks outside my father's condo, and during those walks, which were quite meditative, I could "hear" her if I truly listened. The words I heard in my mind were not my words but hers. I do not remember the exact words that I heard telepathically because when you are in a meditative state, you are in another dimension. She reassured me that she would never leave me and that I would be okay. Those walks became my nightly ritual for over a year, and to this day, when I walk, I often feel her comforting presence and continue to hear her. I know that if I trust and pay attention to the signs, dreams, and my inner knowing and shut off my rational mind without questioning the validity of these experiences, I can maintain my connection with my mother.

When I do ask for signs, they are not always there, because you can't really summon a divine experience. You merely have to be willing to embrace it when it occurs. I have seen license plates with the word *Mother*, dreamt of her, and felt her hands on mine. I cherish those moments, and I still try to keep myself open to receive her love in whatever form she chooses since I know it is not up to me. If it was, I would summon her every day.

I have learned through trial and error how to integrate my mother into my daily life and share my sorrows and joys with her. I have a photograph of her holding a coffee mug with her hand held high. Each morning, as part of my morning ritual, I pick up my coffee cup and tell her, "Good morning, Mom." My office is full of her artwork, and my desk is covered with pictures of both of us. Every day, I wear the necklace she gave me inscribed with the words "You got me!"

When someone you love dies, it is not uncommon to feel that an integral part of you has died with them. However, they do not leave you, because your bond of love continues to exist even after death. My mother was (and is) my teacher and my biggest fan. She taught me to believe and trust myself and my life's path, and she has helped me know that our love, like the love you share with your mother, is eternal. Anyone who has lost a mother (or a significant loved one) knows the grief journey well. It is not pretty. You may not recognize yourself and feel empty, as I did without my best friend. Punctuated with periods of deep despair, isolation, and the inability to sleep or eat, I soon realized that this was not only a devastating journey but a significant emotional passage. The hole in my heart was deep; however, years later after she took her last breaths, I am happy, married to the love of my life, and grateful for the gifts she shared with me.

My journey was emotionally wrenching, and at the time, I didn't believe that my life would improve in any area, but that was not the truth. I was hired to teach at a prestigious medical school in Fort Lauderdale the same afternoon I gave the keys to my father's condo to the new owner. This was no coincidence. I believe my mother was watching over me to make sure I could take care of myself financially since I had spent all my savings when I took care of her. Working at the medical school gave me profound insights into the medical community, insights I wish I had when my mother was so ill. I dedicated my life to work and only work and did not even consider that I would have a partner, much less a husband. I know that my mother had a hand in me meeting him because the circumstances were so extraordinary.

Surprises and a Different Life

I discovered happiness eight years ago when I remet my former teenage boyfriend and first love on a business trip in Rhode Island. We bumped into each other in a consignment store that was once his favorite aunt's tailor shop, where he worked as a teenager in the 1960s. After decades without any contact with him, it certainly was more than a synchronistic meeting. I have no doubt that my mother (and dad) took part in making that reintroduction possible. Our families were well acquainted, and my parents, especially my mother, knew him well from his frequent visits. He is my husband now, and I regularly tease him about my mother's remarks when we were dating. They had differing views about something important, probably the shifting politics at the time, and she told him that she hoped that he never married me because she could tell he would be a "pain in the ass." He was a badass and gorgeous and just as opinionated as she was. I wonder what she would think of our marriage now.

Synchronicity or Magic?

There were so many other unexplained events that occurred months before my wedding that chance as an explanation does not really fit. My husband told me that before he met me at the consignment store, he looked me up on the professional network LinkedIn on April 26. This date is significant because it was my mother's birthday. After reading my professional profile, he decided that he had no intention of contacting me, wished me well, and sent me an energetic kiss.

Meanwhile, around the same time, I was in my apartment in Florida, and his name popped into my head, so I looked him up on social media. I was going on a business trip to Rhode Island, where we both grew up, in a few weeks, and I had no idea that he was now living there, alone. Last I knew about him was that he was working in Los Angeles in the film industry and was married. A few days before my trip, I received a telepathic spiritual message (probably from my mother) and was told that I would meet him on this trip. I usually trust my messages, but this time, I was very dismissive because the thought of seeing him after all these years seemed highly unlikely. Any experienced intuitive will tell you that messages you receive for yourself are difficult to discern because of the wish factor, the desire to influence a specific outcome, but I can honestly say that I never thought I would see him again. It had been decades, and my connections with his family vanished many years ago when his parents passed away.

The universe, however, had other plans. What I did not know was that he had returned years earlier to take care of his sick mother, abandoning his film career of creating sets for movies and television. Although I had visited Rhode Island on several trips for business and vacation during the previous years, I never ran into him. Timing, as they say, is indeed everything. The last day of my business trip, after teaching all week at a local hospital (the program I created in honor of my dad, the Sidney Project in Spirituality and Medicine and Compassionate Care™), I felt like I was coming down with a cold because the weather had been miserable, chilly, damp, and rainy. A massage sounded perfect, and I called a local spa where I knew a great massage therapist. To be honest, I considered cancelling the appointment several times, thinking I could get a massage when I returned to Florida, but every time I picked up the phone to cancel, I heard a voice, perhaps my mother's voice, telling me not to cancel, and I listened.

I arrived early and was not in the mood to wait, so I decided that I would visit a consignment store down the road. I love consignment stores and thought it was curious that I never noticed this one before. What I didn't know at the time was that this building was previously owned by my husband's relatives when he was a child. I tried to dodge the rain, since I did not have an umbrella, so I ran into the store, then walked into an adjacent room. Within minutes, I heard his distinctive, sexy voice as he spoke to the manager of the shop. I knew it was him, and I did what any woman who had not seen an old boyfriend in years would do—I looked in a mirror on the wall; primped my hair, damp from the rain; took a breath; and walked to the main room where he was and called his name. He walked over to me and kissed me, and the rest, as they say, is history.

Santa Fe Wedding of Someone Who Never Wanted to Get Married

When I gaze at the photographs taken at our wedding ceremony in Santa Fe in 2017, I notice that my face is beaming. One picture stands out—the picture of me looking into the sky with longing. I realize now that I was making sure my mother would know I was happy and had finally found love. I never dreamed I would marry, because it never was a priority for me. In that photograph, I look at peace, and I am grateful I still enjoy that comfort. The wedding was bittersweet, because although I was joyful, I wanted *her* to be with me. But I believe she was and made herself known to me during this time in many ways.

All aspects of the wedding were quite extraordinary, and I know it sounds ridiculous, but we planned everything in just five days, and all the needed components fit neatly into place. I was visiting Santa Fe to give a lecture at a conference, and I was excited that my future husband would accompany me and I could show him the town. I know the area quite well and had been a frequent visitor for many years because Santa Fe was a special place, and I wanted to share it with him. We attended a dinner organized for the conference presenters, and the coordinator for the conference, Denise Forlizzi, mentioned during a conversation that her partner, Reverend Ann Rea, often performed wedding ceremonies, and if we wanted to get married, she would introduce us. At the dinner, our seats faced an enormous black-and-white framed photograph of a woman dressed as Joan of Arc with her sword held high in the air. Synchronistically, the entire reason for my trip to Santa Fe was to lecture on my research with oncology patients using arts-based medicine methods I had developed in a book I wrote about Joan. Santa Fe is a sacred city; however, the divine icons that permeate the town are of Our Lady of Guadalupe or St. Francis of Assisi, not Joan of Arc. I believed that Joan's picture was a sign from my mother that she approved of our relationship and in fact had helped make it happen. That evening we decided to get married in Santa Fe. My husband purchased "Joan" for me as a wedding gift, and she is displayed in our home as a reminder of that evening.

My Mother's Presence

Reverend Rea was wonderful and helped us to design a beautiful ceremony replete with music and sacred texts. She also introduced us to Leslie Slavin, a local wedding photographer. I told her how much I disliked posey pictures and was grateful that she took photographs unobtrusively. Her pictures were beautiful, and when I look at our wedding album, I am filled with joy remembering how special that day was. We met Leslie for the first time a few days before the wedding to review last-minute plans and prepare photographic logistics. We walked through the garden where the wedding would take place, and after talking at length and touring the inn, she hugged me and we said our goodbyes. I never mentioned my mother.

On her way out, Leslie turned around abruptly and said, "Don't worry, Janet. I will be here before the wedding and will take good care of you. I will help you get dressed and do your make-up and hair." She paused, then told me, "Your mother wanted me to tell you that." This was a blessing, and I knew my mother was speaking through her. And she did just that on my wedding day.

The point of this charmed story is that it is possible to find love after deep grief and loss. I know that this meeting was not a fluke but magic. After my parents' deaths and other personal tragedies, I resurrected my life professionally and regained my balance, but I never really felt joy. The contentment and love I have in my marriage are gifts, and I know my mother had her hand in our meeting. I still yearn for my mother, and my husband and I often speak about her. He knows as I do that the place she has in my heart can never be replaced fully. It is a place that only my mother can fill.

My feelings of desertion were the most difficult for me. I continue to speak with her daily, and this ritual helped me understand that she has not abandoned me, nor have I abandoned her. I often find myself repeating phrases that she would have said to my husband, and when I notice, even at his expense, I think it is hilarious yet comforting.

Research on Mother Loss

Although I experienced various visions that helped solidify that my mother was with me, I wanted to know more about what other daughters did to heal and what helped their grief journey. The grief of mother loss never really goes away, but it does change. I looked at the published literature and could not find what I needed and was surprised that metaphysical encounters are rarely mentioned in this research. I decided to create my own research study and ask questions that were important to me.

* * *

The next chapter contains results from this research, and I believe it is an important yet often neglected topic. This chapter also documents advice that daughters kindly shared with me as a result of this research. Their words helped me, and I hope you find the same result.

Chapter Two
What Does the Research Say?

In this chapter, I share the results of a grief survey I designed and sent to interested daughters in an attempt to learn their coping and resilience strategies. I hope their suggestions are helpful to you and can offer you some hands-on tools during your journey.

Grief is part of the human experience; however, the grief of daughters whose mothers have died is significantly different than other losses. Research is needed that does not quantify nor reduce the suffering women experience into only numerical findings but includes tools for grief empowerment. According to the National Alliance on Caregiving, over 53 million baby boomers are now attending to their ailing parents, and 61 percent of caregivers are women taking care of a female relative, most likely their mothers.[5] According to a fact sheet issued by the National Partnership for Women and Families, more than 65 million women provided unpaid care in the form of childcare, family care, and eldercare in 2020.[6] Because caregiving is considered a "woman's job" (i.e., unpaid), women often suffer emotionally and financially from what is referred to in the literature as "caregiving burden." Daughters,

---
5. "Caregiving in the U.S. 2020."
6. "Women Carried the Burden of Unpaid Caregiving in 2020."

including myself, know that taking care of their mother at the end of her life is noble and a privilege, but it does have its price.

Angelina Grigoryeva, assistant professor in the department of sociology at the University of Toronto, shared research documents about how caregiving responsibilities usually fall into daughters' hands, and this is not a surprise. During her presentation to the American Sociological Society, she cited that "daughters provide an average of 12.3 hours of elderly care per month compared to sons' 5.6," adding that "sons reduce their caregiving when they have a sister, while daughters increase theirs when they have a brother.[7] In my experience and that of the women I spoke with, twelve hours a month is laughable.

The Deepening of Bonds

Many daughters discover that while caregiving their bonds deepen with their mothers; however, this closeness also influences the intensity of loss when their mothers die. Losing a mother at any time is life altering, but losing a mother when you have become her "mother" and especially if you were forced to take care of her at end of life remotely is particularly poignant and heart-wrenching. Although my mother passed away pre–coronavirus restrictions, I understand this emotional significance after spending ten years taking care of her, and there are millions of women like me.

Caregivers and the Grief Experience

My mother and I always had a close bond. She was my best friend (and still is) and edited all my previous books. She was my partner

---

7. Grigoryeva, "When Gender Trumps Everything: The Division of Parent Care Among Siblings."

whenever I needed to do research on a project, and through the years, we visited libraries in New York and Cambridge, and our trips together gave us opportunities to deepen our relationship. After she died, I needed, desired, and longed for the reassurance that she would continue to accompany me in my life.

In time, I learned that it was possible to have a healthy life with her with me in spirit. If you had a close bond with your mother, like I did, and were her caregiver at the end of her life, it is not uncommon to have metaphysical experiences, and often these experiences are more profound because of your closeness. However, because of that devoted connection and the intensity of that spiritual link, daughters have a more challenging time in bereavement. Caregivers are also more susceptible to experiencing psychological issues, including trauma and post-traumatic stress disorder (PTSD), remembering the pain and suffering of their mothers. I did not recognize that the years of caregiving took such a toll on my emotional health, especially because I was always in a heightened state of worry when I was taking care of her. I did not take the time for self-care, and one day, when it was just too much, I told my dad to drive to the Miami hospital without me to visit my mother who was recovering from surgery. I needed a day off and he agreed. I slept the entire day and felt guilty.

Guilt and Caregiving

Guilt is a factor for many caregivers because they may believe they did not do enough or should have done much more, even though they juggled daily obligations, families, and careers at the same time they took care of their mothers. I only had myself and my mother to concentrate on, and I find it dreadful that daughters are expected to do so much more. Even though our caring is heart based, it often forces us to face our own inner shadows and mortality. Caregiving can easily lead to compassion fatigue, which is most often associated with health care professionals. Many caregivers experience this fatigue at some point but don't recognize it as such. They may dismiss their anger, anxiety, stomach issues, inability to focus, lack of patience, and sleeplessness as normal when in fact they are signs of the need for self-care. What they forget is that you cannot be expected to serve from an empty vessel. Daughters often feel guilty if they were less than perfect. This expectation is a myth, although it is a common belief for women who are high achievers. They mistakenly think that they are impervious to the destructive factors that compassion fatigue brings. I know I was.

The Dreaded What-Ifs?

I spent years in torment with what my mother would call the "what-ifs." What if I had taken her to another oncologist? What if she had enrolled in the research program at the hospital in Miami? What if I had done something different to help her? What if…? I spent so much time persecuting myself, and you may be recycling these same what-ifs in your head, but I assure you that it does not help to beat yourself up. This emotional roller coaster will not serve you. More importantly, I know in my heart she would never want me to feel that way. Because I have spent the last decade teaching in medical schools, I now have resources and connections to physicians who could have helped her and myself. Now when I wander into what-if territory, I try to reframe my thoughts into a more positive and kind direction. I remind myself that I did the best I could, and my best was really good!

What Is Missing from the Research

There have been many books on the topic of the mother-daughter relationship, including the wildly successful *New York Times* bestseller *Motherless Daughters* by Hope Edelman. Her book is very helpful. What is often missing from current and past literature, however, is information about the spiritual and metaphysical components of mother loss. Women are often fearful about sharing these experiences with others, especially their health care providers, because they don't want to be labeled as crazy. They frequently conceal how they really feel from therapists and physicians and even family members and friends for this reason.

There is a fundamental lack of understanding concerning grief, and often clinicians do not know how to support their patients and clients for many reasons. They may be uncomfortable with the topic of death, and an absence of training in medical school has left them without proper education. Sometimes, discussing loss brings up painful memories they have not examined before. One therapist I consulted was brutal when she told me in a session, "Janet, I am glad I don't love my mother like you do, or I would be a mess like you." Although many educational programs have curricula that include grief, their treatment of it is didactic. I believe this is problematic because the value of understanding what the grief experience is truly like belongs to the client or patient who has experienced it. It would be beneficial for women to share their grief stories with clinicians to help educate them because contrary to popular knowledge, grief is not one-size-fits-all.

Lack of Grief Education

As a medical educator for over a decade, I can attest to the lack of medical education on the topic of death and dying, and very rarely is grief mentioned in the curricula. Several years ago, I created courses on these topics for medical students, and the feedback remains positive. I am hopeful that when these young physicians graduate and begin their medical practices, they have the necessary compassionate tools to discuss death and dying with patients and their families because they have taken the time to learn how and, in addition, have reflected upon their attitudes surrounding death. This inner reflection is essential so physicians do not project their personal philosophies during the clinical encounter. Their patient's needs, beliefs, and philosophies about death are what matters. If clinicians included spiritual conversations as well as taking the time to ask questions about their patients' emotional and physical challenges, they would be greatly informed. The inclusion of these deeper questions could help patients and clients heal because grief does not just affect one's psyche. It works on all aspects of the person—mind, body, and spirit. For example, insomnia, gastrointestinal (GI) issues, anxiety, and depression can all be symptoms of bereavement, and it is important not to neglect asking patients or clients about how their grief is affecting all components of their lives. Through dialogue, these interactions can also nurture compassionate relationships and help daughters regain their personal power. Finding a practitioner who is willing to learn from their patients or clients is key. Patient-centered medicine is not always available, and far too often women feel unseen and unheard.

Discussing taboo topics in a safe place is one of the keys to improving the medical culture, and grief is one of those taboo topics. When patients are comfortable sharing not only their physical pain but their emotional and spiritual distress with their doctors, they are empowered. Physicians cannot assist their patients if they are not willing to learn the treasures and tragedies of grief. There is an incredible amount of wisdom that can be gained by listening to daughters. I am a fan of bringing topics that are usually off-limits into the light, and the Sidney Project in Spirituality and Medicine and Compassionate Care™ is a program I am most proud of because it offers a safe place for young physicians during residency trainings to honestly discuss their woundings and fears and learn tools for improving the physician-patient encounter.[8] I used my own woundings from my parents' deaths as a teaching tool, and make no mistake, this path was only revealed to me because of the medical horrors that I witnessed. I know I have been led on this journey to teach these challenging topics because of my experiences. I want to prevent another daughter from enduring similar situations.

Grief Research

When I was investigating research on mother loss on PubMed, a highly respected database that contains thousands of peer-reviewed research articles, I plugged in key words on grief and daughters. I was seeking research articles that examined both mother loss and metaphysical experiences and noticed there was an enormous amount of research on grief in general and parental loss. What was missing were studies examining mother loss for adult daughters that included this dimension. I am not a fan of research that is written in academic speak—data and theories—because when it comes to discussing mother loss, it is not helpful to minimize the anguish of daughters into numerical findings. Data gathering is necessary in research, but I am more interested in qualitative research—research that honors the narratives of the participants. I did not find any

---

8. The Sidney Project in Spirituality and Medicine and Compassionate Care™ has been taught in many hospitals in Florida, Rhode Island, and Georgia. I am proud that it honors my father.

research that was helpful to me, so I created my own study. My goal was to learn more about how daughters coped after their mothers had passed away. I was especially interested in knowing more about the visions, dreams, and signs they received. I knew that I was not the only daughter to have these potent experiences. I wanted to know more. The survey I designed asked questions about all the components of grief that daughters may experience physically, emotionally, and spiritually. I wanted to learn from them. I sent the anonymous survey to some of the essayists in this book as well as women who expressed interest in participating.

It bears repeating that daughters are fearful and reluctant about sharing their metaphysical experiences with health care providers and sometimes with their family or friends for fear of being ridiculed. I want to lift that taboo, and this study can help. I believe this initial supporting data proves that spiritual experiences are valid and meaningful. One of the hallmarks of grief empowerment for daughters is their disclosure of this phenomenon.

Background on Grief Survey

This study can help you understand how other women experienced mother loss and, more importantly, how they regained their equilibrium. The survey also includes questions about what or who helped daughters during their grief process, and their responses offer practical advice. This guidance, I might add, can also inform health care practitioners as well as daughters. I understand that when a daughter loses their mother, especially when they have had a strong connection with her, there is not a definitive end point when grief will vanish. It does transform into a lesser wound in time, but it is a wound nevertheless.

This survey is the first of its kind because it incorporates the areas of physical symptoms as well as metaphysical occurrences that women have experienced, topics that are often off-limits and not validated or discussed. One of the failures of the medical system is that patients who are grieving are often given pharmaceuticals when they do not need them.[9] Some daughters will benefit from drugs, but there are other tools, such as acupuncture, Reiki, naturopathy, and somatic and massage work, that can be very nurturing. Integrative medicine physicians understand the holistic components of health. However, many integrative medicine physicians are expensive, and only those who can afford their services benefit.

Below I have included the sample survey as well as some of the results and commentary. I wanted to create a new model for healing revealed by those who know the pain of grief. I hope you find it as helpful as I did. I have identified key results from the survey, and this information is insightful and profound and can assist health care professionals as well as daughters in understanding mother loss. Results by category follow with the actual words as written by participants. You may also benefit by completing the survey and sharing the results with someone you trust.

Sample Survey: The Eternal Bond Survey

1. When did your mother die?
2. How did she pass away?
3. What key words would describe your grief process?
4. What or who helped you during your grief process?

---

9. Pharmaceuticals can often help women in bereavement; however, drugs will not take the grief away, but they can assist in a better quality of life, particularly when a daughter needs assistance.

- family member
- friends
- clergy
- spiritual leader
- community leader
- motherless groups
- grief support groups
- other pharmaceuticals
- integrative therapies
- acupuncture
- Reiki
- energy healings
- aromatherapy
- Bach flower remedies
- nature
- psychotherapist
- social workers

5. Do you believe that the grief process ever ends? If so, when?
6. Have you experienced mystical experiences after your mother passed away?
   - Visions? Inner knowing that she was still with you? Dreams of your mother?
   - Communications with your mother? Can you explain?
7. Did you experience any of the following during your grief process?
   - GI problems
   - appetite issues
   - depression
   - inability to function
   - lack of interest in life

8. Were you able to be with your mother when she passed?
   – Did this opportunity give you some peace?
9. What advice would you offer other women who have experienced mother loss?
10. How are you doing in your life now?
11. What have you done to incorporate your mother into your life now?
12. Do you have certain rituals that you practice that help you feel close to your mother?
13. What has brought you the most peace with her death?

Results from the Survey
What key words would describe your grief process?

- Participant 1: *Process, lifelong adjustment.*
- Participant 2: *Carnal, visceral, indescribable, immobilizing, never-ending.*
- Participant 3: *Agonizing, horrific, terrifying, gut-wrenching, painful.*
- Participant 4: *Anger, relieved, guilty, disappointed.*
- Participant 5: *My sister passed the same year, so I have some comfort in knowing they were together.*
- Participant 6: *All the grief stages—denial, anger, bargaining, acceptance, depression.*
- Participant 7: *Where was she?*
- Participant 8: *Painful, sad. Depressing.*
- Participant 9: *Angry.*
- Participant 10: *Scattered like sprinkles on a banana split sundae. Sprinkles are the surprises of the impact of her loss on each decade so far.*

Commentary: The responses are emotional, which can be expected, and depict painful feelings. It is important to notice that the process is lifelong, an element that is often overlooked by grief theories. I was particularly interested in knowing daughters' responses to the following question.

Does the grief process ever end?

- Participant 1: *Do not know if it ends. Adjust your life. Mom was my best friend.*
- Participant 2: *No.*
- Participant 3: *No. I've learned how to manage it. Miss my mom terribly.*
- Participant 4: *Never ends. I still miss her every day.*
- Participant 5: *No.*
- Participant 6: *No. It softens. The tears become less when the joy of your memories start taking over.*
- Participant 7: *No. The void of a mother's love is always there. Just got better at coping.*
- Participant 8: *No. Never ends, although the pain does dull.*
- Participant 9: *Not really. Mourning a death never ends.*
- Participant 10: *Sorrow can quietly find its way into special moments. My mother's presence during my childhood allowed for a heart full of love for the rest of my life. When every baby of mine was born, every mothering question came to the surface. Every time, I needed motherly arms around me. I felt that pain, that sting of loss and grief.*

Commentary: All respondents believe that their grief process does not end, although some participants stated it does improve, recognizing that the feelings of grief never completely go away.

Anniversaries, birthdays, the birth of a child, holidays, and important milestones often trigger a grief event many years later.

Did you experience any of the following during your grief process?

- Participant 1: *Horrible nightmares. Could not eat or sleep. GI problems, depression, inability to function, lack of interest in life.*
- Participant 2: *GI problems, depression, inability to function, lack of interest in life.*
- Participant 3: *GI problems, depression, inability to function, lack of interest in life. Sleep problems.*
- Participant 4: *No physical symptoms.*
- Participant 5: *GI problems, depression, inability to function, lack of interest in life.*
- Participant 6: *GI problems, depression.*
- Participant 7: *GI problems, appetite [issues], depression.*
- Participant 8: *Appetite [issues], depression, having a newborn and not having time to grieve.*
- Participant 9: *Not that I recall.*
- Participant 10: *GI upset. When I was sad or unable to function with zest, I would stay in bed, and it was like a miracle every time. I was listening to my body's needs, and my body would respond the next day with energy.*

Commentary: Significant physical symptoms including GI problems, depression, sleep issues, and loss of appetite were cited. These symptoms are not uncommon but interfere with a daughter's quality of life. Several of the participants were unable to function and had a lack of interest in life. It is worth noting that physicians often prescribe medications (for anxiety, depression, etc.), and sometimes these medications, although useful, can cause side effects. Listening to your body, as participant 10 recommended, is excellent advice. If you ever feel uncomfortable with a suggested prescription from a health care provider, seek another opinion and trust your intuition.

What or who helped you during your grief process?

- Participant 1: *My son. I had to function for him.*
- Participant 2: *Nothing, no one understands, and you push down your feelings and bury them, and it impacts your life. I attempted suicide.*
- Participant 3: *Family, friends, therapist, grief therapy, acupuncture.*
- Participant 4: *Friends.*
- Participant 5: *Nothing.*
- Participant 6: *Family, friends, aromatherapy, being in nature.*
- Participant 7: *Husband, children, energy healing, being in nature.*
- Participant 8: *Friends.*
- Participant 9: *Grief therapist.*
- Participant 10: *My friends, my dad, my friends' moms. Read* Motherless Daughters. *Seeing a therapist. Energy healing, medium readings, running, boyfriends. Nature, acupuncture, psychotherapy, and the family I created helped me open my body to flow.*

Commentary: It is heartbreaking that one participant attempted suicide, and I have been told by other women that they also considered suicide when their mothers died. Their cries for help illustrate the profound connection that daughters have with their mothers, and often a daughter is so distraught after her mother's death that she mistakenly believes she cannot live without her. I have interviewed many women and the phrase *I cannot live without her* often arises, although, of course, many women find ways to cope. Reaching out to family and friends can be quite beneficial, but not everyone has that support. Visiting grief therapists, joining grief groups, or consulting energy healers, naturopaths, or acupuncturists can be helpful in bringing the body into balance. However, if you are feeling out of control or have thoughts about harming yourself, please seek immediate help or call 911.

Have you experienced mystical experiences after your mother passed away?

- Participant 1: *Dreams of my mom, and when I am in nature, I can feel her with me.*
- Participant 2: *Dreams and I often call out to her in my sleep. Every day at 1:11, I seem to stare at the clock, and I believe it is a sign from her that she is with me.*
- Participant 3: *My radio went off, and when I asked for a sign a year later, the radio went off again. I believe it was her.*
- Participant 4: *Had a vision and she told me she was taken, and she was not ready.*
- Participant 5: *I feel her presence and a warmth comes over me. I talk to her in the car and feel her presence in my garden. I have her walking stick, and I can feel her energy in my hand when I touch it.*
- Participant 6: *My daughter spoke with her when she was two years old. The same year she died, I was on vacation and walking up some ancient stone steps, and I saw her name literally spelled out on the steps. In my dreams, I asked her if she hears me when I call out to her, and she said that she*

> *could not hear any negativity and is in a place of beauty and positivity, but she would come to me when she missed me. My daughter was the only one to see her.*
> - Participant 7: *I felt her presence when I went to a religious park with my daughter.*
> - Participant 8: *She shows up in dreams, and I pay close attention to nature, and I can feel her all around me.*
> - Participant 9: *She had a near-death experience and said she was blissfully happy.*
> - Participant 10: *Songs on the radio would magically come on like clockwork. Recurring dreams about her. I was in the woods, and I could not find her, and she would be walking away. I felt abandoned, and a mystic told me her death was a choice. (She was killed in an automobile accident when she was thirty-nine.) When I was college hunting, she told me to go higher on the bleachers to choose the "gold schools" and not settle.*

Commentary: What is extraordinary is that all the participants uniquely identified their connection with their moms whether it was through dreams or an inner knowing that she was with them. These described "signs" are unique and only understood by the daughter who received them. Remember that if you have shared these signs with other people and they are dismissive, that is okay, it is their belief. You know how your mother communicates with you.

What advice would you offer other women who have experienced mother loss?

- Participant 1: *Allow your soul, mind, and body and spirit to take in this new information. You are on your own timeline.*

Grieve any way you find possible. This process can last a lifetime. Hang out with supportive people if you want, but it is okay to be alone in your thoughts. Never rush anything.
- Participant 2: *Seek help immediately. Talk about it as much as possible. Do things that remind you of her and make them part of your life.*
- Participant 3: *Get all the help you can, and tell her how you feel every day.*
- Participant 4: *Cherish the memories.*
- Participant 5: *Talk about her often.*
- Participant 6: *Allow grief, give yourself the grace to go through all the feelings. We all walk the path of grief differently. Someone's grief could be so different than yours. Find something that reminds you of your mom and put that into your life. That is the ultimate compliment. I want to remember her and be open to the signs. I have little scarves of hers that I tie on my purses like she did.*
- Participant 7: *This is a very difficult experience that is part of life. Only others who have experienced this loss can relate to your pain. With a good support system, you will be able to continue to live your life.*
- Participant 8: *I wear her earrings, chain necklace, and wedding band every day.*
- Participant 9: *I do not feel qualified to give advice to anyone.*
- Participant 10: *My best advice would be to put an arm around them. Losing a mother is like losing the keys to who you are, and it can be lonely to navigate life. My best advice would be to ask yourself a lot of questions, questions you might otherwise ask your mothers, and to find the resources that you resonate with for joy and comfort.*

Commentary: Seeking help when you need to reach out for support is important, and the participants were brave enough to know when they needed help. Incorporating activities that your mother enjoyed and even wearing her jewelry can be a source of comfort. "We all walk the path of grief differently" is true. Talking about your mother may provide some solace, but be aware that some friends or relatives may be uncomfortable and not know what to say. One of my so-called friends told me that I was the "saddest person she ever saw," which did not offer a safe space for me to share my feelings. I urge you to find supportive people, therapists, and other women to share your stories with who will honor your bond.

How are you doing in your life now?

- Participant 1: *Fine.*
- Participant 2: *I have much stronger faith now, and it is because of her. She was a very devout Catholic, and I felt closer to her as I explored my faith. When my spouse left me seven years ago, the cruelest words he said to me were "You changed ever since your mother died."*
- Participant 3: *I am doing well but many times wish that I could still call my mom to share all the good and the bad things that have happened in my life.*
- Participant 4: *Grief is never-ending. It just changes and shifts into a different mindset for me. Now that I am a grandmother, I sometimes say, "Mom, I wish you were here to know them." I am happy that my kids knew her and her light.*
- Participant 5: *I started a company in my mom's name.*

- Participant 6: *I am doing well and still think about her often and miss her a lot.*
- Participant 7: *I try to uphold the traditions around the holidays that she taught me, and I cook from her recipes, and I have an alarm on every day to talk with her.*
- Participant 8: *Not a day goes by when I don't think of her. I have grown spiritually and evolved as a person so that makes me sad. But I have had to adjust.*
- Participant 9: *I am okay and am writing a biography of my maternal grandmother, and I thought it would be honoring my mother and keeping my mother's memory alive for my descendants.*
- Participant 10: *Married with five children. I am a registered nurse and yoga instructor, and lactation education connects me with other mothers. I manage two health conditions and rest as needed, and my body, mind, and soul are important, and I feel healthy.*

Commentary: I am struck by the wisdom and the healing aspects mentioned by the participants. They honor and acknowledge the sacredness of their connections with their mothers and actively participate to try to transform their grief process without negating the fact that they miss their mothers daily.

What has brought you the most peace with her death?

- Participant 1: *I sometimes feel communion with her when I contemplate the important turning point in her life, decisions she made, and the legacy she left.*
- Participant 2: *Talk with anyone about her who will listen. I have a marker in my backyard, and it has this description*

- *after her name: "radiating love, devotion, and kindness for all eternity."*
- Participant 3: *Make her live on though creating traditions associated with memories and things she did and talking about her so other people can get to know her.*
- Participant 4: *I still struggle with the fact that she is gone. I do not know if I will ever be at peace. I do know she was suffering and that is the only solace I have, knowing that although she is not here, I would never want to see her suffer, so God called her home.*
- Participant 5: *Knowing that she lives on in me, seeing her in me. I take such pride when I am called Momma B. I am told that my house has a certain smell, and Mom had a special perfume. I have candles burning all the time like she did.*
- Participant 6: *Talking about her.*
- Participant 7: *I go to the beach often, which was my mother's happy place.*
- Participant 8: *Learning more about my faith, and I believe that I will see her again and that she can somehow see me and my daughters.*
- Participant 9: *As you enter my home, you will find one of my favorite photographs of her, which I enlarged, and I have many videos of her and my children.*
- Participant 10: *Her love (memories) and seeing my kids resemble parts of her. It makes my heart swell, something that my body needs to do naturally for healing to happen, just like any other wound.*

Commentary: Making peace with your mother's death is a personal journey, and each of us must find our own way, which is, of course, challenging. Allow yourself to discover what is right for you.

* * *

The following chapter is about the honor of grief. I wrote this chapter because I often felt admonished and even dismissed by many people who were close to me, and it infuriated me. I believe that those who have not grieved often have a difficult time understanding what grievers experience. It is imperative to discuss how this process, although painful, is honorable, significant, and sacred.

Chapter Three
The Honor of Grief

I had some heart-wrenching experiences when I was grieving and felt abandoned by those close to me who didn't understand or make any efforts to listen to me. I never felt so alone. This sense of desolation was unnecessarily increased by my feelings of being forsaken by almost everyone in my life. I knew my grief for my mother was sacred and honorable, and my tears were a testament to that fact. This chapter includes an interview with Dr. William Frey II, a renowned scientist and expert on crying behavior. It also includes my thoughts about Dr. Kübler-Ross's grief stages, the phenomenon of "womanly hysteria," and how the pharmaceutical industry has profited off women.

Death Is an Uncomfortable Topic

It is not uncommon to be dismissive of grief because—let us be truthful—death makes us uncomfortable. The medical students and residents I have worked with often tell me how difficult this topic is to discuss with patients and their families, and that is their job! Although the United States' population is truly a melting pot of diverse ethnicities, backgrounds, and beliefs, the practices surrounding death, grief, and mourning often reflect one's spiritual or religious upbringing. People who grieve are often encouraged to "move on" and "get over it," yet this advice, although well-meaning, is harmful. Often, these encouragements are part of the dialogue because the non-griever has their own limitations. They would prefer the griever to return to how they used to be, before they experienced loss, and that is not possible.

A few weeks after my mother died, one of her close friends arrived at my dad's house and told me, "No one will want to be with you, Janet. You have to snap out of it!" I did not appreciate her lack of empathy. She did not ask me how I was feeling or if there was something she could do to help. I was furious. I thought she would know as a mother how to listen to and console me. After she left, I told my dad that I felt alone and ostracized. He didn't know what to say to me that would bring me comfort. I understood years later that he didn't know how, and in his way, he tried. Witnessing his daughter fall to pieces was terrifying for him because he always viewed me as a strong woman who could handle anything. After all, I took charge of my mother's health issues for years and navigated all the ugliness that he was unable to address. My vulnerability was difficult for him, especially because he was experiencing his own ache of loss. What I needed, though, in those early months was his support and love and, most importantly, a reminder from him of how much *she* loved me. I am sure hearing him tell me that would have eased my pain, but I am also aware that I only wanted to hear *her* voice and comforting words and no one else's.

I would have benefited from loving understanding from my family and friends and a safe place for me to discuss my heartache, visions, signs, and dreams as part of my healing. I did not have that opportunity. I felt empty and abandoned not only by my mother but by most of the people in my life who clearly did not demonstrate to me that they understood the complexity of my despair. As the months went by, I was able to confide in a few friends who provided a listening ear when I needed it, and I am grateful to them. This was new territory for me. I was scared. I'd never lost anyone I loved that much.

Grief has its own wisdom, rhythm, and waves of emotions, and it is different for everyone, regardless of gender identification, because it is so personal. No one can really understand this journey if they have never traveled it before. In retrospect, I remember how excruciating it was. I often felt like I just wasn't courageous enough to live without her. I couldn't bear it. I have always considered myself to be powerful, but during that time, I lost my power and was terrified. I finally accepted that it was impossible for me to imagine a life without her, nor would I have to. Love cannot die. My bond with my mother can *never* be severed, because the truth is—this is the eternal bond. And this is a truth for you to hold close.

On Crying

Consider that crying is a profound act of emotional surrender and is a mysterious and private experience. St. Catherine of Siena, doctor of the church, dictated the following while in an ecstatic trance in 1370.

> I wish you to know that every tear proceeds from the heart, for there is no member of the body that will satisfy the heart so much as the eye. If the heart is in pain the eye manifests it.[10]

If you are grieving the death of your mother, crying is probably part of your daily experience. The crying process is unique, and

---
10. Catherine of Siena, *The Dialogue of St. Catherine of Siena.*

what may spur a crying jag for you would not necessarily be the same for me. Our tears summon us to pay attention to our bodies, although we may not listen. When we watch a sad movie, recover from a painful physical injury, or mourn the death of someone we love, we cry. You may be surprised to discover that your tears contain medicinal properties. In fact, the types of tears we shed are distinctive, and the chemical components that are released when we cry vary accordingly. We are all familiar with the phenomenon of crying when we are chopping onions and may be surprised to learn that physiologically they are not the same type of tears we shed in grief. Our psyche has its own computer that punches in the correct type of tears to release for the proper occasion.

Research on Crying

Recent research on the effects of tears in social environments suggests that "the possible mood benefits of crying for the crier depend to a great extent on how observers react to tears."[11] I found that sentence particularly compelling. If someone witnesses our tears and believes crying is a healing act versus something indicative of emotional instability, their reaction would have profound effects. If we feel judged when we cry in front of others, we may decide not to cry at all. In another interesting research paper that Lauren Bylsma wrote with several others, the authors included that the production of tears (crying) is "both an arousing distress signal and a means to restore physiological balance (and perhaps also psychological), depending on how and when this complex behavior is displayed."[12] I am not a scientist; however, I do believe that crying does help to restore our balance and is a healthy purging.

---

11. Bylsma et al., "The Neurobiology of Human Crying."
12. Bylsma et al., "When Is Crying Cathartic?"

Because crying is often considered to be a womanly trait, research about tears was not considered important for a long time. Charles Darwin expressed his contempt for crying as early as 1872 and wrote in his book *The Expression of Emotions in Man and Animals* that emotions were a hindrance and a protective device.[13] He was never able to make the important connection between human tears and *being human*. I know that the demonstration of strong emotions can open our hearts to be kinder and more compassionate human beings because we truly understand suffering.

Sadness is an emotion that is abhorrent to many, and it is one of those forbidden topics. Grievers often believe they need to make conscious efforts to hold back their tears so other people won't feel ill at ease. Often, they pretend they are just fine when they are clearly not. Consider that if you saw a person bleeding, you would not rebuke their cries for help. Crying is a form of emotional bleeding, but it does contain recuperative powers. Crying is permissible and acceptable at funerals, during weddings, in hospitals, and in therapeutic milieus but not welcomed elsewhere. This banishment forces people to hide, dismiss, and stuff down their emotions, contributing to both psychological and physical problems.

Tears pulse with meaning. They are valuable and an expression of the vitality of our love for our mothers. The act of crying is healing and a demonstration of love for others, and sometimes that "other" is us. Crying can offer great gifts if we are willing not to judge the packaging. It is also important to choose whom you would share a crying experience with as well since the display of tears illuminates our vulnerability. It is key, when possible, to select compassionate crying companions.

---

13. Sidebotham, "Viewpoint: Why Do We Cry?"

Dr. Frey, author of *Crying: The Mystery of Tears* and the research director at HealthPartners Neuroscience Center in St. Paul, Minnesota, is an expert on crying and has studied the chemical, emotional, and psychological aspects of tears. His research opened the door to new scientific insights about crying behavior and, more importantly, emphasized the importance of crying as therapeutic. When I was a journalist in San Francisco, I had the opportunity to meet him and discuss this topic at length in preparation for a book I was researching.

According to Dr. Frey, one of the initial challenges when he began his research in the early 1980s was the reluctance in the scientific community to examine emotional stress and crying. I asked him why that was. "It is something that cannot be quantitatively defined to everyone's satisfaction. Shedding emotional tears, even by Charles Darwin, was viewed as a trivial activity." I asked him if he thought the lack of research on crying was related to the fact that it is usually associated with women, and he agreed. "Most things that relate to women have not been studied very well in the scientific community, and science has mostly been in the purview of men with some exceptions, and it has been so male dominated for so long."[14] This negative association continues to promulgate the belief that if you cry (and especially if you are a woman), you are emotionally weak or out of control. I believe that this idea is changing.

---

14. Frey, interview with the author, 1998.

Recuperative Powers of Crying

The concept of feeling better after a good cry has always fascinated me—particularly because in my experience, I do not feel better. I feel exhausted and drained. According to Dr. Frey,

> we know that people do feel better after crying. In fact, 85 percent of women and 73 percent of men report that they do feel better and that they feel less angry and less sad. It differs. Some people have told me that they feel exhausted and drained and go to sleep after crying, while others have said that they feel relieved. Crying may alleviate stress by removing chemicals that have built up. Exactly what those chemicals are no one knows for sure; it has not been proven, but it is my theory. People did not think that there was any relationship between tears and emotions and stress until my work. In my research, we have discovered results, which are consistent with the theory that suggests that all tears are not the same. When you cry from emotional stress, those tears are different from other types of tears. When you cry emotional tears, the tears themselves have a higher protein content than other types of tears, such as irritant tears. Previously, people thought that "tears were tears," and the importance of this discovery is that something unique is happening when we cry emotional tears.[15]

When I asked him about why crying might be difficult for some people, he told me that

---

15. Frey, interview with the author, 1998.

> crying has a lot to do with self-disclosure, and when you cry in front of another person, you are truly disclosing yourself and express your vulnerability and your real feelings. This disclosure is not so much that you are disclosing your feelings to another person, but you are disclosing these emotions to yourself. Crying is the ultimate emotional experience, and it is a very intense process. When you cross that threshold of intense feelings, it triggers an automatic crying response, and it does not matter what the emotion is above a certain intensity. It triggers this alleviation of stress through the crying response.[16]

You may have difficulty crying, and you are not alone. Dr. Frey told me that it is not unusual, and his theory of why it may be challenging is because everyone is unique.

> I think that some people develop a type of fear and a belief that if they allowed themselves to cry, they would not be able to stop, and they are fearful of having a breakdown and truly letting go. Some people who don't allow themselves to cry have an emotional wall up, and it is often somaticized, and they may get a stomachache instead because they can't cry.[17]

Grief can be a mystical experience and an important somatic release. When Martha Graham, considered the mother of modern dance, performed a short piece called "Lamentation," choreographed in 1930, she showed audience members what grief looked

---

16. Frey, interview with the author, 1998.
17. Frey, interview with the author, 1998.

like inside and outside a woman's body. Her beautiful choreography is still relevant almost a hundred years after its creation, and I urge you to watch it on YouTube.

I am trained as a dance therapist, and I know the importance of somatic expression. During the first year after my mother's passing, I had weekly massages from a trusted friend that helped boost my immune system. Her weekly therapeutic, hands-on treatments enabled me to release pent-up anger I could not verbalize. Grief is chronic stress on the body, and when we are in mourning, we are vulnerable and more susceptible to being sick. Women are notorious for not practicing good self-care in the best of times and often put other people first. It is your right to acknowledge your needs—physically, spiritually, and emotionally—not only during your initial grief but throughout your life.

The Myth of Hysterical Women

Weeping is usually associated within the purview of female traits, and we have Sigmund Freud to thank. He linked the phenomenon of hysteria to women, but what is seldom revealed is that he also suffered. According to authors of the article "Women and Hysteria in the History of Mental Health," Freud had an emotional breakdown in 1897.

> After a period of good humor, I now have a crisis of unhappiness. The chief patient I am worried about today is myself. My little hysteria, which was much enhanced by work, took a step forward.[18]

---

18. Cecilia et al., "Women and Hysteria in the History of Mental Health."

Women who spoke out and shared their ideas and opinions about their lives (and their marital status) in the late 1890s were often sent to asylums. They were locked up for their "bad behavior" and were labeled by the medical establishment as hysterical. It is frightening when you consider that husbands held the authority to commit their wives at will. So dangerous were these asylums that chloroform was used to silence women, as well as other barbaric procedures, including the use of straitjackets. It is hard to believe that the use of chloroform, a highly carcinogenic substance, was given to women until 1976, when it was banned from use by the Federal Drug Administration. One can only wonder what the long-term effects were for the women who were forced into silence by this drug. I wonder because women have not always had "permission" to express strong emotions and have been bullied into accepting the label of the hysterical woman. This is not only dismissive but misogynistic thinking. Your emotions are valid, appropriate, and healthy!

A Short Anthropology of Crying and Crying Behavior

The word for sadness in Latin is *saed*, or sated, meaning "enough."[19] If the original meaning of sadness was to "have enough," or even "too much," I wonder how the word evolved with such a negative connotation. During medieval times, the Catholic Church's aversion to crying was obvious when they attempted to outlaw weeping in public by creating a law that contained the concept of "contemptuous mundi." This decree prohibited mourners at a funeral from crying. It is believed this doctrine was passed because the church elders thought that if mourners cried during the funeral,

---

19. Online Etymology Dictionary, "sad (adj.)," accessed November 8, 2024, https://www.etymonline.com/word/sad.

the person they were burying would not receive their place of glory in Heaven. Historically, during the same time, it is interesting that clergy urged their parishioners to cry as a substitute for their confessions.

Many cultures recognize that crying and mourning rites hold a prominent place and can offer comfort for the bereaved. For example, some people believe that communication with the spirits of the dead is possible and that these spirits can travel to and from the afterlife to visit the living. This communication is encouraged depending on the customs. Women have always been the primary mourners for the dead, and little girls from the Osage tribe learn during childhood how to mourn properly, while other members of the community erect sacred rituals for their departed.

In the Celtic tradition, "keening" was an important vocal expression of mourning. Women led the chanting at funerals and vocalized their pain of loss through sound. The term originated from the word *caoineadh*, which means "to cry."[20] Author Angela Bourke wrote eloquently in her research article about the tradition, describing it as "a highly articulate tradition of women's oral poetry. The lamenting woman led the community in a public display of grief."[21] The tradition has faded, although I would imagine that the presence of these women vocally mourning gave permission for the funeral attendees to join in.

---

20. The word also means "crying and lamenting" and "an elegy." WordSense, "caoineadh," accessed November 9, 2024, https://www.wordsense.eu/caoineadh/.
21. Bourke, "The Irish Traditional Lament and the Grieving Process."

Grief Rituals

Rituals after death provide mourners with a sense of community and shared grief so mourners do not feel alone. Every religion has spiritual practices and rituals for mourning, but that doesn't mean you can't create your own way of honoring your mother. Celebrating her birthdays, lighting candles, or inviting her friends and family to share stories, photographs, and memories are rituals that do not have to end at the cemetery. On my birthday, I choose a card from her and sign it "Mom" to help me feel more connected with her.

While we do permit grieving rituals for a requisite period, mourners are quickly expected to stop. There are many reasons for this hurriedness, including people's inability to be present with someone in emotional pain, embarrassment, and the triggering of feelings about their own death. However, when grief is not acknowledged or permitted, that doesn't mean that it will not exist. If we believe and support the myth that crying is a barometer of weakness, it victimizes the daughter, who is legitimately entitled to express her grief.

One of the tragedies of the coronavirus is the fact that thousands of mothers (albeit millions across the globe) died alone, without the comfort from their daughters at their bedside. The psychological toll is enormous for daughters (and their families) because they are denied the expression of shared grief that occurs at graveside. They also have to forfeit the opportunity of attending meaningful rituals of celebration at their homes or in sacred places. They have purpose. Women were left alone to not only deal with the loss of their mothers but the loss of grief rituals. Anyone who lost a mother during Covid can testify to these deprivations and their subsequent psychological costs.

Ancient Philosophies About Tears

Ancient cultures believed that water was the noblest of all the elements and that shedding tears was a sacramental act. Water was considered the source of all life, and it is little wonder that the mention of tears occurs in all the creation myths. The ancient Egyptian word for weeping is *rem*, "to weep," and Rem-Rem is the realm of weeping, a place we have all visited.[22] You may be familiar with the Bible verse "They that sow in tears shall reap in joy."[23] Death and resurrection are important themes found in ancient myths and biblical texts, and they echo the fact that after death, the griever can resurrect themselves.

Images of tears recur throughout mythology, and sometimes the tears themselves take on colorful hues. Freyja, the goddess of love and fertility in Norse mythology, wept golden tears when her lover was killed in battle. Tara, one of the most important Buddhist goddesses, was born from the divine-colored tears of her father. These stories remind us that we are not only suffering on earth, but the goddesses also suffer and weep with us.

I was heartened to read about Seneca, the philosopher from the fifth century BC who wrote at length about grief in the literary tradition called *consolation*. This tradition included a series of letters that were written to comfort loved ones. He wrote to his mother several letters. Among them, he penned these wise words: "All your sorrows have been wasted on you if you have not yet learned how to be wretched." There is wisdom in this advice, for until you traverse the process of grief with all its ugliness and darkness, healing will be challenging. I assure you that suppressing your emotions or trying to run away from feelings of deep grief, although preferable

---

22. Rem was also an Egyptian fish god who fertilized the land with his tears. Massey, *Ancient Egypt*, 373.
23. "Psalm 126:5."

in the moment, will not help your journey. If you choose to censor those feelings, they will still erupt—and often when you least expect it.

The Sacredness of Tears

Tears have always held a sacred place, especially in Hispanic culture. I love the idea that the *curandera*, a spiritual and physical healer in the community, was pre-chosen for her role before birth. It was believed that a curandera was able to cry in the womb and was given the gift of healing through her tears. According to the famous curandera Elena Avila, a nurse and healer, the foundation for *curanderismo* teachings is that

> it is not enough to diagnose a physical problem without looking into what is going on with the heart and soul of patients. Each illness is a story, and it is only the patient who can tell that story. True healing can only be effective if it has some kind of spiritual basis.[24]

This honoring cannot take place until we tell our stories of grief to reframe our losses and regain our equilibrium.

The Bible is also a rich source of stories about crying. Mary Magdalene's ritual when she washed the feet of Christ with her tears was an expression of her devotion. Crying was considered an act of "affective piety," and when she bathed his feet with her tears, it was the ultimate expression of her love. This act was also considered the ultimate violation of social norms since, historically, she is mistakenly considered a prostitute instead of an acolyte. Magdalene was so popular in poetry and literature that texts specifically written to

---

24. Avila, *Woman Who Glows in the Dark*, 37–38.

stir or inflame the soul of the reader were called "affective literature" and were also quite popular. In fact, the word *maudlin* (from Magdalene) passed into the English language from the French and is still used to describe someone who is tearfully sentimental.[25]

The DSM Labels

Until 1980, the *Diagnostic and Statistical Manual of Mental Disorders* (*DSM*) listed hysteria as an illness. Chlorpromazine, a popular tranquilizer, was available to doctors in 1954 and later replaced with the popular prescriptions for women: Miltown, Valium, and Librium.[26]

> By 1968, the "minor" tranquilizer Valium (diazepam), marketed as an antidote for socially dysfunctional women—the excessively ambitious, the visually unkempt, the unmarried and the menopausal misfits—was the best-selling drug in the world as well as one prescribed overwhelmingly to women.[27]

Prozac later emerged as the drug of choice for both sexes and was (and still is) a popular antidepressant, although it has its side effects. Feminist icon Betty Friedan, one of the cofounders of

---

25. The word is derived from the Middle English name Maudelen, which was a variant of Magdalene, a variant of Mary Magdalene. It's interesting that in many definitions I found, she is referred to as a sinner in an attempt to devalue her. The word *maudlin* is usually associated pejoratively and reflects the idea of being overly sentimental or tearful.
Better Words, "maudlin," retrieved November 9, 2024, https://www.betterwordsonline.com/dictionary/maudlin.
26. Valium and Librium are still used, and now Prozac and Zoloft are the favorites.
27. Tone and Koziol, "(F)ailing Women in Psychiatry."

the National Organization for Women (NOW) and author of the groundbreaking book *The Feminine Mystique*, was an articulate spokeswoman against pharmaceutical abuse targeted toward women. At the time, drugs were often prescribed for women who were discontented with their traditional roles as wives and mothers without other options. Suppressing their unhappiness and often rage, they were given "happy pills" (mother's little helpers) and made to feel as if there was something terribly wrong with them if they complained about not being fulfilled by those roles.

Friedan's book was published in the 1960s on the sea of cultural change that would bring women's rights and civil rights into the mainstream. Her words sparked a new consciousness for women and articulated the beliefs that many women had but were too afraid to share or kept deeply submerged for fear of ridicule. The book sold millions of copies and validated that the feelings of discontent women were experiencing were not singular, and it gave them much-needed consent to speak their truths. Although she has been criticized for focusing only on the malaise of white, middle-class women while ignoring women of color, that was not her intent. "We had to create ourselves.... There was a lot of rage in women.... And [women] therefore are entitled to the equality of opportunity and their own voice."[28] Friedan was often condemned for not including women of other races; however, during the formation of NOW, and in later years, she worked alongside women of color. After she left her position as president of NOW, Aileen Clarke Hernandez, an African American woman became the next president, and the early New York chapters of NOW were founded by two African American women: Florynce Kennedy and Shirley Chisholm.

---

28. Friedan, "Women's Rights," interview by Mary Parkinson, 9:52–15:44.

Friedan coined this feeling of unease the "problem that has no name," her label for the kind of fatigue and feelings of emptiness that many housewives were treating with popular tranquilizers, and argued that "women's predisposition to nervous illness had less to do with anxiety and depression than their failure to live fulfilled lives."[29] "You have to say no to the old ways before you can begin to find the new yes you need."[30] Her words continue to inspire me and speak to the discovery of yes within our own psyche necessary during our reconstruction of our lives during and after grief. This recognition of the sacredness of your journey to regain a "new life" during and after grief is not included in Dr. Kübler-Ross's explanation of the five stages of grief. This is a huge mistake and an ignored opportunity.

Dr. Kübler-Ross Made a Mistake

Clinicians can offer great comfort, psychological understanding, and support for daughters. When they blindly adopt Dr. Elisabeth Kübler-Ross's stages of grief as the only model, they contribute to the lack of acknowledgment that grief belongs to the griever, and it is a sacred act of love. The respected work of Dr. Kübler-Ross's many stages, although compelling, does not depict the actual stages of grief despite the fact it is universally accepted as *the* model. Denial, anger, bargaining, depression, and acceptance has been the universal gold standard, but it negates the fact that every person has their own experiences with grief, which may or may not mirror those stages. More importantly, those stages should not be used as a checklist of dictated emotions that women should use to judge how they are doing. These stages may bring comfort to those

---

29. Prewitt, "Take Some Pills for Your Hysteria, Lady."
30. Friedan, *The Feminine Mystique*, 514.

who want validation for their feelings, but I believe it is a false analysis. Reducing the multilayered grief process to five words does a disservice. Daughters may feel as if they are not experiencing the grief process correctly if they do not travel through these stages or, even worse, they remain stuck in one of those stages. It is insulting because it is formulaic and reductionist. It does not acknowledge my experiences or yours.

Grief is a dance, and we may also feel guilt, sadness, lack of interest in our lives, joy, and celebration. Dr. Kübler-Ross also never mentions any occurrence of visions, dreams, or other signs that the bereaved may experience. The point I am making is that you cannot quantify how you should feel or will feel. The wisdom of suffering that one learns during grief is formidable wisdom, and one learns what truly matters in life when someone you love is taken away.

After the death of her mother, writer Ada McVean wrote in 2019 an insightful article stating that Dr. Kübler-Ross's model "is not science based, does not describe well most people's experiences, and was never meant to apply to the bereaved."[31] According to McVean's research, Dr. Kübler-Ross created this model after she interviewed two hundred dying patients to learn about their psychological beliefs about death and that this model was not based on empirical or systematic investigations but a collection of case studies. What I think is compelling is that her research, although merited, did not consist of interviewing those who had lost loved ones but was based on those who were facing death, and those populations are very different. McVean ends her article with sound advice:

---

31. McVean, "It's Time to Let the Five Stages of Grief Die."

There is not a "right way" to grieve. There is not a "wrong way" to grieve. And I hope that when you experience grief you can take some small comfort in knowing that however you are feeling is just fine.[32]

The Danger of Labeling Grief as a Mental Illness

In March of 2022, the newest disorder to be added to the *Diagnostic and Statistical Manual of Mental Disorders* (*DSM*), a publication of the American Psychiatric Association, included prolonged grief disorder. They defined this "disorder" as "intense yearning or longing for the deceased (often with intense sorrow and emotional pain)."[33] Adding further insult to those in deep grief, clinicians could bill insurance companies for the treatment of this "disorder," and pharmaceutical companies now had further permission to manufacture drugs that grievers would now "need." This addition was not without controversy, and Joanne Cacciatore, an associate professor of social work who is an expert on the grief experience, stated,

> when someone who is a quote, unquote expert tells us we are disordered and we are feeling very vulnerable and feeling overwhelmed, we no longer trust ourselves and our emotions. To me, that is an incredibly dangerous move, and short sighted.[34]

When someone is unable to function at all for long periods of time or threatens to harm themselves, they need professional care,

---

32. McVean, "It's Time to Let the Five Stages of Grief Die."
33. American Psychiatric Association, "Prolonged Grief Disorder."
34. "The DSM-5 Adds a New Diagnosis."

and in this case, I am not referring to those circumstances. If you are interested in reading more, there is an abundance of materials on PubMed and in the *DSM* online.

Grief Is Not Pathological

Daughters who are grieving after one year or "long for" their mothers are at risk of being labeled and medicated. The only boon would be for pharmaceutical companies to help psychiatrists medicate their patients when these daughters are not mentally ill but experiencing deep grief. Grief is not a mental illness or a pathology but a natural process. The grief process will include intense longing for your mother, and the physical separation from her often creates emotional distress. These are natural human responses and not a mental disorder. Many research papers on grief characterize this normal experience as problematic if grief does not resolve within a year. This is just ridiculous. I wonder if the authors have ever lost a beloved. Find support, allow yourself to mourn, and reach out for help when you need it.[35]

Who Decided This Diagnosis and Why

The financial conflict that surrounds this diagnosis and the task force that created the initial diagnosis for prolonged grief disorder in 2012 are alarming because 69 percent of the members of the task force reported financial relationships with pharmaceutical companies.[36] There is a justification for prescription drugs when they are needed, and they can be beneficial. I do not believe drugs are an antidote for grief, but I know they can often help

---

35. If you are unable to function, have severe depression, or have thoughts of suicide, please seek out professionals who can assist you.
36. Styx, "Prolonged Grief Disorder."

some women to ease their distress. Antidepressants and antianxiety medications are the usual pharmaceuticals chosen by clinicians who may not know that natural therapies can also assist. Homeopathy, naturopathy, acupuncture, nutraceutical support, massage, and energetic practices are very valuable. If you choose to work with any type of integrative medicine practitioner, naturopath, or energy healer, seek out those who are clinically trained and have credentials. Resist the urge to self-medicate because all medications, including natural remedies, have side effects. It is always prudent to work with someone you trust who also possesses the proper qualifications.

* * *

The next chapter offers information on how grief can provide us with great spiritual and metaphysical opportunities. I discuss these opportunities and share some of my experiences.

Chapter Four
Unlikely Companions
Grief and the Other Side

This chapter documents the gifts of grief, which can be received if we are open to them. I discuss how grief can open daughters to metaphysical connections, and I hope that this chapter will give you some solace. Included in this chapter is the topic of psychic connections that health care providers frequently experience with their patients. However, often they are reluctant to share those experiences because it is a taboo subject, even though it is a common occurrence. I want to normalize these moments because they are not confined to just those in grief.

Grieving is a form of prayer—a prayer to be retrieved from the land of sorrows and a prayer to reunite with our loved ones. Grief is a voyage to the underworld and possesses many gems of wisdom. These insights cannot be told or taught; they must be felt and experienced. This process can last a lifetime and also possesses various degrees of power—sometimes it will feel shattering and frightening and other times quiet and bittersweet. I cannot tell you that it has an end point, but although it never truly ends, it changes as the sting of grief transforms into grace. Typically, grief has a negative connotation that encompasses great suffering, and that is true. It is painful, but it is always a potent teacher. The emotional descent we experience heightens our senses. We feel so much, and it is natural to feel unsteady. Initially, the grief process is full of darkness; however, further along the passage, color returns to life. I have survived profound grief and can attest to its underlying treasures. Admittedly, when one is in the throes of grief, anything that could be seen as a "gift" is not remotely recognized.

Leaning on My Mother

I understand the concept of "leaning on other people," but I always knew that I could take care of myself. However, when I was in an emergency room in a Boca Raton hospital in 2021, I decided I wanted to lean on her. I was experiencing sepsis, a life-threatening condition, after an elderly cat that my husband and I had rescued bit me. My husband was quick to recognize the symptoms and drove me immediately to the emergency room and saved my life. If he had not known the warning signs, I would be dead. As I was lying on a gurney waiting for a hospital bed (alone because of the coronavirus restrictions), I was told by the clinically efficient physician who had no bedside manner that I could die if I did not receive antibiotics immediately. I was already terrified, and his lack of compassion did not help. It was four in the morning, and although I do not remember everything that happened, I remember pleading out loud, "Ya know, Mom, this would be a perfect time to show up!" I wanted only her.

Although I did not see her, I knew she was there. I could feel her reassuring presence, and that internal knowing helped me through the next twenty-four hours of IV treatments. I pictured her next to me in my hospital room, which was ironic given all the years I had spent in hospitals when she was the patient. Now I was in the same hospital, and my room was on the same floor where I had visited her so many times over the years.

The vulnerability of grief (and serious illness in my case) has a profound effect on the psyche and often presents opportunities to experience psychic connections. My core knowing and faith that my mother was with me in the hospital has been echoed by many daughters who told me they heard their mother's voices, received visions or signs, or simply experienced a deep inner wisdom that she was with them, usually when they needed her most. I believe the reluctance for women to share these sacred experiences with others stems from the idea they will be considered irrational and ridiculed. The essays in part 2 further illustrate those spiritual and metaphysical connections and are written by those who know they exist.

Psychic Connections in Health Care

Psychic connections are common in health care, especially for hospice care physicians and nurses. Unfortunately, it is often a prohibitive topic because, like daughters, they fear reprisals. One of my colleagues, a palliative care physician, told me she could see auras around the bodies of her patients and often felt a presence in their rooms that she could not explain. When I asked her if she ever shared those experiences with anyone she worked with at the hospital, because she may not be the only one, she replied that she would "never tell anyone." She mistakenly believed it would erode her status as a competent doctor.

There are research studies on this phenomenon documenting that the bedside visions patients experience at end of life do occur, and they are reassuring to patients and, I would add, to their families.

The dying may see or sense others in the room with them and will sometimes hold conversations with these invisible presences. They may tell you that they are perceiving those who have died before them. Sometimes they describe light or scenery.[37]

When you consider that connection to the next world is experienced by health care workers, then why wouldn't that bond continue for those who shared a cherished relationship?

Metaphysical Connections

You may have experienced metaphysical connections with your mother—an image out of the corner of your eye, a song that is suddenly on the radio, lights switching off and on, or the smell of her fragrance. I wish I knew the exact mechanism for why or how this takes place, but I do not. However, these experiences validate that she is with you, and those magic moments are therapeutic. Although you may know people who dismiss supernatural phenomenon because they have never had those experiences themselves, their beliefs do not negate the power of those experiences. A few weeks before I was planning on visiting Rhode Island, one of my favorite places, I had a vision of my childhood friend's mother who has passed away. She was insistent that I "find Paula!" We had lost touch over the years, although I thought about her often. I had no idea that she owned a house close to where I was going to stay during my trip. After spending hours tracking her down, I was thrilled to find her contact information and called her to share my revelation with her. Paula was delighted, and we spoke for a long time about our lives as if we had just recently talked. It was familiar and comfortable. I know that

---

37. Pearson, "End of Life Experiences."

her mother wanted us to reconnect, and our relationship continues today. I have her mother to thank.

The Wonderment of Visions

According to a book I discovered titled *Treatise on Ascetic and Mystic Theology: For the Use of Seminarians and Young Priests*, written in 1913, my vision of Paula's mother was defined as a bodily vision or "exterior vision with the help of sight." It was further described under the category of private revelations as "graces of light and love." I don't know who the author or authors were since they are not cited, but I appreciate that these definitions offer credence that this phenomenon can occur. Different types of visions were explained as bodily, imaginative, and intellectual. Imaginative visions "have a material form; but they are perceived only by the interior sense of the imagination." Visions during the dream states are also described, including the idea that these visions can also be received when one is awake, an apt explanation of my vision of my friend's mother.[38] I believe intellectual visions occur when we experience deep inner knowing that our mothers are with us.

You cannot force any type of metaphysical connection to occur. They arrive when they arrive. However, they can occur through ritual, meditation, or sacred ceremony or even when you are doing mundane activities, such as walking, cooking, or gardening. These spiritual insights are a *nes*, which is a Hebrew word for a miracle. A nes can also be signs of a higher reality. I believe that there is a purpose to these insights to not only help us to heal but to transform our consciousness because they serve as a mystical initiation.

---

38. *Treatise on Ascetic and Mystic Theology*, 277–79.

During the time I was experiencing visions, I did not understand their significance, particularly because many of these visions had strong links to Catholicism. I am Jewish, so it was strange to me but not unsettling because I have a long history of metaphysical encounters. One of my close friends suggested that I talk to her priest, who had a PhD in psychology. She thought he would be able to help me understand what I was experiencing. When I shared my visions with him, he said, "I don't know what is happening, Janet, but you are lucky to receive this gift. It's beautiful!"

This sacred domain is beyond normal analysis because this realm is not in the "normal" range of our everyday lives. I have experienced visions of, excuse the words, "dead people" and have also seen family members, friends, and clients' loved ones. It was not out of the ordinary for me to see or hear them, and I wrestle with the fact that I have not "seen" her. But I have dreamt about her, felt her energies, and received what psychotherapist Carl Jung would describe as *big* dreams, or dreams that have qualities of authenticity that transcend normal dreaming. The messages I have received telepathically I have written down in countless journals, and the drawings I have created from my light visions never cease to amaze. Maybe that is how my mother chooses to communicate with me. One day when I was especially missing her, I asked my husband where she was, and he replied that she was around, and I should not doubt her presence. That afternoon, I received a form letter addressed to Mrs. Sidney Roseman. This was the first time I received a letter in the mail that specifically had her name. That was her sign.

My Mother's Vision

My mother never talked about spirituality or mysticism, but she was supportive of my interest and my seeking. When I shared my metaphysical experiences with her, she listened without judgment. One afternoon when I was in Florida taking care of her, she surprised me when she woke up from a nap to tell me about her mystical encounter and was very animated. She told me that she saw a figure in front of her who was "dressed in priestly clothing," and she said she was a little startled at first. She recognized the presence to be my dear friend Alonzo King, the founding director of LINES Ballet in San Francisco. I sent him an email and asked if he had appeared to my mother, because he is a mystic and walks a strong path with Spirit. It made perfect sense to me that he would want to check in with her since he knew she was so ill. He told me that it was not him but Yogananda, one of his numinous teachers, adding, "She is so blessed. I do not want to dilute it with words but know that she is loved and protected."[39]

Throughout my mother's challenging medical journey and years later, after her death, Alonzo was an enormous support for me, and his words continue to inspire me.

> Be strong, Janet, and no matter how it appears, remember that your mother is not this body, she is Spirit. Always has been. Try as best as you can to see what she really is, a shining being of light and love. Be confident that she is loved and being taken care of, infinitely more than we can ever attempt to. The Holy Ones were with her. Suffering has ended for her. But not for us. She is completely immersed and surrounded by an endless sea of love and joy. Why would she want to leave that? After years of physical suffering, she has dropped the troublesome body and is wearing her real Self. Hope at last. We are here to accelerate our vibration so that we too can enter that

---
39. From personal correspondence with Alonzo King.

sphere, even while here. This is our real work. But please know, the loss that you feel is deeply painful. I understand. The Masters with all their spiritual knowledge in the world still suffer when loved ones depart. Send your mother love and joy. Never stop speaking to her. Include her in your prayers and meditations. You will see her again.[40]

I believe him.

A Sacred Gift

When I was living in San Francisco, a few years before my mother's diagnosis, Alonzo gave my mother and I a wonderful gift. She was visiting me, and I was thrilled to spend time with her. I was a dance critic at the time and a dedicated fan of his choreography. I was touched by his work—dance making that elevated performance from the decorative to the sacred. In one review, I wrote that

> I am sure in a former life that Alonzo King was a priest... an archbishop or even a pope. King's choreography has such a devotional quality that no matter what you watch; each piece retains his signature; elegance of movement and purity of line that you feel blessed by just the watching.[41]

When he invited us to attend a rehearsal, we were both excited. I knew that she loved dance and dancers as much as I did. After an hour or so of watching the dancers, we decided to leave and said our goodbyes. We thanked him for this wonderful experience. He asked us where we were going, and I told him that I didn't want

---

40. From personal correspondence with Alonzo King.
41. Roseman, "Alonzo King Creates Amazing Grace in 'Lines.'"

to interfere with his rehearsal with his dancers. He replied, "Wait, there is something for both of you. Please stay." After a short break, the members of his company began to dance to one of my favorite ballets. This choreographic piece was not included in the repertoire for the next concert; however, knowing how much I loved the ballet, he wanted my mom to see it as his gift. He was and is a blessing to me and to my mother, and I will always be grateful to him for that beautiful afternoon!

Spiritual Emergency

Grief is emotionally shattering, and we are energetically wide-open because our physical energies are so depleted. This psychological state can be described as a spiritual emergency. The concept of a spiritual emergency was initially coined by psychologist Stanislav Grof in 1989. He defined the symptoms as "experiences of extrasensory perception, disorganized behavior and unusual or illogical thoughts or beliefs with strong spiritual content."[42] What Grof did not realize is that "extrasensory perception and beliefs with strong spiritual content" are the elements that are revealed in visions, signs, or dreams, and they are not illogical. I am not referring to a psychotic break but to the extrasensory occurrences that often arise after the death of a beloved. It should be noted that his contributions of research with his wife, Christina Grof, are quite impressive because they were willing to challenge the philosophies of modern psychiatry in the late 1980s.

> Since modern psychiatry does not differentiate between mystical or spiritual states and mental diseases, people experiencing these states [spiritual emergencies] are often

---
42. Muller, "When Spiritual Crisis Shows Up in the Mental Health System."

labeled psychotic, hospitalized, and receive routine suppressive psychopharmacological treatment.[43]

They also believed that these states of consciousness can result in "emotional and psychosomatic healing, positive personality transformation and consciousness evolution."[44]

Mystical encounters are baffling and extraordinary and often cannot be described in words. One of my favorite Jungian scholars, Robert Romanyshyn, wrote,

> grief, if it is endured, can restore to us a sense of the sacred and the holy.... Perhaps at the core of our grief, just beneath the skin of depression, is deep hunger for an epiphany of the Divine.[45]

You may find that speaking with a spiritual leader or healer in your community can shed light on your otherworldly experiences, and if you decide to do that, choose a spiritual leader who is familiar with this phenomenon. It is important to mention that when daughters have these mystical encounters, they seek more of them. Remember that the numinous world is not always accessible.

More on Hallucinations

Bereavement hallucinations, as they are called, are quite common, although the term *afterlife communications* is more well known. These experiences are usually described as occurring during sleep and when we dream. In one study, the authors included other

---

43. Grof, "Psychology for the Future," 6.
44. Grof, "Psychology for the Future," 6.
45. Romanyshyn, "Robert Romanyshysn."

ways of knowing that loved ones were present through "sensory modalities of touch, sight, hearing, smell, and sense of presence that externalized the phenomenon," adding that "they were typically regarded by the participant as deeply meaningful and comforting."[46] I also take issue with the word *hallucination* because it is automatically discrediting. My experiences of visions, auditory dialogue, and dreams defy real-time definitions, and the women I spoke with who experienced visions confirm that I was not alone. Consider all the saints who experienced revelations, including my favorite: St. Joan of Arc. Were they all hallucinating?

Dr. Julie Beischel, the director of the Windbridge Research Center, has been studying after-death communications for decades and is an expert in the field. One of her articles caught my eye because her pioneering research verified that one-third of adults in the United States have had after-death contacts. She further explained that these reported incidents are "mostly consistent across genders, ethnicities, education levels, incomes and religious or non-religious affiliations."[47] Her work legitimizes and validates that they occur. I hope that her research is read by mental health practitioners who may not understand the frequency of these manifestations and, more importantly, the healing aspects they provide.

Indigenous Practices

Indigenous cultures know the value of consulting shamans, curanderos, and healers in their communities because they are trusted and looked upon with great respect. The appropriation of

---

46. Elsaesser et al., "The Phenomenology and Impact of Hallucinations Concerning the Deceased."
47. Beischel, "Spontaneous, Facilitated, Assisted, and Requested After-Death Communication Experiences and Their Impact on Grief," 1–32.

these sacred practices is unfortunate, and it speaks to the desire and need for non-Indigenous peoples to receive knowledge and guidance that addresses their soul yearnings and their interest in receiving spiritual medicine. This thirst reflects the dissatisfaction that many people experience with the current health care system. They are seeking other ways for wellness that mainstream medicine may not understand.

Although they may be appealing, short-term trainings in spiritual medicine practices that promise to award the participant with the title of "healer," "shamanic healer," or a variation of that theme are disingenuous. The ancient systems of medicine that are passed down for generations cannot be mastered in a weekend. True Indigenous healers understand that knowledge is acquired through years of experience, and the oral tradition of imparting this wisdom is not just given to anyone who seeks it. It is a lifelong commitment. Author Tom Cowan states,

> only with extreme care and sensitivity to the spiritual integrity of native people do we dare to adapt their spiritual traditions.... Doing so requires training and permission from the elders.... Any attempt to lift those customs out of the cultural and theological matrix that makes them sacred would be an act of desecration.[48]

This is true for all Indigenous medicine practices.

Shamanic Journeys

Shamanic journeying is a beautiful practice and enables the shaman and client to interact with their ancestors, discover their animal

---

48. Cowan, *Shamanism as a Spiritual Practice for Daily Life*, 14–15.

spirit, and obtain potent energetic healing through soul retrievals. Shamans understand that death is part of a continuum of life, and the shamanic journey offers opportunities to connect with those who have passed, and healers often receive messages. These journeys are profound and honoring of the dead. Soul loss occurs when there are misplaced or lost energies that leave the physical or emotional body because of physical or emotional loss, trauma, shock, or anger. Returning these energies or soul fragments to the body can assist in healing all aspects of the body—mind, body, and spirit. When soul fragments are returned, the client feels better because those missing pieces of themselves are restored.

My dear friend Jyoti SaeUn, who was a healer and the creator of Clearing Clouds, believed that

> your body's wisdom reflects imbalance and attempts to communicate through emotional, physical, and mental pain or a sense of spiritual disconnection. The SaeUn method of clearing and balancing the bioenergy field aligns with the body-mind for access and gentle release of unresolved feelings or energetic interferences from the past.[49]

She discovered the concept of soul fragments in her professional energy practice, and when she taught or worked with clients, the intentional gathering of these energies was incorporated to raise the bodies' vibrations.

---

49. *The SaeUn Method*, 24. Jyoti SaeUn, the creator of the SaeUn Method, or Clearing Clouds, was an amazing healer and friend. She taught me her method of healing, and for that I will always be grateful. Permission to use text from her unpublished book was granted by her daughter, Lisa Haney.

> As the soul fragments integrate, they can increase frequency, and deeper more subtle levels may come to the surface for clearing. The Body is increasingly uncomfortable with separation in all its guises and leads us elegantly back to wholeness as we listen and respond to its messages.[50]

Animals who share their protection and powers play an important role in the shamanic tradition of journeying, and this is an integral part of authentic shamanic practices. If you are interested in a shamanic healing session, seek out someone who is well trained and talk to them about their philosophies before you schedule an appointment, and ask for referrals from someone you trust. As in any profession, there are exemplary practitioners. Avoid anyone who tells you that "only they" can help you and charges exorbitant fees. This is a manipulation. Esoteric philosopher Rudolph Steiner believed that the natural laws of the universe would not allow any esoteric knowledge to be imparted to anyone who was not qualified to receive it. That may indeed be true; however, there are psychics, mediums, and other healers who may have knowledge but seize the opportunity to take advantage of their bereaved clients, and when you are grieving, you are especially vulnerable.

Vision Quests

You may be familiar with the concept of the vision quest, or a journey to the spirits and ancestors to obtain advice, spiritual wisdom, strength, and insights. In some Native American traditions, vision quests take place away from one's home and usually in nature and can last for a day or longer. Prayer is a fundamental requirement for engaging in a vision quest, and often fasting, bathing, and placing

---

50. *The SaeUn Method*, 14.

yourself in an environment away from your daily life is necessary. Black Elk, the well-known Sioux holy man, spoke about the idea of "crying for a vision" in the spirit of lamentation. "The most important reason for 'lamenting' is that it helps us to realize our oneness with all things, to know that all things are our relatives."[51] When we are grieving, we *are* lamenting and want to reach not only Spirit helpers but particular Spirit helpers—our mothers. I believe that our sorrow is the conduit for this connection, although I have been told by healers in the past that my emotional pain would prevent my mother from communicating with me. This idea is false. I have trouble believing my mother would refuse to be in connection with me because I was sad. That never made any sense to me. Why would my biggest ally, who I adored, stop that bond of love? I know she would not want me to suffer, and if she could help alleviate my pain in life, would she not do the same even in death?

Vision quests should not be undertaken without the guidance of an authentic healer who understands the rigors of this journey. It is important to respect their teachings. It is not appropriate to try to conduct a vision quest without a guide. Without their direction, you will not have the proper understanding of what is required. You do not have to undergo a vision quest for days on end. Most of us are not prepared to do that, nor do we have the proper education and guidance from an elder who knows the process. However, I believe that we do have the capacity for a vision of our mothers through intention. We can amplify that intention through meditation by setting aside a time that is dedicated to making that connection with her. You may want to invoke an intention during meditation that you are open to receiving her in whatever way she decides is right. She may choose to connect with you through your

---

51. Brown, *The Sacred Pipe*, 84–86.

dreams, give you a sign, or send wisdom to you through your inner knowing. During your meditation, you may receive an image, a word, or even a message. I suggest that you record your experiences in a journal so you can reread the information over time. Refrain from asking other people what your experiences mean, because only you can ascertain what these images, words, or messages signify. It is wise when conducting any type of vision questing that you do it when you are feeling strong and at ease. This process is sacred, and when we are upset or emotionally distressed, we do not see or experience things clearly. You may find the following exercise helpful as a conduit for making connection with your mother. I have found that this exercise is valuable when you are yearning to align yourself with her.

Exercise
Mother Connection

This exercise not only offers relaxation and calm but also opportunities to connect with your mother using visualization and breath work. The benefits of this inner peace are enormous, especially when you are feeling overwhelmed and anxious.

Purification ideas: Lighting a candle and burning or spraying sacred herbs as purification can assist you during this meditation and other inner work you are doing. Herbs used for smoke cleansing include sage and palo santo, and if you do use these herbs, purchase only ethically harvested products from a Native American retailer. Smudging is a Native American tradition used for ceremony, and if you are not Native American, it is inappropriate to replicate ceremonies that you are not privy to or do not understand. Smoke cleansing can be quite effective in removing negative energies. I am not suggesting that sadness is "negative"; however, when you cleanse with herbs and smoke, their properties can help you feel more positive.

Preparation: Before you begin, ask for protection from your guiding spirits that reside only in the light and surround yourself with benevolent energies. When we are in anguish, it is easy for other types of energy to make themselves known because we are vulnerable. I want to make sure that you are protected.

1. **Choose your space.** Make sure you choose a space either inside your home or outside in nature where you will not be disturbed. Allow yourself to relax and focus on your breath for ten to fifteen minutes. You may want to place your hand on your heart. It can also be helpful to lay your hands on your stomach to form a V and breathe into your hands. This will help you relax and reduce or eliminate any feelings of fear during your breath work. Continue to breathe and visualize the comfort of peaceful energies circulating throughout your body. If you are still feeling anxious or fearful, you can repeat the breath work and revisit the exercise when you are feeling more emotionally balanced.
2. **Set intention.** You may use this exercise as a tool to connect with your mother, and regardless of the outcome, know that you are empowering yourself spiritually, physically, and emotionally. Of course your intention is to communicate with your mother, but remember that she is also part of this

experience, and she can choose when she wants or how she wishes to appear to you.

3. **Record your intention or memorize what you wish to say.** It is helpful to record your intention out loud so when you are in meditation, you don't have to open and close your eyes to read what you wrote on a piece of paper. You can play back this recording as a guide. If you are conducting this exercise with another daughter, you can also take turns reading each other's intention and later share what you've experienced.

Suggested Intention Narrative

The following is only a suggestion. Feel free to edit or change any of the wording or create your own. Only you can decide what feels right to you and what you want to say to your mother.

> *I want to connect with my mother, and I am surrounding myself with only divine energies, and I ask to be protected. I am asking my mother to come to me in a sign, word, or symbol that I will recognize according to what she feels is best for me right now. I know that we can continue to make this connection because of our eternal bond. I trust that she will reveal to me only the highest and best information for my own healing. I am grateful.*

4. **Document your experience.** Before you document the information that you received, take some time to reflect on the meditation, and when you

are ready, write it down so this knowledge won't be forgotten. Write down what you experienced, whether you heard a voice, saw an image, or received any other key information. It's easy to forget when you are deep in meditation, so this is a helpful tool. In addition, keeping a record of your meditation may also reveal further insights when they are looked at after a significant time period—perhaps six months or a year. Sometimes, partial messages appear across several meditations, and reading the results over time may offer you insights that a singular meditation did not.

Conclusions: At the end of this exercise, you may experience feelings of tranquility. Some women have told me they received direct messages as well as images of their mother's face, which gave them an enormous sense of peace. Everyone will experience this exercise differently.

Gifts from meditation: The insights you experience during your meditation are gifts and should be treated as such. You may be guided to action—perhaps to make a call to someone you have not thought about for a long time—or receive reassurance. The symbols or words or messages you receive may not be clear to you immediately and drawing these images can help. Artmaking takes us out of our rational mind, allowing our subconscious to speak with us, and we often depict feelings and ideas that we cannot articulate. Resist the urge to analyze what you experienced and just be present.

During one of my visions, I saw a woman's face. She held her hand over her lips, illustrating that I was not to reveal any information I received to anyone, and I never have. Pay attention and release any expectations of how you think your visions should arrive. Accept what it is. If you have regular meditative practices, you can include your intentions during this time.

In the beautiful book *The Spirit of Indian Women*, I found a passage I consider particularly poignant that explains in detail that the spirits appearing to a child during a vision quest are lifelong companions.

> The spirits … in the form of an animal or an object … spoke about how the spirit would help him or her in future life, especially … in times of distress. It sang its spiritual song for the child to memorize and use when calling upon the spirit guardian as an adult.[52]

I love the fact that the spirit guardians the book describes can accompany us throughout our lives. I am sure that my mother was and continues to be my spirit guardian. She has always been my protector and guide, and that will always remain. She is my medicine. My mother may not physically inhabit my world, but that does not mean that in death she cannot accompany me in mine. We are partners in spirit and in life.

A Word About Psychics and Mediums—with Apologies

Often daughters seek out psychics or mediums to obtain information about their mothers. I certainly did. I am not against that quest, but be cautious of whom you consult. I have had many positive

---

52. Fitzgerald and Fitzgerald, *The Spirit of Indian Women*, 117.

experiences over the years with psychics and mediums, but I have also had distressing experiences. Communicating with the higher realms is sacred; make sure the person you are working with is recommended by someone you respect. Please avoid anyone who guarantees a particular outcome.

Another important consideration is that psychic or mediumship readings can be addictive, especially if you believe that the medium or psychic you are consulting is the only one who can make connection with your mother. That belief is dangerous because it gives your power to someone else. You are the best judge of the information you receive. Does it resonate with you? Did you feel better after the reading? Did the psychic or medium urge you to have a series of sessions? That is always concerning. Trust your judgment. If you do schedule a reading, wait until you feel emotionally strong.

* * *

The next chapter offers practical tools for making connections with your mother through dreams and includes a short history of the prevalence of dream temples dedicated to Asclepius, who was considered the father of medicine during ancient times. The chapter also includes tools that you can utilize for your personal dreamwork.

Chapter Five
Sacred Connections
Dream Healing

After my father passed away, I had the opportunity to teach a course in dream healing at Pacifica, a Jungian graduate school. The opportunity came at a perfect time because I needed to find my academic footing again. Teaching the course was a significant healing experience for me. The location of the school was gorgeous, and after I taught my all-day class, I spent a lot of time walking around the campus and sitting by the waterfalls. It was so peaceful! The topic of dream healing was inspirational for me and fascinating. I share some of my work in this chapter, as well as that of other experts in the field of dream healing.

In her book *Bereavement Dreaming and the Individuating Soul*, Jungian therapist Geri Grubbs wrote:

> The need to connect with the dead, especially following the loss of a loved one, is innate. It has been with us since time immemorial, despite modern attempts to suppress it. What people instinctively sense about the dead transcends anything doubting skeptics or logically minded thinkers may assert.[53]

---

53. Grubbs, *Bereavement Dreaming and the Individuating Soul*, 1.

After mother loss, daughters have a deep yearning for that connection, and dreams can be the perfect medicine. When I had the good fortune to teach the course Ancient Ways of Healing, it gave me the opportunity to delve deeply into the process and history of dream healing. This immersion provided much-needed grounding for me because I was still quite traumatized from the deaths of my parents. The prospect of teaching again helped me regain my confidence. The students enrolled in this course were eager to participate. They were smart, open-minded, and willing to share their dream experiences with me. During the semester, I was struck by the fact that most of them spoke about not only dreaming of their ancestors but receiving messages from them. Their comments were inspiring.

Throughout the class, we explored the phenomenon of Asklepion healing temples. You may be familiar with the caduceus symbol embroidered on physicians' coats, depicting two snakes on a staff. However, this was not the actual symbol of Asclepius. He was half man and half god, and his staff was called the rod of Asclepius and only had one snake. Symbolically, snakes have great powers for healing (and for causing death), and it is fitting that this representation for medical care illustrates those powers. Asclepius is often compared to Jesus because of his ability to heal and to raise the dead. Shamanically speaking, the snake is a powerful figure and can be a symbol of protection and guardianship and indicates a transformative process.

Shape-Shifting Through Grief

Transformation is one of the elements contained in Asklepion healings—a transformation that occurs when the patient changes from *who they were* to *who they can be*. This is an apt metaphor for the grief process, an unfamiliar journey that frequently offers unexpected surprises. We cannot achieve this shift without walking in the dark with a willingness to accept *what is* as we shape-shift into a different identity—a person who knows some of the secrets of death. We learn these mysteries when we accompany those we love during their end of life. If you are familiar with yoga, you will understand the concept of kundalini, an energetic system that, once aroused, leads us to enlightenment. These energies are sometimes referred to as serpent power. Our grief can initiate us into new energetic shifts and alter our consciousness.

Short History of Asklepion Healing Temples

I love Asclepius (and his daughters), and considering the proliferation of healing temples in ancient Greece dedicated to Asclepius, I am not alone. Remains of the temples built in his honor, which date back to 350 BCE, can still be found. These temples were sacred places of healing and were the prototype of what we would now consider holistic medicine. Pilgrims would journey to these temples in the hopes that they would receive a healing dream from Asclepius that would be instructive for their physical or emotional challenges. The temples were located near freshwater springs because it was believed that immersion in these waters would help to remove any emotional and physical obstructions that would hinder one's healing process. Devotees had great faith in divine healing, or they would never have been able to attempt the often-perilous journey to reach the temples and were usually desperate. Those who could not make the journey often sent proxies who would dream in their place.

Healing Rituals

Patients would participate in various stages of preparation before they were allowed to enter the temples and had to undergo various purification rituals. These therapeutic modalities included bathing, eating healthy foods, singing, dancing, and listening to music. Rituals of prayer were held each night during the "hours of the sacred lamps."[54] The sleep trance the pilgrims experienced was called "enkoimesis," or sleep induction, and opioids were often used to help induce sleep.[55] According to the narratives inscribed on tablets found near the sites, poppy flowers were frequently used. There are also descriptions of the removal of tumors from pilgrims, which we would identify today as psychic surgery.

The Asclepiads, or the priests and priestesses inside the temples, were especially trained to decipher the dream messages the pilgrims received. They were not allowed to serve in the temples until they had studied extensively and were knowledgeable about the energetic systems of the body. In fact, many of the prescriptions they offered mirror integrative medicine protocols, including the use of herbs, fasting, plant-based medicines, and other natural remedies. I would imagine they were also compassionate and knew how to listen without judgment, much like contemporary therapists today. As Mary Ellen O'Hare-Lavin wrote:

> The etymology of the word "clinic" comes from the Greek word *kline* (pronounced cli nay) which means couch or bed, the place where dreams take place.... The Asklepion healers relied on beds and couches for dreams in the healing process.[56]

---

54. Personal curriculum notes, "Pacifica Dream Healing Course," 2010.
55. Askitopoulou, "Sleep and Dreams."
56. O'Hare-Lavin, "The Practice of Dream Healing," 8.

Who Was Asclepius?

Depending on what sources you consult, the genealogy of Asclepius often credits him with being a gifted mortal physician who later passed into legend as a healing god. When he was an adult, he was punished to death by Zeus for raising the dead. His father was Apollo, the sun god, and his mother was Koronis, a mortal princess of Thessaly. While she was pregnant with Asclepius, she had a liaison with Ischys, who was also from divine lineage, and her indiscretion caused both of their deaths. Angered by her infidelity, Apollo commanded Artemis, the goddess of the hunt, to kill Koronis. As Koronis lay on what would soon be her funeral pyre, Apollo had a change of heart and attempted to save her from the flames at the last minute, but it was too late. He removed his son from her body and named him Asclepius, which literally means "to cut open."[57] Riddled with guilt, he gave his badly burned son to Chiron, a teacher and physician who lived in the underworld. Chiron was knowledgeable about physical misery because he was fated to spend his life in pain after being wounded by a poison arrow. The Greek word *traumais* means "a wound," and both Asclepius and Chiron were physically and psychically traumatized; however, their wounds gave them the gift of understanding what suffering entails.[58]

Wounded Healers

The strength of the wounded healer lies in the dismemberment of the psyche (and often physical challenges), which is destroyed to create something new and beautiful. The Portuguese word *medalha* signifies this disintegration and can mean both medal

---

57. Atsma, "Asklepios."
58. Online Etymology Dictionary, "trauma (n.)," retrieved November 9, 2024, https://www.etymonline.com/word/trauma.

(of honor) or bruising.[59] This bruise cannot be removed entirely and is omnipresent; however, you can learn to live with it. Chiron taught Asclepius how to feel, acknowledge, and receive greater consciousness because of his wound, not despite it. When we embrace our emotional injuries and align with their teachings, we can live in greater peace. Further pain occurs when we refuse to acknowledge our struggles and fight to return to who we once were. This is not possible because we are not the same. Accepting this inevitability is difficult; however, wounding is not without its rewards. It teaches us the lesson of compassion—not only for others but for ourselves.

Asclepius's story may appeal to you because his strength, like yours, originates from emotional damage. The psychological complexity that is required when taking care of mothers can cause additional wounds, and those scars do not go away, but they do dull in time. Anyone who has taken care of a mother knows how difficult this can be. These daughters are also healers because of their love, dedication, compassion, and patience. There is a reciprocity that occurs in this exchange between mother and daughter that I did not realize could take place during the caregiving relationship. I took care of my mother for many years, but during that time, she also took care of me. We were very close before she became ill, but through the years, my devotion to her was ignited. Decades ago, I was told by an astrologer that the most important lessons I would learn in my life could arrive through my understanding of and experiences with death. I never understood that message until much later in my life. You may have had a similar experience. Do you relate to the concept of the wounded healer? Have you always

---

59. Balch, "'As with a Poem, Each Patient Is Unique.'"

felt that healing others was part of your journey? Do you have a call to heal?

Asclepius's Daughters

Scholars differ on who wrote the original Hippocratic oath, which was penned during the fifth or third century BC, depending on what source you consult. The oath not only swears alliance to Asclepius but includes allegiance to two of his daughters, Hygeia and Panacea. The inclusion of Asclepius's daughters in the original Hippocratic oath is important because women (even female goddesses) did not always get their due, and both mythological women offered wisdom that is still beneficial centuries later. According to several sources, the Greek word *hygeia* means good health, well-being, and wholeness, which makes sense since optimum health is the balance of mind, body, and spirit. According to author Elizabeth Brooke, Hygeia was known as "the glorious" or "the light of day" and had a cult of her own, and many homes included a shrine dedicated to her.[60] Although she invokes images of hygiene and cleanliness, she is much more. She offers clarity and discernment, which are essential ingredients for balance. When you invite her into your life, as her followers did, she can help you access the clutter in your life—clutter that can be literal or psychological. Hygeia's wisdom can begin with a simple question: "What or whom can you remove from your life that would bring you solace?" The actual act of cleaning your house of clutter is also useful and can occur in small stages. Cleaning out room by room is a good start to this process.

Her sister Panacea brought universal prescriptions to those who summoned her. Her formulas included herbal medicines and

---

60. Brooke, *Medicine Women*, 97.

medicinal salves that could cure any health problem. Panacea is a steadfast ally if you allow her healing powers to touch you during your healing journey. Ask her, "What remedy do I need right now?" Sometimes a universal remedy can be found by reviewing your past. What did you or do you find helpful during times of stress? How did you heal yourself? Would that solution work now? You can also call on these goddesses during your dreamtime or through meditation. If you do, ask for their guidance, and expect an answer.

Dream Healing

All cultures invoke dreams as a healing form. Shamanic journeying is a form of this dream process, although it happens in real time. The term *dream walker* from Native American beliefs respects that dreams are powerful and during your dreams you have the ability to go anywhere and speak to anyone, especially the elders. The images in your dreams may be archetypal, such as the magician, father, mother, priestess, or guardian, or they may take their form as angels, power animals, or other helpers. Because we are in a different state of consciousness when we dream, there are no restrictions on whom or what we can contact. The limitations of our daily life have been lifted. This gives us opportunities to exchange information and receive messages.

One of the benefits of practicing dream healing is that it offers you opportunities to discover your own dream guidance as part of your self-care. Taking care of others while ignoring your own needs is not a badge of honor. This can perpetuate a loss of self because you are not paying attention to what you need, and that information may not be conscious. Although there may be a part of us that honors the truths revealed from our dreams, there may be another voice that doubts the authenticity of those revelations. Remember that the process of dream healing is a practice in trust. Trust that you will receive the dream you ask for and trust you will remember. There are many ways to dream, and you can decide what method works best for you. It will take patience, but you can remember your dreams through practice and intention. You can also invoke a Dream Guide to assist you, and in part 3, you will be guided to "how" you can do this.

Retired psychologist Gary Seeman has written at length about dreamwork and has categorized dreams. Guiding, repetitive, archetypal, lucid, and predictive dreams may occur, as well as nightmares.[61] It is important not to dismiss any of the images you see or messages you receive because they all have meaning for you.

- *Guiding (or guidance) dreams* can connect the dreamer to a person or experience that can help them transform their lives.
- *Repetitive dreams* repeat themselves in an effort to get the dreamer's attention.
- *Archetypal dreams* often include images of deities, symbols, and metaphysical images.
- *Lucid dreams* occur when you interact with the dream because you are not completely asleep.
- *Predictive dreams* can also be paranormal and predict life events for the dreamer or those close to them. Not all predictive or paranormal dreams are about death. In fact, these dreams can give you a sense of a positive future through a new job, a new home, new friends, etc.
- *Nightmares* are not necessarily bad omens as many people may think. Although they may be unpleasant or even upsetting, they have the ability to awaken the dreamer to situations that are not being addressed and need to be.

---

61. Seeman, "The Transformative Power of Dreams," 2–3.

A Word on Dream Diaries

You may want to keep a dream diary to record your dreams every night. It doesn't matter if you can't write down the complete dream because you don't remember it all. Even fragments that stay with you in the morning or during the day can be helpful. I like to think of my dream diary as a psychological tool I can use to check for self-reflection. Often, I have discovered by reading my dream recordings that I needed to pay attention to some area of my life that I was dismissing. A dream diary can be a potent teacher and guide. Keeping a dream diary is quite beneficial because the symbols you encounter may not reveal themselves to you immediately. You are the best person to decode what your dreams mean, and please avoid at all costs the dream definitions that are written in books or those you find online.

Dialogue with Your Dreams

I have found that some of the most revelatory information from a potent dream can be found when you dialogue with the images that appeared to you. This exercise is often used by therapists because it is so beneficial. Ask questions, including "Who are they?" "Do I recognize the symbols?" "What do they want to tell me?" I have found that drawing the images helps a great deal because I have a concrete depiction of what I saw and I can have a conversation with these illustrations. You can also re-create the images in your mind's eye as well. Dialogue and wordplay can be fascinating. When you ask your questions, consider that these symbols are real and can speak to you if you give them a voice.

When I dream of my mother, it is bittersweet. I am so happy that she has appeared to me, but I am sad I cannot touch her directly. I always want more connection with her. In one profound dream she told me that after you die, "you get to keep your heart." She also thanked me for helping her to "get rid of the pain." These dreams did not feel like dreams but a tangible connection. I felt her energy. I felt her love.

Dream Sticks

I was introduced to the concept of "dream sticks" at a conference I attended many years ago. The instructor told me that the creation of a dream stick can help access the dreamworld. I was skeptical at first, but I found that when I placed my dream stick next to my bed before sleep and included my intentions (guidance, protection, cultivating peace of mind, or clarity), it was enormously helpful. In the following exercise, I will describe the steps needed to create your own. Although I formed my dream stick from a piece of wood I found while walking in a nearby park, you can choose any particular object that you prefer.

Exercise
Creating a Dream Stick

The first step when making a dream stick is to find an artifact that resonates with you. You may find an object from your belongings or, even better, from your mother's. It may be a piece of wood, a crystal wand, or a ceramic stick. The second step is to choose colored thread of any color or many colors. Wrap the thread around your dream stick. I was told that the thread is important because it makes a pathway for those in the nonphysical world to reach us. You can also use ribbon, velvet, or embroidery thread if you like. A dream stick that I keep by my bed is wrapped with ribbon from a gift she gave me for my birthday.

You can create more than one dream stick to use, and if your dream stick appears in your dream, record those images in your diary. Although dream sticks are a potent tool to help you access the nonphysical world, I believe that setting your intention for connection with your mother before you sleep will not be ignored regardless of whether you choose to use one. Any dream healing ritual or artifact that you decide to use will be of assistance.

* * *

I have dreamt of Mother Mary many times, especially when I was in psychological pain. She is the ultimate goddess figure and the personification of the mother image. In the next chapter, I discuss her importance to me and share interviews with women I met who told me about the gifts that she brought into their lives.

Chapter Six
The Ultimate Mother
Mother Mary

I choose to include a chapter on Mother Mary because she is the ultimate mother symbol whether you recognize her by her Christian name or not.[62] I wanted to document how she helped me through the years and share her spiritual and historical significance. She has always intrigued me.

Mother Mary has led me on my spiritual path, and this is a fact that I find rather astonishing considering that I didn't know very much about her growing up. However, I experienced a strong connection with her early in my life. When I was a little girl, I asked my mother to take me to Holy Land in Waterbury, Connecticut, a huge outdoor pantheon of enormous religious structures that re-created sacred Christian sites. It was not a request that you would expect from a child, but she agreed. During the visit, I wandered off. As I walked through the site, I felt as if there was a presence with me, but I was unable to articulate it at that time. I believe Mother Mary has been with me since that day, and I was simply not aware of her until decades later.

---

62. I am using the term Mother Mary; however, she is also referred to as the Virgin Mary.

Meeting Mother Mary

Through the years, although I saw her image countless times, I never really paid much attention until early one morning when I was teaching a class for a college in the Bay Area. I tried to muster as much energy as I could at eight in the morning, and the steam heaters did not help. I opened the windows to let some air in, to feel the cold air rush through my nostrils and lungs to help me wake up. After the class ended, I paused in the second floor stairwell across from the classroom, and there she was! I literally was face-to-face with Mother Mary appearing in the form of a five-foot-tall life-size statue of pink marble. The look on her face was serene, and she was completely at peace, but it was not her expression that I was interested in—it was her hands. They were beautiful. Intuitively, I placed my hands on her long fingers and stood in silence for a long time. Students wove around me on their way to their classes, but I could not move out of their way. I was drawn in and hypnotized by her. It was a memorable encounter.

Mother Mary is the ultimate archetype of healing for women of all faiths because she is the Great Mother regardless of how she appears—Our Lady of Guadalupe, Black Madonna, Kwan Yin, Sophia, Mother Nature, Mother Earth, or White Buffalo Calf Woman. She offers healing and a listening ear to all women, whether they are spiritual, agnostic, or religious. As one woman told me, "She accepts you, loves you, and comforts you. She is the Eternal Mother. She brings comfort in her energetic embrace." As my fascination with the myriad faces of Mary gained momentum, I discovered that she was a calming presence for me because she is the embodiment of compassion, offering well-being and healing. Wherever I found her, I always felt that she was listening to me. Her pillar of support helped me not only through my mother's illness but after her passing. She is mother to everyone regardless of what their financial, spiritual, or cultural background may be.

Looking for Mother Mary

Fascinated by her different manifestations depicting various ages and a variety of skin tones, I began to visit churches in the Bay Area to see her, and soon those pilgrimages expanded to other areas of California. I have amassed a huge collection of photographs that I took of her image in paintings, statues, and drawings that are incredibly beautiful. As my interest grew, I wanted to know more and continued my quest. I was particularly interested in the apparitions and healings attributed to her because I was in need of healing. It seemed as if the universe supported my quest because I received unsolicited calendars and articles on Mother Mary in the mail at the same time. One afternoon, I visited Grace Cathedral in San Francisco and was drawn to a small statue of Mother Mary. The statue was not a complete head-to-toe statue, the kind usually seen in churches, but a small image of her head carved in stone. I looked at her for a long time while I rested on a prayer kneeler in front of her. Telepathically, I heard a voice revealing that I would write a book about her. I am ashamed to admit it, but I laughed and replied out loud, "You have the wrong gal." I thought it was some type of divine joke because who else but a whimsical Mary would send me all over the map to meet her, a woman I hardly knew. In time, I would begin to know her well, at least from my limited perspective. She was correct. Years later I completed graduate school and published my doctoral thesis on the spiritual choreography of Isadora Duncan, Ruth St. Denis, and Martha Graham, icons of dance and feminists who all created dances in her honor.

Whenever I had the opportunity to travel, I would visit churches, shrines, and gardens. I read scholarly articles, purchased books, and talked to religious clerics. I found out I was in good company when I learned that Marilyn Monroe was also her fan and visited the Ave Maria Grotto, a Marian shrine located at the St. Bernard Abbey in Alabama, and signed the guest book. When I told my friend Sister Madeline, she replied, "She is our mother. Grace-infusing and knows our troubles and sorrows." And certainly Marilyn had her share of troubles. If you decide to seek Mother Mary out, you are led on a spiritual journey. I do not know if it is faith, belief, a mystical encounter, or wish fulfillment, but in my experiences, she is real. I believe that unless you have had personal experience with her, she remains unknown and a historical figure without any resonance.

California Encounters

I was intrigued when a stranger at a church I was visiting urged me to visit an outdoor shrine in Watsonville, California. She told me that Mother Mary's image mysteriously appeared in a tree trunk at Pinto Lake County Park. I was excited to see for myself, and when I arrived, a young woman walked with me from the parking lot to the sacred spot where other visitors had placed religious candles, rosaries, and photographs of their loved ones on the tree. She explained that the image was Our Lady of Guadalupe, the venerated icon in Mexico City, and told me that "only those who had faith would be able to see it." I did see her, and honestly, I expected that everyone could.

Palo Alto Shrine

Through word of mouth, I was led to an ad hoc shrine in the basement of a house in Palo Alto, California, created by a group of women from various religious and spiritual backgrounds. They met each month to write poems, create art, and discuss Mother Mary's influence on their lives. I asked one woman why she attended the meetings, and she told me, "She listens to what you need and reminds you to be kind to yourself. When you ask for her mothering, she is available." At the time, I didn't realize how important that message would be for me. Now, I know that a mother's love for her daughter is eternal and timeless, and nothing can interfere with this flow of love. Mother Mary reminded me of that love, and the need to mother myself.

Mission Dolores
One of the most beautiful images of the Virgin Mary I have ever seen was inside the Mission San Francisco de Asís church, built in 1776, often referred to as Mission Dolores. Her image fills an entire wall, and the first time I saw her, I was captivated and lost in her image because when you look into her eyes, she looks right back. Her depiction is created from hundreds of mosaic tiles, and I watched the light rays that radiated from her hands dance in front of me. She was glorious. I visited this church often because I always sensed that she was with me, although I cannot really explain this feeling with words. I discovered that when I meditated on her hands and focused my attention only on her light, I felt calmer and grounded inside of my body. This image of Mother Mary reminded me of the goddess, who manifests her healing gifts to those in need. She certainly helped me. I have always wondered if Mother Mary was able to conduct healing through the laying on of hands when she was alive. Is it possible that she taught Jesus how to heal? Although I have not found documentation that she utilized the

concept of "laying on of hands" directly for healing, St. Bernadine of Sienna, a Franciscan, wrote:

> All gifts, virtues, and graces of the Holy Ghost are administered by the hands of Mary to whomsoever she desires, when she desires, and in the manner she desires, and to whatever degree she desires.[63]

This certainly applies to her healing prowess.

Energy Medicine

The concept of laying on of hands is found in many religions. Depending on the religious affiliation, it is practiced differently, but it is always a spiritual act. I remember that when I was studying Reiki, one of my teachers told me this form of energetic medicine is a centuries-old tradition that originated with Jesus, who healed the sick with and without his hands. Reiki practitioners seek to help their clients restore balance and regain optimum functioning through the reception of universal energies that are energies of love. Some critics mistakenly claim it is to be avoided because it is part of the occult, implying that it is not an honorable practice. Before anyone can offer Reiki to others, they must obtain certification from qualified master practitioners to earn different degrees of proficiency during immersive training programs for each level of prowess. I studied with a wonderful teacher for several years who challenged me, before I earned my Reiki master designation.

---

63. "Did Mary lay her hands on all the Apostles in the Upper Room to pour out the Holy Spirit anointing?"

Thornton, California

When I lived in the Bay Area, I found out about a statue of Mother Mary in the small town of Thornton, where it was reported that the statue not only cried but moved. There was an investigation by the Church authorities. They did not deem these occurrences miracles, but that did not deter an influx of visitors, including me. When I traveled to the church, what seemed miraculous to me was not the statue (although she was beautiful) but the fact that I watched a woman crawl on her knees from the back of the church with a look of devotion that I had never before seen or experienced. I thought I was time-shifting into another century. I never spoke with her, since I thought it would be dishonoring, but I always marveled that she didn't notice my presence. You do not have to be a Catholic to believe in Mary, and for me, she is the healing mother, the one who understands, who can listen and help to ease internal chaos.

Although the numerous churches I visited were beautiful, I was interested in *why* women sought her out and what they gained from their interactions. At that time, I was hoping their faith would rub off on me. Based on many conversations I have had over the years, it was clear that Mother Mary speaks a common language—a language of protection and love, and I wanted to experience the same.

Oldest Marian Shrine in America

When I moved to Florida, my parents drove me to St. Augustine to visit the Shrine of Our Lady of La Leche, the oldest shrine dedicated to Mother Mary in the United States. After I interviewed the church leader, he directed me to the small chapel near the main church. Before I entered, I could hear the voices of women reciting the rosary, and their chants were melodic. I took a seat and listened quietly. When they were finished, I introduced myself as a journalist and hoped they would allow me to speak to them about their devotion. They agreed.

I asked them about Mother Mary's significance in their lives and what she offered them. One woman told me:

> She is the most perfect human that was ever on the earth. She will guide you, but most importantly you will find peace with her. We all have struggles in our lifetime. She helps you through prayer and trust. I could not count on a hundred hands how many times she has helped me. And sometimes you must be patient. Do not expect an answer the next day.

She told me that she would send me a rosary, and a few weeks later, I received it in the mail. I was surprised and quite touched. She insisted that if I was devoted to Mary I would "always have complete and total peace and that this peace was within me, always," adding, "Janet, you are going to be very powerful working with our Lady by your side." My mother was in the early stages of cancer. I knew I would need all the support I could get, and Mother Mary was the perfect companion to accompany me on a very turbulent journey.

Another member of the group jumped into the conversation and told me that after her first visit to this chapel, she cried for days believing that her tears washed her soul, and she felt healed. This is called the "gift of tears." We continued to talk for a long time, and I asked the group why they thought Mother Mary appeared so differently in the shrines I visited, appearing in all shapes, colors, and sizes. You can see that diversity in shrines where she appears with different hair colors, and her skin tone is variable, usually reflecting the images of the community. I was told "because she is mother to all, no matter what you look like, she is your Heavenly Mother. There is only One Lady. She is a woman who understands what you have been through."

After a few hours of discussions and questions, three women in the group showed me tokens of their adoration to Mary. An older woman with dancing blue eyes gave me her personal rosary ring, which was discolored from overuse and held her faith. I still have it. Another woman gave me her medal from her trip to Medjugorje, which she said was blessed by Mary, herself. A third woman removed the Our Lady of Guadalupe medal from her necklace and handed it to me. She told me she bought the medal when her son was born, who was unable to walk or speak, and she believed that "Our Lady brought him to me for a special reason." I was so moved that three women, perfect strangers, would offer their most cherished objects of devotion to me, someone they barely knew. They told me that I was now part of Mary's group, and although I didn't believe them, now I do.

Santa Fe Shrines

In Santa Fe, New Mexico, there is a beautiful church dedicated to Our Lady of Guadalupe that I have visited on numerous occasions, particularly when I needed emotional support. What is especially striking is the fact that her image is at the center of the church, defying the custom of having Jesus as the focal point. Outside the church is a beautiful and enormous statue of Our Lady, and it is common to find visitors praying regardless of the weather conditions. La Conquistadora, or Our Lady of Conquest, was brought to Santa Fe in 1625. She resides in the Cathedral Basilica of St. Francis of Assisi, one of the most popular churches in the area. Her name is also cited as Our Lady of Conquering Love for

All People, which speaks to why she is the ultimate embodiment of compassion for all.

Religious Connections with Mother Mary

The saints have written about Mother Mary, and I thought it was meaningful that St. Thérèse of Lisieux wrote about her after her mother died when she was quite young. She wrote,

> I remember that, when my mother died, I was fourteen years of age or a little less. When I began to realize what I had lost, I went in my distress to an image of Our Lady and with many tears entreated her to be a mother to me. I believe it helped me; I have been conscious of her aid; and eventually she has brought me back.[64]

And she was not alone. Hildegard de Bingen, abbess, composer, poet, medicine woman, and mystic, saw Mother Mary in one of her many visions during twelfth-century Germany and experienced the sacred vibrationally. She described what she saw:

> I listened as a voice said from the radiance: These are great secrets. Now, behold the crystal-clear radiance bathes the woman in light from the crown of her head to her throat. She therefore *blossomed to full strength*. This is indicated by the red light which glowed about the figure.[65]

It's so fascinating that Mary was seen in red light, because the colors most associated with her are blue and purple.

---

64. "Introduction to the Life of St. Teresa."
65. Benz et al., *Color Symbolism*, 90.

Psychologically, the color purple speaks to the "psychological unity with the mother," and what greater unity can there be than with the Mother of All?[66] I especially align with the image of blossoming to full strength, something I have not achieved yet but aspire toward. It is so interesting that this iconic mother has so much spiritual potency.

Many years ago, I had the opportunity to interview Father Jozo, the famous priest from Medjugorje who gained prominence when he supported the revelations from children in his community who insisted they were not only seeing the Virgin Mary but receiving messages from her daily. After he was convinced they were telling the truth, he was imprisoned and tortured by the secret police when he refused to back down and deny their visions. This site is sacred, and the village continues to be a popular destination for millions of pilgrims seeking spiritual experiences. The movie *Gospa*, based on Father Jozo's experiences, was later released starring Martin Sheen.

I met Father Jozo at a conference, and his charismatic presence was difficult to ignore coupled with his movie star good looks. I remember people following him around to touch his robe and reside in his orbit. We spoke through an interpreter, who I later discovered was one of the visionary children, now all grown up. When I asked him if he ever saw Mother Mary, he told me he had experienced many visions of her, which sustained him during his imprisonment. "She is much more beautiful than I can say.... That we do not know in our regular life cannot be described." We spoke about her different cultural depictions at length, and then he told me, "If she hadn't spoken Croatian to the children, then she would always be foreign. She is a mother and that is her greatness. She is

---

66. Fincher, *Creating Mandalas*, 63.

Mother of All."[67] I didn't share my visions with him, but it was as if he already knew. Months after we talked, I received a postcard in the mail that urged me to continue my spiritual quest. I never shared my address with anyone at the conference, so it was quite a surprise and comforting.

Ancient Goddess Worship

One of the reasons for Mother Mary's appeal is that she is the symbol for the goddess, regardless of how she is named. She is the manifestation of ancient goddess worship, and many scholars believe, as I do, that all of these ancient goddesses are indeed one woman: Mother Mary. She artfully changes form and age—adolescent, middle-aged, or matriarchal—and there are numerous names for her all over the world, including Our Lady of the Rosary, Our Lady of Perpetual Help, the Queen of the Universe, the Lady of La Leche, White Calf Buffalo Woman, Kwan Yin, and Sophia. I have seen statues of her in strange places—in an old garage, on top of gravestones, in gardens—and hidden in unexpected locations. Her image has been carved on walls and made from wood, metal, and bronze. Russian icons of the Virgin Mary are a revered art, and there's the belief that she is not "simply a representation…but is intended to actualize the Divine, to make visible and palpable as a living presence." Her magic is indicated when you consider that "when an icon was old and faded or broken, it was not thrown away or burned, but buried in the ground like a body."[68]

Women who flock to her are seeking an authentic form of worship that respects womanhood, and she is the ultimate icon for that

---

67. My interview with Father Jozo was later published in the *San Francisco Examiner*, 1996.
68. Schaup, *Sophia*, 119.

honoring. During the fourth century, the Collyridians worshipped her, recognizing her as the essence of the divine feminine. They ate cakes called collyrides and danced in her honor.[69] This idea that women would worship a woman was heretical, and they were condemned by the Church—most notably because they allowed women to become priestesses and chose a woman to celebrate. Epiphanius, the Bishop of Salamis in Cyprus, called their members "silly, weak, and contemptible" to discredit them, although the cult spread widely.[70] Sites that were previously dedicated to the goddess Diana or Ceres were now dedicated to the Virgin Mary, particularly after she was named "Mother of God" by the Church. This interchange between goddess images and the Virgin Mary "was a keen acknowledgment of the mystical and divine powers of the sacred feminine."[71] The Montanists were another ancient goddess sect that granted women previously unknown freedom and autonomy and believed that Jesus was a woman. Whether she is depicted as a goddess in stone images or as a Minoan goddess with a snake in her hands, it doesn't matter because she speaks the language of her followers and appears in a way that is familiar to each culture.

What is important is that she is available and can help ease suffering. The noted mystic St. Bernard of Clairvaux, a devoted follower of Mary, wrote the Memorare, a prayer in her honor to remind her followers that she will indeed answer prayers. One of the most memorable lines of the prayer is:

---

69. Roseman, *Dance Was Her Religion*, 20.
70. Roseman, *Dance Was Her Religion*, 21.
71. Roseman, *Dance Was Her Religion*, 24.

> Remember, O most gracious Virgin Mary, that never was it known that anyone who fled to your protection, implored your help, or sought your intercession, was left unaided.[72]

It is this promise that is universally appealing because her healing forces are fierce. No mention in this prayer is made of what religion one must follow, and her enduring face of love and acceptance is the key to popularity. Regardless of what you choose to call her, she knows your wounds from the inside like any compassionate mother would.

Mother Mary's Universal Appeal

She is mother to everyone, and during grief, she can be a calming presence. When I visit her, I always feel that she is listening, and I am not alone. My beautiful friend Christine Anastos, a cancer thriver and founder of Connect & Thrive, Inc. (CAT), an organization to empower women through their journey with cancer, shared her calling to Mother Mary with me.

> My mother and I felt a very strong connection to the Virgin Mary so much so that I had been calling my mother Mary since 2006 when she had her allogeneic transplant and was given the gift of a new immune system and life. I prayed to Virgin Mary every night to heal my mother. It was my faith in Virgin Mary, in particular, the mother of all mothers, that sustained me through my own mother's lengthy illness through her death and thereafter. As my mother lay dying,

---

72. "The Memorare."

she conjured up enough strength to tell me that she would live in my heart forever, and that she did.[73]

* * *

As you get ready to advance to part 2 of this book, I hope that you found the previous chapters revelatory and insightful and that the information contained in part 1 offered you some consolation. Part 2 of this book is a compendium of narratives about mother loss written by women of different ages and from different backgrounds. Their stories helped me, and I hope the same for you.

---

73. From personal correspondence with Christine Anastos.

Part Two
Healing Narratives

Narrative Medicine

The narratives in this section are healing stories because they articulate authentic journeys written by daughters who know what it is like to lose a mother. Although each essay chronicles a personal experience, collectively they contain universal elements not only of bereavement but of hope, recovery, and often discovery, regardless of the authors' backgrounds and spiritual and religious philosophies. I am honored these women have agreed to share their stories. Their words address the power of the eternal bond between mother and daughter. These stories are therapeutic to read and confirm that we are not alone in our suffering and rebirth.

All cultures respect the oral tradition of sharing stories and telling tales of suffering, resilience, and resurrection. Although the details of the stories may differ, they are powerful teachings because they validate that we are not alone in the human experience of living life and witnessing the death of those we love. As mere mortals, there is no escape from the beauty and tragedy of existence. Indigenous cultures recognize that storytelling is profound wisdom and often use talking circles that enable the participants to listen to and learn from the voices of the elders. Their voices are what we would term *narrative medicine*. So important is the oral tradition that narrative medicine is now being taught at many medical schools to not only help physicians young and old understand their patients' stories but also provide opportunities for them to share their heartbreaks and joys in doctoring. Dr. Lewis Mehl-Madrona's contribution to the use of narrative medicine is quite compelling, and I am a fan of his work. In one of his insightful books, he writes:

> We treat by telling a story.... The term *narrative medicine* arises from the impossibility of separating treatment from the stories told.... In the indigenous worldview... each person is the sum of all the stories that have ever been told.[74]

The metaphysical dimension of their narratives is profound medicine, providing comfort and spiritual validation. I wish that health care practitioners would take the time to listen to their patients' stories because they are of enormous clinical value. These accounts are inspiring because they do not negate the tragedy of losing our mothers. They offer revelatory examples of resilience and courage—necessary during the grief process. The most important component found in these stories is the power of love that continues to exist—whether a daughter has lost their mother last year or twenty years ago. I have no doubt that you will recognize yourself in their stories, as I did. May their words bring you peace.

---

74. Mehl-Madrona, *Narrative Medicine*, 6, 17.

Valerie Remembers Frances

A friend once described the relationship I had with my mother as "idyllic." We loved each other tremendously and had an extremely close relationship. In fact, we talked on the phone every day for as long as I can remember. There were days where we could talk on the phone three or four times if something big was going on for me. She would joke around and say something like "What else, sweetie? Haven't you told me everything yet?" or "Didn't I just talk to you, cookie face?"—always said in a lovingly teasing tone. I think you could say I worshipped my mother, but in a healthy way because we each had our own lives. She was my best friend, confidante, fashion consultant, recipe adviser, companion, and sounding board, and I loved her with all my heart! I was forty-four years old when I lost her, and she was seventy-six years old—a very vibrant, active seventy-six-year-old.

My mother's death came fast and furious. One minute we were celebrating my birthday, and a few days later, she was taken by ambulance to the hospital with an irregular heartbeat. Up to this point in her life, she was very active, involved in life, and in good general health. I met her at the hospital, and after much testing, the doctors determined that she needed an emergency quadruple bypass surgery. My anxiety level was high, but I remained confident, and I was happy she did so well after surgery. When I visited her the next morning, I was amazed because she was sitting up in her bed, and her green eyes were sparkling even though she was in the intensive care unit and just had major surgery. She told all the nurses and health care workers that when she was feeling better, she would come back and visit, and they would see just how fabulous she looked! Even at seventy-six years old, my mother was a fashion statement and was always perfectly groomed, and her shoes and purses always matched. Her doctor told me that she would live to be 106 since she had such an incredible attitude about life, and I believed him. After all, she was the Commander, my nickname for her.

After a few days, she was moved out of the intensive care unit into a regular room, but the nursing care was not as good as the intensive care unit, and it was concerning. One evening when I was visiting her, she started complaining of terrible pain. She was not a complainer, so I knew something was terribly wrong. I could not find a nurse anywhere, and I was starting to get frantic. Desperate to help her, I had to scream to get the nurses' attention. Finally, they came into her room, and eventually her doctor showed up and told me that he thought her pain was from complications from the surgery and wanted to do another surgery. My heart sank, and I did not want her to go through two open-heart surgeries in one week because it sounded very risky to me. She had her second surgery and survived. I went home after her surgery, around midnight, but I had a terrible feeling, and I was feeling very frightened. At three thirty in the morning, I received a call from the hospital, and they told me that she had gone into cardiac arrest and died. It was October 18, 1999. I was beyond devastated. The analogy of a tornado like the one in *The Wizard of Oz* is apt, and I felt like Dorothy when she experienced Auntie Em's house flying into the air and crashing down. The roof was blown off, but the foundation of the house was intact, although it needed to be rebuilt. I knew I had to repair the foundation of my life and build anew.

The first three days after she died, I did not eat or sleep after the initial shock of her death, and I soon realized I had a big problem. I began to take sleeping pills and would go to sleep around eleven at night, and I would wake up at one and stay up throughout the morning hours. I could barely eat anything at all and quickly lost ten pounds. I did not feel very well, and the sleep deprivation also created a lot of anxiety for me. This destructive pattern continued for about three months, and I was a wreck. A friend of mine recommended acupuncture to help me, and normally, I would have dismissed this idea, but I was desperate, and it helped a great deal.

I remembered that before my mom's passing, we had discussed all her wishes regarding her death and talked about how we would communicate after she died. I had asked her specifically to please try to communicate with me after her death, and she assured me that she would do everything possible to make that happen.

During the first month after her passing, there was a strange occurrence in my home. I lived alone and noticed that suddenly the CD player would turn on and her favorite CD would play. This startled me, and it continued about five times. I asked my brother to come over and check the electrical panel to see if everything was okay, and he told me that everything looked fine. There was no logical explanation for what happened. I realized that this was her way of letting me know she was with me. Several months later I had a dream, a dream that had an enormous impact on me. In the dream she told me, "It is difficult for me to come see you, and I will not be able to come back for a while. But I am fine, and I want you to live your life fully, and I will see you when you get here, but it will not be for a long time," adding that she wanted me "to have a wonderful life and enjoy myself."

Years later, although I still miss her, I have gone from grief to gratitude! I think of her almost every day, and most of the time, it is with beautiful memories. Sometimes, if I am feeling sad, I can hear her say to me, "Just keep going and do something. God helps those that help themselves." This message always propels me into action, and instead of moping around, I take positive action.

Several years after my mother passed, every year, a few months before the anniversary of her passing, I would get depressed and gloomy. I started thinking that I could not do this every year and that I needed to come up with a new plan. Instead of agonizing over my loss, I decided that I would begin an annual tradition in her honor. I call it the Celebration of Life. I organized a fundraiser in honor of my mother with the proceeds going to the American Heart Association. The plan fell together magically. A friend of mine had a magnificent yacht and offered to let me use it, and all the food and drink was catered. I invited my closest friends and family and asked everyone for a donation. Each year, I anticipate this event, and I no longer dread the anniversary of my mother's passing. My mother was a free spirit, and I sometimes think of her as a bird or butterfly, free to fly around wherever she wants. The first year of the Celebration of Life, we took the yacht down the Intracoastal Waterway, and a butterfly followed us all the way down to the water for about two hours. I really think it was my mother's spirit with us. I also think of the butterfly as a significant symbol for my own transformation because I had the ability to evolve from a caterpillar, to blossom into something colorful and beautiful.

At some point in my healing process, someone told me that I would realize a blessing from my loss, and I remember thinking that they were crazy. But they were right. I have become a more compassionate human being, and when someone else is going through a difficult time, I can offer my sincere compassion because I understand challenges. I love that one of my closest friends calls me "the angel of compassion." I can also feel real elation for my friends or colleagues if something great happens in their own lives.

I have learned to be grateful for the time I had with my wonderful mother, and if I do feel sorry for myself, I always hear her soft voice telling me, "Sweetie, just keep on going, and you will feel better. Don't be immobilized." I went from grief to gratitude, and I want to encourage other women that they can too. I always think about how my mother would want me to enjoy my life and would be angry if I had not moved forward in my life. I do believe that with faith, all things are possible! Now, I know that I can make it through anything if I could survive such a devastating loss. My mother's words always stay with me, and she continues to guide me. I believe that we all have eternal life, and I know I will be with her at some point, but for now, I am going to honor her and create a wonderful life.

Valerie Benton retired from her thirty-year television career. She plans on producing films, and one of them will focus on motherless daughters and how they dealt with their loss. She hopes to offer hope and encouragement to women and let them know that they will not only survive but thrive.

Monica Remembers Ann

My mother died in September 2007, ten days before my fiftieth birthday, sixteen years ago. I still go to visit the grave where her body is given to repose. Close to the stone that bears my mother's name, I sit in the coolness of spring, the bright sun of the summer, the crisp of autumn, and in the warmth of my car on cold winter days, considering life, my childhood, and family. I pray a rosary, and I am filled with gratitude for this beautiful woman who was my "Momma."

I will always have that empty space in my heart that only she could occupy. It is not bad, painful, or tragic. The sense of emptiness, to my mind, is evidence of having loved deeply. To be a daughter and be void of that would be the real tragedy. I grieve and mourn simply and precisely because I loved her, and I knew she loved me. The intensity of grief has lessened over the years, as is normal, but I still mourn for what I no longer can experience in the physical.

The memory I cherish most is holding my mother, 5 feet tall, 135 pounds, against my chest, my head resting on hers, and hugging her, to feel secure and cherished, simply because I loved her. We both knew and wanted to bathe in the joy of that. This one gesture we shared held more than words ever could; in that connection, that form, the union, there existed an indescribable sweetness. We were typical mother daughter—separated by diverse generations but beautifully joined in the life journey. She was my mother, my guide, my spiritual mentor, my critic, my cheerleader, my heart.

My mother and I had our conflicts. We disagreed in perspective about many things. We would work and at times struggle to understand each other. We would debate and argue and keep at it because each was so incredibly important to the other that understanding and being understood was worth the frustration and emotion of it all. I laugh to think how well she demonstrated to me what it was to be passionate about something, to take a stand and defend it because it was part of your core values. This has served me well in life. We were so much richer at the end of the verbal fencing mothers and daughters so often do. Both of us willing to grow enough to let go of angst, to return to our mutual love, maybe not agreeing but learning a bit more about the other and loving still deeper.

I realize now, when I contemplate this relationship, that there is an "allowing" that must happen between mothers and daughters to have what my mother and I had. Pride or the need for victory will cripple the ability to verbally fence with finesse, to accept to be challenged while maintaining respect, to defend without destroying. My momma pulled no punches. She was direct and clear but open to worthy discourse, and I learned to step up to her standard. Neither one of us was interested in arguments to inflict pain and wounds. My mother did not seek the "win." We sought to understand each other and be understood as well. We shared who we were honestly, and we each allowed the other person "in." There were no shadows between us. I just know she lives in a reality much beyond my ability to fathom, and I am confident that she is aware of and involved in my life. I am sure she knows how much I love her, and we both take time to remember the connection felt in those hugs.

Eternally loving you, Momma.

Monica Martin is a woman of many facets and interests. She is a mother to three beautiful daughters and three granddaughters, so the privilege and legacy of creating eternal bonds will continue. She has a long career as a nurse and is active in her Catholic faith community.

Lisa Remembers Jyoti

When I was still a girl, my mother told me that I should no longer think of her as a mother but as a friend. She cared for me as both, the best of mothers and friends, then and until she died, just three days before my sixtieth birthday. She was also one of my favorite traveling companions. Sometimes, on a lunch date, we would make believe we were two young women on a road trip, escaping from some small town somewhere to see the world. On actual summer adventures to Montana, we sang Willie Nelson's "On the Road Again" at the top of our lungs as we sped along in our Volkswagen Bug.

For one dreamy month, we traveled together across India with her mother, my grandmother Connie, taking up Hindu chants at the ashrams we visited. A perpetual seeker, my mother found what she felt to be her true name on one of her solo journeys to Nepal. Jodie, a nickname since her childhood, became Jyoti, Sanskrit for "light," capturing beautifully the radiance and warmth that emanated from her very being. Her chosen last name SaeUn, which, loosely translated, means "clearing clouds" in Japanese, was bestowed upon her by a Zen Buddhist monk who said that a healing session with her had cleared the clouds from his heart.

In December of 2020, I met her at the airport in her home state of Montana for one of our final trips together. It was a sad time in the world, and a hard time for Jyoti. Sadness showed on the faces of my aunts who had gathered her up from her assisted living residence on the shores of Flathead Lake. I could not tell from my mom's still-brilliant green eyes exactly what she was feeling, though certainly sadness, too, coming through in tearful goodbyes, exhaustion from the move, and that mix of fear and excitement that travel brings. I wheeled her through security, and we barely managed to catch our next flight on our way to Mexico, where I had arranged a new assisted living home for her so she could enjoy nice weather and receive greater care. Less stringent quarantine policies meant I could be close to her when I visited. Snuggled up against each other on the plane, my mom and I marveled at the direction our lives were taking and laughed together like children.

When she was still healthy and strong, Jyoti would sometimes talk about her death, not with worry or fear but with a characteristic playfulness and a wish expressed. "I want the end of my life to go like this," she would say. "Happy, healthy, happy, healthy, happy, healthy, dead!" Jyoti's death haiku came back to me often during our time together in Mexico. Though her mobility was compromised, she was in good physical health. Her mind, however, was fading, and this was exacerbated by isolation during the pandemic lockdown. I visited as often as I could, traveling from Oakland every six weeks and staying three weeks, working early mornings virtually, then spending afternoons with her. We would sometimes take trips to the village and lake nearby but mostly would sit shoulder to shoulder in her room or in the garden, relishing physical contact, sharing memories and funny stories as love and sunlight poured over us like honey. She was grateful for my company, delighted about the change, and curious about how this all fit into the larger story of her life.

On my last visit in the summer of that year, I noticed how much more her mobility had diminished, how she seemed so much smaller. She would doze off rather than talk as she sat next to me, and there was a growing distance in her eyes. I could feel her quietly grieving all that she had lost. I did all I could to brighten her spirits, and several days before I was to leave, two dear friends joined me in taking her out to lunch. It was the Fourth of July, and while no one, including us, was celebrating this holiday, there was a festive feeling on the streets and in the square. We ate delicious tacos, chips, and guacamole and enjoyed the colorful scene around us. Wheeling her down the crowded, narrow sidewalks and getting her back into the car was challenging, but she clearly enjoyed the ride home, reminiscing about our visits to many of the sites we passed. When we returned, I helped her into bed for a nap, and then I walked down the hill to the small cottage where I stayed during my visits. I was just on the edge of sleep when I got the call that she had fallen out of bed and injured her hip. I rushed back. Seeing my concern as I entered her room, she reached out to touch my face. "Ah, Lisa," she said, "this is the end that was waiting to happen."

After being transported to the small hospital nearby and getting X-rays, she rested comfortably and made friends with the nurses while I stepped outside to make calls, asking advice from loved ones about what to do next—transport her to a larger hospital an hour away in Guadalajara for hip surgery or bring her back to her new home and begin palliative care. I remember swallows winging through the sky over the lake as the sun set when my oldest and dearest friend, an emergency room doctor who had lost her own parents the previous year, asked, "Are you ready to lose your momma?" The tears finally came then. I was not ready to lose her, and yet I could not imagine how she could endure this surgery as well as months of painful rehabilitation. I talked with Jyoti about the two paths before us, and while we did not make any decisions until the morning, looking back, we were already beginning to say goodbye. I hardly slept at all on the small couch at the foot of her bed; as dawn came, I knew in my bones that I could not support putting Jyoti through surgery and recovery.

My mother had spent a lifetime attuning herself to the wisdom of her body, developing her own energy healing practice, eschewing the quick fixes that modern medicine prescribed. She also had stated wishes for a quick death after a healthy, happy life. When I shared with her my certainty about the best way forward, she said, "Many have gone before me." I held her hand tighter as we sat in silence for a moment, and then she offered these gracious words that became my mantra and my prayer: "It is done. It is said. It is brave. It is blessed."

I barely left Jyoti's side for the next two weeks. She was mostly still because pain medications eased her into a peaceful sleep, yet we both journeyed far and wide. Her blessed words echoed through me as I was buffeted by storms of grief followed by a strange and deep calm. Then feelings of resistance, frustration, anger, doubt, guilt, and even shame came over me in waves, leaving me exhausted. I was grateful that I had companions, the sweet staff at her residence, the sometimes brusque but mostly helpful doctor, her loving community, our Montana family, my own closest friends, and my husband. Even my brother, who suffers mental illness, was grounded and supportive, calling often to check in.

Jyoti and I were also companions to each other. I sang her favorite songs, played the native flute music she loved, gave her sponge baths with essence of lavender, wet her lips, and read her poetry. My heart broke open ever wider in witnessing her beauty and courage and in receiving her rarely spoken words, whispers of "Thank you" and "Will you hold me for a while?" and "Take care of yourself" and "I love you." One night, ten days after her fall, she opened her eyes wide and, with a voice strong and sure, asked, "Could you call in some light?" Without thinking, I said, "Yes!" and brought my arms up into the air. I immediately felt energy surge into my being as if all whom Jyoti had touched were reaching out to her through me. Touching her, I became a conduit of their gratitude and love. Hours passed, and she spoke again. "I am moving toward the light." I urged her forward. Much later that evening, she said simply, "I am the light," and I could feel her beginning to return to her true home. The following evening and for several days afterward, a bird native to the area, big, black, and brash, began to appear outside her window, calling in raucous counterpoint to her slowing breaths.

The morning before Jyoti died, I made the decision to leave her bedside. My aunt had suggested that one of the reasons she was holding on so long was because I was taking such good care of her. I don't know about that, but I could feel that her spirit was only barely present. Before I left her that evening to spend the night with my husband, I told her it was all right to let go fully now. I would be fine. It was time. She passed away several hours later, her two favorite nurses by her side. They later shared with me that the bird outside her window called even louder as Jyoti took her last breaths and then became silent after she passed, never to return.

One of Jyoti's friends used to say that her voice was like mother's milk—it was that warm and nurturing and full of love. While I no longer have her company or hear her voice, I have the memories of our travels together and apart, and I have her words: hundreds of pages of letters she wrote to me during our travels as well as her own journals. They are words wise and rich, which provide their own comfort and connection.

She comes to me in dreams, beautiful as ever and with important messages to share, and appears when I am alone in nature. Her spirit speaks to me especially strongly through birds—in any song that echoes that black bird that called her finally on. She speaks to me through hummingbirds that buzz and chirp in flight around my head and then perch nearby, calling me to stillness, and the bald eagle that circled three times over my aunt and I as we swam in Flathead Lake near the medicine wheel where we scattered her ashes. Even as I write this, I feel her presence in the red-tailed hawk that circles above my home, its wing tips illuminated by the sun, ascending in spirals away from me into the clear blue sky.

Jyoti and I would often talk about how we were on parallel paths, making our own ways through the world, encountering similar or very different challenges but either way discovering common truths. I see us now as moving in more of a double helix, together for a time, then apart, always connected in deep love and returning before too long to meet each other again.

Lisa Haney has dedicated her career to the transformative potential of education and taught literature for over twenty-five years at the Athenian School in Danville, California. She continues to support and empower educators as executive director of the California Teacher Development Collaborative, recognizing the significant influence teachers and leaders have on the lives of their students and communities. A current student of liberation psychology, her essay reflects her deep love for her mother and the belief they shared in the power of storytelling to foster healing and growth. She lives with her husband in Oakland, California, as part of the cohousing community she helped to found, and takes frequent trips to Washington, DC, to visit their daughter.

Ann Remembers Ann

Like so many daughters, I had a challenging and complicated relationship with my mother. She liked routine, structure, and predictability. "Just take one step in front of the other," she liked to say. But I tended toward diagonals, zigzagging through life in ways she found disconcerting and upsetting. In this way, I was more like my father, who she was deeply drawn to and who maddened her regularly!

My parents met in the seventh grade. They were assigned the last two seats in the back of the classroom, as they both missed the first day of school that fall. My mother's family had just moved to Pennsylvania from Virginia. And my father's family came home a day late from the Jersey Shore. According to my mother, though she had been warned by neighbors "not to fall for one of them damn Yankees," she was smitten.

A decade later they married and started a family. Within ten years, they had five children. Despite that, their focus remained on each other. This was good and bad for us kids. We were sometimes ignored, sometimes batted like Ping-Pong balls between their decision and indecision. I was the middle child and a loudmouth. Speaking up meant I didn't get trampled underfoot in all the hubbub of our household. I had my own point of view and opinion about everything and everyone. My mother responded to my dramatic outbursts by calling me "Sarah Bernhardt" in a tone of exasperation.

Ultimately, the five of us kids went off to college. We drifted apart into our separate adult lives. As my parents began to age, none of their children remained nearby. Some had moved West; some had headed back East. No one was there as the old barn and farmhouse began to need more than they could give. In November 2011, my mother was admitted into the ICU. Her adult children rushed to the hospital in Milwaukee. My father looked dazed. What next? What now?

As my mother went into a rehab hospital to regain her strength, we agreed it was time for our parents to sell the farm in Wisconsin and move near one of us. My parents chose to come to New Mexico, and in 2012 they moved into a home about five minutes from where I lived near Santa Fe.

My feelings were mixed. Why me? I was the unruly daughter. The one my mother had called pigheaded. The one who had come out as a lesbian in my early twenties, causing my mother grief and anxiety about what kind of life I could possibly have. The one who had managed to graduate high school in three years and left home at seventeen to start college. The one who had never come back to the farm.

I had these questions, but I was also excited to rekindle an adult relationship with my aging parents. Who were they anyway? How could I help them in the next chapter of their lives? Once they settled into their new home, they joined a local church. At their invitation, I attended the official church-joining ceremony and took joy in their joy. My spiritual path had veered away from Christianity, but I was happy in their happiness.

One Saturday afternoon they rushed over to my house after watching a matinee at the local movie theater to tell me what a great film they had seen. I was taken aback by the lack of boundaries. They didn't call first. But what the hell. Here we were. I made them hot tea and listened to my father talk about the movie.

My father was my mother's caregiver, the driver, the leader of adventures. And my mother went along. Then suddenly, nine months after moving to New Mexico, my father fell ill and died within weeks. It was shocking, and my mother's grief was unbearable. She had no direction, no desire to live, no idea what to do or how to do it. I took her to grief counseling and learned to accept the process she was going through. My partner bought her the book *Good Grief*.[75] In it, my mother found the advice she needed. After reading it she said to me, "Once you lose someone close, you must decide to live again. You must make a new life for yourself. You cannot live in the past." This insight helped my mother find her way forward

With incredible courage, my mother joined the local senior center and made new friends. For a few years, I took her to church on Sunday mornings. Then I helped her find another member of her church, a widow who lived nearby, so they could drive together. Occasionally, I attended with the two of them, singing hymns off-key and listening to the stories about Jesus and the apostles that the minister told. Then in 2019, the day after Thanksgiving, my mother died.

I was standing in the small ER room next to my sister and brother when my mother, eyes closed, laying in the hospital bed, exhaled softly. I felt her rush past us, charge down the hall, and fly out of the building. She wasted no time lingering. My sister clenched

---

75. Westberg, *Good Grief.*

my hand as she cried. My brother stood by quietly. I swayed between them, aware that our mother was off to find our father and reunite with her one and only lifelong love.

Two months later, the global pandemic arrived. As a college president, I was managing rapid institutional change and crisis. I was responsible for students, faculty, and staff. Everyone's lives were upended, including mine. One afternoon, after an intense Zoom meeting, I went outside to my Ceremonial Circle. In my belief system, nature is the temple. In our forest home in the mountains outside of Santa Fe, I had found a simple open place among the pines and marked it for ceremony with a circle of stones. This is where I pray to Creation each day and reorient myself for whatever comes next.

I have stood countless times in that place nestled in the Sangre de Cristo Mountains, overlooking the forest, listening to the raven call, feeling the wind. This is where I sing and pray, where I sit and meditate. That day, for some reason, I felt moved to open the stones to the west. The Circle had an Eastern Door for entering the Circle. Then one moves sunwise around the inner space in these sacred circles, pausing to pray at each direction. But that day, following an impulse, I moved the stones and made a second door or opening in the West, opposite the entrance in the East. In my spiritual practice, East is considered the direction of conception and beginning, the direction of inspiration and insight, whereas West is the direction we walk in this lifetime, following our Sun Trail or Life Purpose. West is the direction of completion. When we leave this life, we move out the Western Door into the next world. East and West, birth and death. I didn't have a logical reason for opening the Western Door that day, but I felt compelled to do it and simply followed my intuition.

That night, for the first time since my mother's death, I saw her in a dream. In fact, I saw both of my parents. My father was walking toward me through a farm gate, waving his arm and calling my name. My mother was close behind him in a long, flowing skirt, waving and smiling. They were strolling toward me on a green farm lane like the one at my parent's old farm.

I woke up with a feeling of calm reassurance. Despite the upheaval and chaos of the pandemic, my parents were all right. I had opened the Western Door of my Ceremonial Circle, and this action somehow opened the door between my life among the living and their lives among the dead. Maybe by opening the Western Door, I had opened myself to welcome them back from the other side, that mysterious next place beyond this life. I felt they had made the dream journey to assure me everything would be okay.

I believe the ability to connect via dreams to our ancestors and the people we have loved who have made the transition out of this reality into another dimension is an inherent ability that we all share. I believe that dreams offer us opportunities to engage with those who are no longer living. In this way, through these dreams, these relationships continue. They continue to influence and inform us, shaping our lives from the inside. This is a powerful, meaningful connection. In waking consciousness, when we recall the dream images and experiences, they are no less real, and sometimes more real, than daily life.

Recently in a dream I am rushing to pack for a trip to China. I find my mother patiently hanging clean sheets on the clothesline outside of the mud porch of the old farmhouse. I slow down, notice the ripple of white sheets in the fresh, sun-filled air, see her hands carefully stretch the damp sheet against the clothesline, notice the wooden clothespins she holds in her teeth. I tell her I have to get my luggage from my bedroom upstairs. She nods, smiling, and I keep moving.

This dream gave me the gift of remembering that even as I travel through the world, I am balanced by a sense of home. My mother's steady routines grounded me as a precocious and imaginative child. Despite my desire to run from home and race into the world, she provided a place I could return to. Despite our differences, we loved each other.

The relationships we have with those we love do not end at death. They continue through that radical change and persist as long as we live. Different from memory, these dream encounters are new. They bring new dimensions of awareness to these abiding relationships. Developing understanding, compassion, connection, and love through our dream relationships with our mothers allows us to continue to grow and mature with our mothers even after they are no longer physically alive. I am grateful for the ability to dream and recall my dreams. I wish you the same gift.

Ann Filemyr, PhD, has served as faculty and as the dean and VP of Academic Affairs at Antioch College, the Institute of American Indian Arts, and Southwestern College in Santa Fe, where she also served as president for six years. She is the founding director of the PhD in Visionary Practice and Regenerative Leadership at Southwestern. She is the author of six poetry books, countless essays and articles, and a few book chapters. She studied traditional healing and lifeways with the late Keewaydinoquay Peschel, an Anishinaabe Mashkikiwe (Ojibwe herbal medicine woman), for twenty years.

Debbie Remembers Rosemarie

My mother, Rosemarie Ferrante, was an amazing woman. She had a strong spirit and a passion for life, yet her body was plagued by many ailments. She was a source of joy and love to those around her, and I believe her appetite for laughter gave her extra years to live, defying what medical experts predicted. In April of 1991, I awoke to my mother's screams. She was in bed with her eyes closed and screaming, "Someone get the principals now." I did not know if she was having a nightmare, and I could not wake her up. Panicked, I called 911 and then my brother. He arrived at the same time as the ambulance, and when they took her to the hospital, I wondered if I would ever see her again. I was only nineteen years old.

The doctors told us that she had a severe brain aneurysm, and she underwent nine hours of brain surgery. She was only fifty-three years old at the time. After several weeks of rehabilitation, she came home, but our worlds would never be the same again. I was deeply affected because she was not the mother I knew. She could not process information effectively or remember much of anything anymore. The brain damage she experienced produced a significant personality change, and our roles were now reversed. She was now the child, and I was the mother. I assumed all responsibilities for her doctor's appointments and managed her medications.

She became the focus of my life because I only wanted to keep her alive. She apologized for everything she put me through, although she did not remember the details of her surgery. In the years following her surgery, she was diagnosed with coronary artery disease and underwent many procedures, including having stents placed in her body. She also developed angina and could not walk very far. She was not a suitable candidate for open-heart surgery because she was too fragile.

Over the years, I was heartened when her memory improved, and although she still behaved like a child, things were better. She loved to play bingo and Pacman on her Nintendo. I was always amazed that she was still a great card shark and easily beat me at poker all the time. Even though she could not remember many things, she still laughed, yelled at us, and enjoyed life with my father.

After a multitude of serious health problems, including breaking her right hip, a mild heart attack, a blood clot, and diabetes, she was taken out of the hospital to what would become her permanent residence—a nursing home. It was not until this point that I realized that she was going to die, and I had to let go. I wondered how her countless health situations had now become so bad. Although she had a horrible health history, she had managed to survive and in some cases thrive, and even her doctors referred to her as a "walking miracle." When I visited her in the nursing home the week before she died, she had IVs in her arms and oxygen in her nose, yet she asked me if I wanted to play cards with her. Poker—her favorite! My mom always managed to surprise me, and for someone so ill, she gave me one last gift.

She was also given a harsh medication that I thought was too strong, and it paralyzed her. I was angry and alarmed and asked my husband and son to come with me to visit her. When we arrived, she was unable to move, and I shouted, "Mom, we are here. Look who came to see you!" After several tugs and shouts, she opened her eyes for a split second and looked directly at my son. Then she closed her eyes. That was the last time I saw her.

When the doctors phoned me, it was the worst call of my life. I was in complete shock. I threw the phone back to my husband and fell to the floor, crying. This was the beginning of a new chapter in my life—life without Mom. I was so angry when hospice called that I never called them back and believed that they killed her with medications that took away her ability to fight. I kept telling myself that if she did not take the medication they gave her, she would still be here with me. My husband believes that everything happens for a reason and that her passing was her body's way of saying that she had been through enough. I realize now that her body and spirit were calling out to release her from her pain to find peace. After her death, I could not visit her home or call her house, and even though I saw her casket lowered into the ground, I wondered if she would be able to breathe. I waited by the phone for her to call me so I could hear her voice again.

A month after her death, I searched for a group to join but came up empty-handed, so I formed my own women's group. The women in the group were incredible and so were the stories they shared. We met monthly to grieve together and pay homage to the women who gave birth to us. Although our feelings of loss will never go away, we had the chance to truly know each other and witnessed our collective pain, and I am proud to call each of these women my friend.

I have watched my son grow, and when I look at him, I miss my mother and wonder what she would say about him to me. I miss having her take pictures with him, and I yearn for the moments when she smiled at him as if she were the most blessed woman on earth. My daughter will never meet her grandmother. I wish my mother could see both of my children and give them kisses. I feel cheated and robbed that my mother died so early. I look at those people who still have their parents with them—you know them—and I cannot help but feel jealous.

Everything reminds me of her. She loved old music from the 1950s, Elvis, the color purple, bingo, Lucille Ball, and Pepsi. She loved watching planes and became giddy when she saw one in the sky. Her grave is near the airport, and she would really be pleased about that. There are other things that remind me of her. I smile every time I see a watermelon, which may sound strange, but I think about the time I fed her watermelon when she was unable to do so on her own in the nursing home. Whenever I hear a Josh Groban song, I think of her and feel chills up and down my arms because when I received the call that she had passed, he was on television. His music has taken on an entirely new meaning for me.

Until my mother's death, I never thought much about the afterlife. I never thought about communicating with the dead. I know that she can see me and my children each day. I realize you have to look at what is right in front of you—and I look at my children knowing she is part of them. And on many occasions, I not only feel her presence, but I know she protects each one of us. She is there at just the right moments during the day when I need her. Sometimes I see a bird in my yard that lands at the most perfect time. Or something comes up out of the blue that gives me the wisdom and guidance I need. I know in my heart that it is her. Most definitely I feel her all around me.

I live without a mother in my life. When I look back at the times we shared, I feel so lucky. I have no regrets and consider myself fortunate to have shared those special moments with her, even during doctor and hospital visits. I miss those moments deeply. She was the most amazing woman I ever met, and when I look at her pictures, I see a beautiful person who chose me to be her daughter. My heart bleeds for not having her in my life physically, yet her spirit lives on inside of me and inside my children. I am blessed for that.

Debbie Abazia worked in New York City on Wall Street and was the director for investor relations for a New Jersey semiconductor company. She has worked as a model since 1998 and continues to work on a variety of movie sets as an actor since 2019. She lives in New Jersey with her husband, John, their two children, Hayden and Sabrina, and dog Mozart and cat Linus.

Kristen Remembers Lisa

Sometime last year during shavasana at the end of my yoga class, I was overtaken by the sensation that my mother was with me. I felt her energy swirling like golden glitter in a purposeful, gentle breeze. The feeling hummed in my ears and swept around my body, finally settling into my open palms.

With tears streaming down my cheeks onto my mat, I imagined her energy absorbing into my hands, warming my whole body. A vivid picture of her at age forty formed in my mind. Since her death almost twenty years ago, details of her appearance sometimes become fuzzy, but at that moment, her healthy pre-cancer self was overwhelmingly clear. When my mom, Lisa, died from metastatic breast cancer, I had no way of knowing all the ways I would carry her with me and see her around me.

I have written quite a lot about the different ways my mother's loss has changed me. The shape of my longing for her continues to change and evolve with each new phase of my life. Thankfully, the pain of losing her has become less acute, albeit ever present.

Every so often, I find myself trying to imagine who I would be and what I'd be doing if my life hadn't been punctuated with such a deep loss, but it's nearly impossible to imagine. While I deeply miss my mother—most especially the feeling her presence afforded me—I don't think I want to give up the understanding and the humanity I've found through my experiences. And yet, I put in effort daily to stay connected with her, actively looking for signs of her as I move through the world.

I have found reminders of Lisa in the profound and the mundane. My grief felt especially persistent when my children were small. I had them not too long after her passing, and the din of emotional anguish was the background of every joyful moment of being a new parent. New motherhood, an incredible life experience, without her was the definition of bittersweet. Her love for my children would have been an incredible positive force in their lives, and her steadfast guidance would have eased many of my own challenges. I still sometimes find, like on the day we found out that my son got into the high school he wanted, that I picked up my phone to call her with good news.

Now, there are mostly sweet visitations, such as when a ladybug landed on my arm last week or when I heard her favorite song playing from the car next to me at a stoplight. These encounters feel like a gentle, sentimental breeze—like walking through a cloud of Lisa's perfume. I can breathe it in, but I can't find a way to grab hold. I try to remain open to every ephemeral way to find her.

My mother was outwardly very pragmatic and composed. Her executive functioning remains unparallelled; I have never seen someone get more done in a day. Yet it was easy for those of us close to her to see that she recognized the magic around her. And with the rosy glasses of hindsight, I enjoy conjuring up her memory and imagining her in my life now. I can picture what it would be like if she were playing a board game with us at my table— her smile lighting up her face and her deep laugh. But I have no idea what she would say, really. Her words were often a surprise or rather from a perspective I had not considered. The incompleteness of these musings leaves me feeling empty.

Lately, I've been reading about grief and listening to podcasts about death and dying. I am comforted to hear other people's stories about loved ones who have passed and that they too feel the pressure of keeping them alive through objects and storytelling. How do I cope, two decades later, with the seemingly cellular shift that took place from profound loss? Is there a way for grief to both break me and heal me? Can I be a better version of myself, a better mom, because of it? While I'm sometimes frustrated that I'm still asking these questions, I rarely feel alone anymore. I have made countless friends who have been touched by loss, and when I think about them, even though their experiences are vastly different, we share several important things.

First, we share our love and affection openly. Second, we laugh easily. Even in dark moments, together with these friends we find a peppering of light and joy. Third, we walk around with an invisible, magnetic pain that pulls us together. Sometimes we forge bonds over pleasantries before revealing the loss that has already begun to knit us together.

Thank goodness for these people. They are the first ones I text when I have a dream about her where I could actually feel the sensation of her hugging me or when I think I saw her in a crowd. The validating way that these friends listen and relate has helped keep my mom alive for me.

Kristen Carbone founded Brilliantly after a decade-long career working in curatorial departments in museums across New York and New England. Brilliantly is a company that offers women with breast cancer a solution for feeling more comfortable post-mastectomy based on the profound shifts they experience in their identities and connections with their bodies after their mastectomies and reconstruction surgeries. She loves writing, public speaking, and problem-solving. She is a member of Dreamers and Doers, the Fourth Floor, HeyMAMA, and Women of Wearables. She lives in Providence, Rhode Island, with her "Junior Staffers," Liam and Sylvia.

Christine Remembers Loretta

In the summer of 2004, the foundation of our family was irrevocably shaken when my mother was diagnosed with Non-Hodgkin Lymphoma. This marked the beginning of my role as her devoted health care advocate and caregiver, a seventeen-year-long journey filled with love, strength, and unwavering commitment. I watched over my mother and her medical care like a hawk. Initially, it was my way of coping. Eventually, it became my way of being. My own health battle began in the winter of 2016 when I was diagnosed with breast cancer. Without a genetic predisposition or family history, my diagnosis was attributed to environmental factors. Having worked as an environmental engineer for twenty-five years at the time of my diagnosis, the irony was not lost on me.

Determined to bridge the gap between conventional medicine and holistic health, I explored various healing modalities, such as acupuncture, aromatherapy, detoxification, massage, nutrition, Reiki, and yoga, while navigating the health care system during my mother's diagnosis and then my own. I immersed myself in nature, spending extensive time in forests and by the sea with my beloved dogs, first Windy and now Aurora, by my side. These experiences catalyzed my physical recovery and inspired a deeper spiritual alignment, culminating in the founding of my social impact company, Connect & Thrive, Inc. (CAT), which empowers women with cancer to begin their healing journeys. My mother was my guiding light and my beacon of hope for CAT, and when I sat with the world's foremost experts in health, wellness, and healing, I received constant signs that she was with me and helping me bring life to CAT.

When I named my company, I selected a cheetah as its logo, inspired by an African safari my family went on many years ago. The cheetah we saw in Kenya left a grand impression on all of us. To see such life amidst a severe drought was exhilarating. Upon our return home, my mother bought two ceramic cheetah statues, one for her home and one for mine, and we each named our statues "Queenie" after the cheetah we had encountered in the plains. While researching the cheetah and its spiritual meaning, I was overjoyed to discover its symbolism of flexibility, determination, patience, and a high capacity for empathy and precise knowledge as to how to respond to the hurt, pain, and suffering of others, aligning perfectly with CAT's vision and mission. The cheetah became a constant reminder of the connection my mother and I shared.

The final chapters of my mother's life were marked by profound intimacy and revelation. During quiet moments, our conversations—full of love and devoid of regrets—offered both comfort and closure. Prior to my mother's peaceful passing on August 2, 2021, she told me to look for a fox—a cunning, clever, and gorgeous creature with dark front legs (which look like opera gloves) and a bushy, white-tipped tail that we both cherished. "I will send one to you, but remember, they are not so easy to come by." Though a release from her suffering, her death left an immeasurable void; she was not only my mother but my best friend.

The loss of my mother ended the daily routine of care and removed the foundational support that defined so much of my adult life. The days following my mother's death were filled with intense loneliness, mitigated only by imagined conversations and vivid dreams where she visited me, healthy and vibrant. In these dreams, we often traveled to remote locales around the world that we had once visited. Each dream was a vivid reminder of our shared dreams and heritage, providing comfort and continuity. Over time, these dreams became less frequent. Though when I find myself grieving her loss, she oftentimes returns to me in my dreams.

A poignant reminder of my mother's enduring influence occurred during a trip to Beth Israel Deaconess Medical Center on September 3, 2021. In the very room where I had supported my mother through countless appointments, I was no longer watching over her; I was now the patient. As I left my appointment with a heavy heart, a red-tailed hawk circled overhead. I immediately interpreted this as a sign of my mother's protective spirit now watching over me. It was a complete role reversal. On another occasion, while visiting my mother's grave, my father and I were greeted by a red-tailed hawk. These majestic birds seemed to arrive when we desperately needed reassurance of my mother's presence, strength, and everlasting love.

After a winter of pandemic-induced isolation, in the spring of 2022, I met with a renowned physician, a pioneer in the use of scientific tools to validate recoveries from incurable illnesses and an expert in spirituality and healing. I was not sure if I should share the story behind my inspiration for CAT and the role that my mother played or just focus on the business aspects. As I was pondering this, we were visited by three gorgeous cardinals, two males and a female. My mother cherished these symbols of hope, love, and comfort that served as a connection to her mother (they are known in the spiritual world to be signs from loved ones who have passed away). They flew in and out of the trees, and I felt that they were harbingers of what ensued. I shared my mother's story with the doctor, which offered profound insight into CAT. At the end of the meeting, only the female cardinal remained, nearly motionless, just watching. I believe in my heart and soul that it was my mother's way of validating that she was with me and inspiring me to carry on with the important work that I was doing.

The loss of my mother brought back memories of her mother, my beloved grandmother, whose passing in March 1995 had left a similar void. Reflecting upon my spiritual journey, I realized its roots lay in the extraordinary bond between my mother and her mother. My mother's father passed away when she was just eight years old, leaving my grandmother a young widow. Despite the hardships, my grandmother was a pillar of grace, resilience, and strength, and her presence taught me the true meaning of unconditional love. For months after her death, I visited her grave daily. On a particularly difficult day, my mother and I went to the cemetery together. The wind was swirling, and the leaves were floating through the air with what seemed like intention. I felt sad and discouraged, longing for a tangible connection to my grandmother. As we approached the grave, my mother and I stopped in our tracks. There, sitting on the grass in front of the rose quartz gravestone, was a rabbit. My mother grew up in the town where my grandmother was buried and had never seen a rabbit. The closest thing to this beautiful creature we had seen was a stuffed animal I had given to my grandmother one Easter, which she was buried with. This rabbit, however, was very much alive. It did not move as we approached, just looked at us as our eyes filled with tears and our hearts with love.

I was named after my grandmother, and my sister was named after our great-grandmother. Losing our mothers and grandmothers compels us to find ways to honor their memories and keep their spirits alive. Future generations will also carry on their legacies. Through our collective memories, the lives of those we have lost will continue to shape us with their love, and the signs they send to us will remind us that they are still present in our minds and hearts.

The months and now years following my mother's death allowed me to truly appreciate the strength and love she had imparted to me—gifts that proved foundational as I navigated my grief. This deep well of maternal love fortified my commitment to CAT, where I sought to infuse her strength and compassion into every facet of the business. While working tirelessly on CAT, I was awarded first prize in the Cancer Journey Institute's Discovery Contest, which included a one-week "Love Yourself More After Cancer" retreat at the Mimosa Retreat on Lefkada Island, Greece. As soon as I looked at the calendar, I knew deep in my heart that this was a trip I needed to make. It coincided with the Greek Orthodox Good Friday, Easter, and Mother's Day. I embraced the opportunity to focus deeply on personal healing and growth while learning to love myself more. This period of introspection and connection with nature allowed me to understand that healing from grief does not mean moving on from the memory of a loved one but rather involves weaving that memory into every day, finding ways to honor that bond in acts of living and being.

I have always had a strong connection to the natural world, and it was heightened when my mother died. I felt that being in nature offered more opportunities to find and receive signs from God to reinforce my faith and my heartfelt belief that my mother and grandmother were watching over me. In a way, I was in a perpetual search for signs from them—and in the case of my mother, the elusive fox. At times, I felt disappointed in myself that I could not simply draw upon the love that my mother told me would always live in my heart. Why wasn't it enough?

Upon my arrival on Lefkada Island, I was informed by the owners of the retreat that they had been visited by a red fox the night prior while preparing for our arrival. I could not have been more excited! That night, after attending the Greek Orthodox Easter service, I reflected upon the meaning of this holiest of holidays and the resurrection and rebirth it symbolized. While saying my prayers under the clear night sky and stars canopying Lefkada, I heard the fox just outside my villa. Its voice was unmistakable, filling my heart with love and longing. I sat in awe as I experienced what I had been waiting two years and nine months for. Its presence reassured me that I was exactly where I needed to be.

Later in the week, during an excursion to Agios Nikitas, I decided to remain in this beautiful seaside town to hike to an isolated beach with breathtaking scenery. While roaming the streets in search of the sign to the steps to this hidden gem, I spotted a Milokleftis chalkboard sign at a local taverna with a fox logo and the hashtag #followthefox. It turns out it was the company that made the first Greek apple cider, and translated, Milokleftis meant "apple bandit." I was apparently headed in the right direction. On the other side of the street, there was another sign that read "Milos Beach." While exploring this stunning stretch of coastline, I spotted a snake, which is a prominent symbol of transformation, rebirth, and healing. And this is exactly what I was doing while I was there—deep in the process of a significant transformation.

The night before I departed from the retreat, I saw the fox's scat. I knew that my mother's spirit was in and around me, but for whatever reason, she chose to remain hidden. By the end of the retreat, I had come to realize that to feel the love of my mother, I needed to take the time to be still in order to feel her presence. I did not need to constantly validate it with the signs I was desperately searching for. This retreat offered me the opportunity to experience the most powerful force in the universe—love. This trip was not just an escape from daily stresses but a profound engagement with my inner self. The spiritual signs around me, including the long-awaited appearance of the fox, reinforced my spiritual connection with my mother. This experience, coupled with the reunion with my family members after the retreat, served as a powerful affirmation of my mother's subtle presence in my surroundings no matter where I was. Each moment seemed orchestrated to remind me of the connections that transcend physical presence.

These moments of connection, woven through the experiences at the retreat and in the company of family, serve as a testament to the power of love and resilience. They offer hope and comfort to those navigating the depths of their own grief, reminding us of the indomitable strength and continuity provided by our loved ones, both seen and unseen. Each sign and moment of connection reiterates the profound bonds that tie us to our past and guide us into our future. They remind us that love does not merely endure; it surpasses time and space, weaving through the very fabric of our lives, offering solace and inspiration even in the deepest despair. These signs were not mere coincidences but threads in a larger tapestry continuously being woven by our interactions, memories, and shared histories. They connect the tangible with the intangible, the past with the present. And for me, they are vital in maintaining the continuity of love and legacy that my mother—and her mother before her—bestowed. This ongoing connection has not only been a source of comfort but a driving force behind my endeavors with CAT. It inspires me to infuse every aspect of my work with the same strength, compassion, and resilience that were hallmarks of my mother's life. Through this work, I aim to honor her memory and extend her legacy, helping others find their paths to healing just as I have found mine.

After I returned from the retreat, I felt a renewed commitment to live fully, not just for myself but in honor of those who have shaped me. This commitment was symbolized profoundly during my stay in Greece, where the natural world seemed to echo the lessons my mother taught me to be resilient, to seek healing, to help others, and to connect deeply with the world around me. I continue to find strength in the signs and messages that I believe are from my mother. Whether through encounters in nature, moments of unexpected guidance, or the supportive presence of family and friends, I am reminded of her enduring love and the eternal bond we share. This bond continues to guide and inspire me, offering a beacon of hope for anyone who has experienced loss and a reminder that we are never truly alone in our journeys. The love we carry and the connections we cherish transcend all barriers and continue to shape us long after our physical presence has faded.

The bonds that we share with our mothers are never lost; they evolve, guide, and comfort us, reminding us of the everlasting impact of love and the enduring spirit of those we hold dear. These experiences have taught me that while physical presence may fade, the love and memories we hold in our hearts remain a powerful source of strength and inspiration. They continue to shape our lives, guiding us through challenges and celebrating our triumphs. I carry with me the lessons and love of my mother, using them to inspire and support others on their journeys. This connection between mothers and daughters is a profound and unbreakable bond. It is a testament to the enduring power of love and the incredible resilience of the human spirit. In honoring my mother's memory, I strive to live a life filled with purpose, compassion, and strength, extending her legacy of love to all those I encounter.

May this story inspire others to find hope and strength in their own journeys, knowing that the love we share with our mothers is eternal and ever present, guiding us through life's greatest challenges and most beautiful moments.

Christine Georgia Anastos is the founder of Connect & Thrive, Inc. (CAT), a social impact company for cancer survivors, patients, thrivers, and caregivers. CAT empowers women on their personal healing journeys by connecting them to a marketplace of reputable practitioners and curated products. She has more than thirty years of experience in the fields of engineering, industry, and consulting. She has conducted over one thousand environmental safety (EHS) compliance, management systems, and due diligence assessments, as well as high profile civil and criminal EHS investigations. She has a BS in engineering and an MS in civil and environmental engineering from Tufts University.

Lavoie Family Daughters Remember Shirley

Pam Remembers Shirley

What I remember most about that cold December Sunday morning at our mother's house was the quiet. My sisters and I gathered at the kitchen table after mass—a tradition we kept all our lives. Generally, with six girls and an array of husbands, grandchildren, and great-grandchildren sprinkled into the mix, it is chaotic. The joke was if you were lucky enough to get a chair, don't get up! Everyone was settling in with a cup of coffee and sweet rolls, and I noticed that Mom was not herself. She was incredibly quiet and fidgety. She blurted out that she had seen a doctor and that a spot had shown up on her X-ray. Bells went off in my head because Mom smoked for forty years; however, she did quit three years before. She decided to wait until after Christmas to continue with the tests. We celebrated Christmas with gusto, and I knew it would be her last Christmas with us.

Her diagnosis came back as small-cell lung cancer. A second opinion confirmed that she had cancer. She was referred to an excellent doctor with a zest for life, and he felt that our beautiful mother had a chance to survive. We had many family meetings, and I always felt pride because when you have six strong type A personalities, disagreements were to be expected, and we successfully resolved our disagreements easily. She had chemotherapy in small doses at first, and we pitched in taking turns to drive her to her appointments, and she always had at least one daughter who stayed with her. Because of the side effects from treatments, she was hospitalized, but the Lord answered our prayers, giving her the opportunity to enjoy ten weeks of good health. She was able to travel and loved going out to lunch, and once again, she was our social and fun-loving mom. We all prayed for a miracle. Although her doctor wanted to start her on chemotherapy again, she refused because she knew that the quality of her life would suffer. She died in our arms at age seventy-five with the help of hospice, our love for Mom, and the strength from God on a dreary November afternoon, just eleven months after her initial diagnosis.

We each had particular jobs to help her. Since I am the oldest, I took care of her finances, and my mom called me her financial adviser. Barb, our second sister, shaved her head when her hair started to fall out and helped her pick out a pretty wig. Jean, the third sister, was the only sister who lived in our hometown, and she picked up prescriptions and groceries for the week for Mom. Mary, our fourth sister, was her medical adviser because of her strong understanding of health care, and her advice helped my mom gain additional time with us because of her smart decisions. Michel, our fifth sister, lived in Texas, and she came home numerous times during Mom's illness and was her vacation planner. At least twice a year, Mom would stay with Michel and her son to enjoy the warm weather in the winter. Mom loved to visit her and especially enjoyed spending time with her youngest grandson, Eli. Our youngest sister, Angie, was Mom's chef and would bring her meals.

The relationship that Mom had with each of us was one of a kind. Although she treated us as unique, she also treated us the same. I still do not know how she loved us all the same, but I never felt she had a favorite daughter. If one of us was going through a challenging time, she always gave us the extra love we needed. She always had a deep love for God. Her life was filled with joy, and she said that these happy occasions revolved around her faith. She even planned her funeral, choosing her favorite songs and the dress she wanted to be buried in. Although she did not have much money, she was specific about her wishes being followed. I was the executor of her will, and she trusted me completely, knowing that I would manage her affairs with love and compassion. She wrote down items that she wanted to give us, and after she passed, I read the handwritten wishes she had for each of her daughters. She asked us not to fight about money or material things, and although the division of her estate went well, it was not easy. There were several items we all wanted, but through a give-and-take process we all received wonderful heirlooms. Her final request was to die at home, and she always had one or several family members by her side for the last six weeks of her life. She slipped into a coma, and on the eighth day, she died in our arms. Every wish she had asked of us had been fulfilled, but it was the hardest day of my life.

While we took care of her, we sang the same songs that she had sung to us when we were little, and several times a day, we recited the rosary and asked for God's blessings. As I look back on those eight days, I cannot help but feel that it was her last gift to each of her daughters because we had not slept under the same roof since I had married years earlier. During that time, I cried so much, laughed so hard, and enjoyed being a Lavoie sister.

From the moment that she passed, I had an empty spot in my heart. How could I—someone with a loving husband, two sons, two wonderful daughters-in-law, four energetic grandchildren, a grandmother, five younger sisters, and all my nieces and nephews—be lonely? Because she is gone. I knew she loved me for who I was.

She was a beautiful woman, very striking, and she had gorgeous, big, brown, and expressive eyes that she passed on to each of her daughters. She told me many times that her happiest years were when we were little girls and she tucked us into bed and gave us a goodnight kiss. How lucky I was to have had such a wonderful mother. The love and traditions that she gave me helped prepare me for my life's journey.

I miss her every day. One minute I am fine, and the next minute, I am reduced to tears because something reminds me of her or I remember a moment I shared with her. One request she had was that she wanted us to say a prayer for her every day. I receive great comfort in reciting the Hail Mary, the prayer she taught me so long ago. Our priest told me that she can hear us and that I should speak with her. In the morning, when I am getting ready for work, I talk with her. I tell her about my day and share my disappointments and joys with her. Not too long after her death, I was having a terrible day. I stomped my foot and told her she better fix things because I could not. I ranted, raved, and cried until I was completely exhausted. I told her I needed her help. I knew she heard me and was with me. I felt an unknown energy, as if the hair on my arms was full of electricity. Later that day, my problem was solved.

Because of her strong faith, I feel great comfort, especially when I attend church services. She always sat in the fourth pew to the left of the altar, and no one ever sat in *her* seat. My sisters have told me that they feel her presence during mass as well. They described it as feeling as if her arms were wrapped around them. Although I have not felt her arms around me, I always feel as if this is the most peaceful time of the week. One of my sisters took over her duties preparing the church for mass. I have taken over her office as secretary for the Council of Catholic Women. Mass is my refuge, and it is as if she is reminding me to keep my faith strong, especially during any struggles I experience. A few weeks ago after mass, the three newest grandchildren were all together. I was watching the commotion and the laughter. Everyone was talking at once, and pictures were being taken of the two little boys and the little girl, only two weeks old. I felt pressure on my shoulder, a hand, and I was filled with great joy. It was Mom. She was there. We always said she never liked to miss a good party. I know she now had the chance to see her three newest grandbabies through eternal eyes. I know that at every celebration Mom will not be there physically but certainly in spirit. She will live on in my heart forever.

Pam Fink lived in central Illinois all her life. She was married to her husband, Dave, for over four decades, and they have two sons. Her role model for a long, happy marriage was her mother. She was a breast cancer survivor and advocated for women to give themselves examinations on a regular basis. She worked for the US Postal Service for over twenty-five years and was the former postmaster in central Illinois. She passed away in 2021. She will be missed.

Barb Remembers Shirley

What a special evening we had planned, and we invited Mom to a memorial service sponsored by the Bloomington chapter of the Compassionate Friends organization. I lost my youngest son in January 2000, and my husband and I were the recipients of the award that year, and we were honored to accept it for all parents who had lost a child. We sat in the front row, and I noticed that Mom was not herself. I later found out that earlier that morning was when she told my sisters about the doctor's diagnosis. She did not want to upset me, knowing how important that day was to me.

I found out the next day, and it made sense why she was so quiet. Because our family has a history of cancer, I knew, as my sisters did, that something needed to be done right away.

Christmas that year was full of emotions for all of us, and we tried to have the strength to have a wonderful time, and as usual, she made it incredibly special. First, the great-grandchildren opened their gifts, then the grandchildren, the husbands were next, and then her daughters. Every year she would buy all six of us something alike. We sat down that year with our eyes closed, and when she told us to open our eyes, the gifts were there, and this memory will stay with us forever.

After her diagnosis was confirmed by several doctors, the chemo began. Mom looked at me one day and said, "Life is all about choices. I chose to smoke, and this is the result of that choice." She added, "God is taking me on a new journey, and it is in his hands where it will lead me." All the sisters took turns staying with her, making her meals, and taking her to her appointments. Mom lived by herself for over twenty years, and this was difficult for her since she was so independent. She was hospitalized from complications from chemotherapy, and in June, she began radiation treatments, and they seemed easier for her body to handle. Mom looked great. She felt good and kept busy spending time with her family and friends. In October, she started chemotherapy again. We had a family meeting, and my mother decided she did not want any more treatments and that she was not afraid to die. She told us she looked forward to seeing her husband, our father who died twenty-three years prior, again. She passed away with her daughters and her sister by her side.

My first thought after she died was that it could not be happening. No one else in this world loves me as much as Mom does. No matter what happened in my life, I knew I could always go to her, and she would give me a hug and a kiss, and everything would be fine. Her home was a soft place to fall. Although there are six daughters, she told us she loved us all the same and was proud of our individual strengths. I believe her because I have children and grandchildren of my own, and I love them the same way. One day when I tucked Mom in for an afternoon nap, she told me that when she was gone to "look to the heavens, and I will look down and say, 'I love you, Barb.'"

We were raised as strong Catholics, and we all believe that our mother is in a wonderful place now. I know she has been with me several times since her passing. When I needed to decide about moving and wanted to know if the house I found was the right home for us, I asked my son, Matthew, and my parents to talk to God and Mother Mary and to please give me a sign so I would know what to do. I asked for a big sign since I didn't think I would pick up on a little sign. I am sure she laughed about that. Later that evening, I just knew that this was the right house for my family. I miss my mom, truly miss her great spirit and giving heart, and she will be forever in mine.

Barb Munsterman was a jewelry designer and the former owner of D's Design. She had three children and lost her youngest son in a tragic car accident and found comfort and solace in Compassionate Friends. She had an eye for color and believed, like her mom, that it was important to create a home that reflected your personality. She passed away in 2024. She will be missed.

Jean Remembers Shirley

My mother prepared my sisters and our families for her impending death from lung cancer. She had a strong faith and passed that faith to all of us. She spoke of being ready to join loved ones who had gone before her. She said she had lived a full and wonderful life and how blessed and proud she was to have us all in her life. She was at peace, and we could not help feeling the same way. What I was not prepared for was the enormous void in my life after she passed. I used to speak to her daily, and I would usually call her on my way to work. "Good morning, Mother Dear," I would say, and she would reply, "Good morning, Jeannie Dear." We would talk about the events upcoming, and we would catch up on what my sisters and their families were doing, and she let me know if she needed anything. On Saturdays, she would get her mail, stop over for a cup of coffee, and we would visit. She could not just sit. She would unload my dishwasher, fold a load of clothing, or dust while chatting with me. She would also dine with us every couple of weeks because she loved my husband's cooking. She would never arrive empty-handed, and that was something she passed on to us. If I was traveling, she would be more than willing to go along for the ride. She was ever present in my life.

I did not know why I had not realized just how much I would miss her. Maybe it was because I took all the small things she did for granted. Maybe I did not realize how much she was the focal point of our family. She was the one who kept everyone updated, and she would always open her home to family and friends every Sunday following mass. She was the one who made all the holidays, birthdays, and special occasions memorable. After she passed, I knew she was in a better place, but I was overwhelmed with grief.

One Sunday my sister Angie and her two children and I were the only family members at church. This was unusual because on any given Sunday, there could be twenty of us. I arrived late. The pew where my mother sat was empty, and I took her seat. It wasn't until later that I saw my sister was sitting two rows behind me. I felt so alone and sad sitting by myself, but gradually I felt a strong presence and a sense of comfort. I could feel sensations within my body; I didn't feel lonely any longer. I felt her presence and was filled with joy.

The last Christmas gift she gave all of us was an ornament inscribed with the words *I am with you because you remember me.* I realize that she is ever present in my life. Everything she taught and shared with each of us influences me each day. She loved and lived life to its fullest, and she loved her family with the same passion. She would never want any of us to be grieving or sad. My "Mother Dear" is always with me! I feel close to her when I prepare to go to church for Sunday mass. It was important to her, and I am continuing that tradition.

Jean Herron lives with her husband in the same community where she was raised. She is an office manager for a busy dental practice. She enjoys cooking with her husband, playing golf, and antiquing. She has two grown children and two grandchildren, who melt her heart.

Mary Remembers Shirley

My mother, Shirley J. Lavoie, left a legacy of love to her family. Not once did she allow us to feel anything but rich with faith, love, hope, and security while capturing our uniqueness. She taught us to dig deep to find out who we were and to find a direction in life that would give us good health and happiness. She would say that no one could take away who I was and where I came from and to be proud of that! And I am. She would tell me to look around and that there were those who were less fortunate to make the best of every situation.

I lost my father when he was only fifty-four years old twenty-five years ago, and he has appeared to me three distinct times. I saw him in a split second as he nodded and tipped his hat, and I have seen him in my dreams. Each time, I felt like he was giving me his approval for how I was living my life without him. I hope that I have a similar experience with my mom because when I saw him, I felt comforted, as if I was touched by an angel's healing touch.

I gave my mother her medicine to keep her comfortable during the last weeks of her life. I knew it was normal to wonder if I did enough and if I made the right health decisions for her, although knowing this did not stop me from going over those last difficult weeks in my mind. One afternoon, I was sitting in the spare bedroom sobbing, praying, and wondering. It was the room where she had slept when she lived with us. My tears were streaming down my face, and I closed my eyes, and for a moment, I felt as if she was tucking me safely into my bed as she had done when I was a child. I felt a warm blanket of comfort and reassurance that she was with me, and this was a gentle reminder to celebrate her life instead of wasting time second-guessing when I know she knows I did my best for her. I have challenges each day, like most people, and I call them "growth opportunities." I thank God for each and every opportunity, but most of all, I thank God for my parents, who taught me to be the best that I can be. I miss my mom, but I see her in my sisters every time we are together, and that reminds me that being a Lavoie girl is truly a blessing.

Mary Quinn is married to a kind and genuine man, and together they raised two daughters who keep her life fun, full of heart, and remarkably busy. She has five beautiful grandchildren. She was the former executive director of the Heartland Spa in Gilman, Illinois, and continues to help women make healthier lifestyle choices to live their best lives.

Michel Remembers Shirley

When my mom passed, I felt a sense of relief because of the agonizing pain that she endured. I wanted to take her pain away when taking care of her, and I think all her daughters did to some degree. We encircled her. We touched her and let her know that it was okay with us for her to go to the Lord. I wanted my mom back, the way she used to be—full of life and, in her words, "piss and vinegar." I had never seen anyone take their last breath, and I don't ever want to see it again. She fought so hard to be brave, and our faith allows us to know that she is in Heaven and that we all have eternal life. I believe she is in Heaven with my dad, looking over us, and guiding me every day. Her life was enormously powerful in the little things that she did—rituals and actions that I observed and felt.

Her memory is even more powerful. Before I make a big decision, I find myself asking Mom if she approves since she was so verbal in her opinions. I have taken Mom's beliefs, broken them down, and made them my own, including birthday celebrations and holiday gatherings, and I am following my Catholic faith in a way I know she would approve of. I know she is proud of me and my sisters, and she would often say so.

I don't know how she did it, but she always made me feel special. I never saw her playing favorites, although she made me feel that I was her favorite. She had so much love to give, and she loved us deeply. I have never felt jealous of any of my sisters, and she taught me that. Loving us all the same yet making us each feel like the favorite had to be her special talent. She never backed down to the challenges of life and that included her death. She embraced the fact that her time was up and made peace with that fact. I believe she couldn't wait to see my father, the true love of her life. My father died when she was in her prime, and she was a beautiful woman, but she never remarried. When I asked her why she didn't date, she told me that she was not "going to take care of another man and do his dirty laundry ever again!" She took over his business with help from my sister Pam, even though it was a man's world, and neither of them backed down from the challenge. I learned this lesson from her, and I have never backed down from a challenge either.

She taught me to treat my friends with respect as she did and to rely on friends for help when in need, and she loved people. I believe I am a good mother to my son because of how I grew up. I tell my son that I love him every day. My mom taught me to never go to bed angry at the people we love. After we moved to South Padre Island, Texas, my husband was diagnosed with pancreatic cancer. She came to my rescue and told me that she knew how I felt, and she did. She cried with me, let me cry more, and then she sat me up straight and gently took a hold of my shoulders. She told me that this was God's will and that I needed to be strong. She said that my husband and God were counting on me to be a good mom and stepmother.

When she visited me, I genuinely enjoyed it. She always called me every weekend to make sure I was taking my vitamins, that I was taking care of myself, and to check on her grandson. I miss those conversations, and I wonder if anyone will ever love me as much as she did. We moved to Austin, Texas, in 2006, and she came to visit and cleaned my house as she always did. My house is clean today because I always hear her telling me, "Michel Marie, are you keeping up with your house?" I will never forget the memories we shared together. I want to tell her that "yes, Mom, I am taking my vitamins, my son is doing his homework, and my house is clean!" I think that she knows.

When she was sick, I tried to visit her every month even though my sisters were taking care of her. I wanted to give them a break, but what I really wanted was to steal time away just for us. I tried to make sure she was comfortable and not in pain. She loved reflexology, and I would rub her feet just like she used to rub mine. I am not a great cook, but I tried to cook for her, and we would laugh about that.

On Mother's Day during the last year of her life, I flew home and surprised her. She was on the phone when I rang the doorbell, and the look on her face was priceless when she answered the door. When she recovered from the shock of seeing me, she said, "Michel Marie, you scared the hell out of me." I told her good, because I knew she would make it to Heaven, and we needed to get all the hell out of her that we could. She laughed and then cried and cried some more. She was a gentle, loving soldier for God and a true mother until the end of her life on earth. I know she looks down on me every day and is still my mother.

I want to dream of her, but I haven't yet. I did feel her presence, though, when my son's grandmother passed away. I could feel her with me. I could almost smell her. I could hear her say, "Honey, be strong for him." My heart and will are strong because she fills them both. I love her and will continue to miss her until we meet again. I don't know when the healing process will stop, but I know that she is in a far better place, but selfishly, I wish she was still here with me.

Michel Lavoie lost her husband to cancer in 2001. She worked as executive staff director at Red River Service Corporation in Austin and is a single parent. She has a BS in human resources. Before she moved to Texas, she worked in the public school system and coached the girls' volleyball program, one of her passions. She attributes her sense of humor, ability to survive adversities, and positive attitude to her mom.

Angie Remembers Shirley

The last few weeks of my mother's life are still vivid. All her daughters stood by her side just like she had asked us to. And even if she did not ask, we would have been with her because it was the right thing to do. Her last week was a struggle, watching her take one breath at a time, and when she finally passed it was bittersweet. The pain and struggle were finally over for her. Her faith was so deep that it made it easier for us to let her start her new life, but I did not realize just how lonely I would feel without her.

I had a dream about her after she died. My husband and I were on vacation, and wherever we went, she and her best friend would be standing side by side and waving and smiling at us. We were in the mountains, and they would wave to us. We would be eating, and they would continue to smile and wave. So, wherever I am, I know she is always with me. I want to thank her for everything she did for me. She will be in my heart and mind forever and ever!

Angela Lavoie Taylor is the baby sister of the Lavoie family. She enjoyed watching her husband and son participate in truck-pulling contests and shares her passion for cooking and baking with her daughter, passing on family recipes. She works as an orthodontic assistant and enjoys drawing, ceramics, and designing baskets.

Frances Remembers Adele

It's the end of the day. There's a slight breeze out of the south; the birds are preparing for the night, and the sun is sinking ever lower in the west. The sky is awash with glowing colors—pinks, oranges, even purples light up the clouds, with patches of deep blue sky peeking through. I take in the coconut palms silhouetted against the brilliant backdrop, and I am in awe. I stop, smile, and say, "Hey, Delly."

Delly was a nickname my grandmother gave my mom, Adele, when she was a little girl. I adopted it as my favorite term of endearment when she was alive. Now that she's passed, I use it whenever I feel her presence or when I want to communicate with her. When there is a dramatic sunset, I'm reminded of her. "Quick, let's get someplace high so we can watch the sun set!" she would say. It is hard to find "someplace high" in Florida, but I could usually get to a bridge over the Intracoastal Waterway, drive halfway over, and pull off at the highest point. There we would sit and marvel at the show nature was putting on. If it hadn't been for my mom's insisting, I would've missed it. In her last years, Delly was my little Zen master.

We hadn't always been close. She was a Scorpio, a water sign; I'm an Aries, a fire sign. Fire and water don't mix very well, and we didn't see eye to eye on much of anything when I was growing up. In fact, we hadn't lived in the same city (sometimes not even in the same country) for thirty-five years. In 1998, she was diagnosed with Alzheimer's. I moved from Denver to Juno Beach, Florida, to be closer to her as she dealt with this horrible disease. The devastating diagnosis for her turned out to be a blessing in disguise for me. We were closer and had better times together than ever before. In addition to the experiences we shared, I had the challenges and joys of learning how to be a caregiver. I was the student, and she was the teacher.

I sometimes wonder if on a cosmic level she volunteered to take on the disease of Alzheimer's so that I could learn some of the valuable lessons caregiving teaches, and she could accelerate her own spiritual advancement. Suppose in that other worldly zone between lives, she made the decision to come back as my mother (teacher, protector, and caregiver) so she could guide me the first part of my life, and then we would switch roles before our deaths, and I would protect and care for her. Sounds bizarre, but if one thinks about karmic law and spiritual evolution, why not?

If you can relate to this philosophy, then the obligation of caregiving can shift from an onerous, weighty chore to an act of devotion. When I think that she might have chosen me to fill that role, I realize she must have loved me very much, and I must be extremely special to deserve such a gift. It was an honor for me to care for her.

I'm no saint. I wasn't the best nurse. Patience is not my strong suit, and I deeply regret all the times I resented the time and the work. There are many things I wish I had done better. However, when I did stop and take a few minutes to think of her as a spiritual being who willingly and lovingly took on the burden of her disease, I could smile and feel gratitude for my good fortune at having such a rare person for a mother.

My mom was smart, earning scholarships to get herself through college during the Great Depression. She taught high school English, Latin, and drama in Fort Payne, Alabama, before marrying my father and raising two kids. She remained a teacher to my brother and me when she shared her love of music, books, sports, and nature. She was gregarious and made friends easily.

When she was eighty-three, she was diagnosed with Alzheimer's disease; however, it didn't cause her to lose herself. Instead, she became firmly grounded in the here and now. She could not remember the near past and therefore didn't mourn what happened yesterday. She had no plans for tomorrow and therefore didn't stress about the future. She just was. During the next nine years, my mom—through her actions—taught me many things, among them:

Lesson 1: Be in the moment; appreciate the little things in life; be grateful for your blessings.

One day as I helped her toward the car for one of her many doctor's appointments, she stopped mid-stride. As usual, we were running late. "What is the matter? We must hurry," I said through clenched teeth. "Look at the sky!" she said. "We don't have time to look at the sky!" She insisted that I stop and look up. I did as I was told, and when I looked up, I was rewarded with the sight of mounds of cumulus clouds reflecting a glorious midday brightness against deep blue heavens. No one could look at that beauty and not be touched to the core. I know now that my mom was telling me that no matter how important I thought my endless "to-do" lists and schedules were, there were more important things in life, such as taking some time to enjoy each day and to be mindful of the gifts we are given. She was saying, in effect, "Take a moment to breathe deeply and look around at the miracles of the universe." What a wise woman.

Lesson 2: Always try to look on the bright side.

My mom taught me not to dwell on the negative. One evening when I came after work to see her, she took one look at me and knew I was feeling down. The first thing she said was "So, tell me the happiest thing that happened to you today." She couldn't fix the problem, but she tried to give me a tool. Most of us live where our minds are, and often, we can choose to hang out in the dumps. Or not. She knew the wisdom of elevating one's thoughts and living in a better place. By changing my focus from the negative to the positive, I managed to feel better and had much more energy to fix the situation than if I had let my problem take the upper hand.

Lesson 3: Respect each person you encounter.

I believe we are here on earth for a reason—that we all have value. My mom had kind words to say to just about everyone she met, and she was grateful to all the people who helped her. Because she was so positive and so appreciative, it's no surprise that my mom's friends and the nursing home staff cared deeply for her.

Lesson 4: Choose to be kind.

Skilled nursing facility staff are overworked and underpaid. Some become certified nursing assistants as a calling, and they are angels. Some become CNAs for the small paycheck, and they do not seem happy. Several times a week, I found some aspect of my mother's care that was lacking or downright incompetent, and I would complain. My mom reprimanded me, saying, "They are doing the best they can. Taking care of all these old people is a difficult job."

Lesson 5: Be cognizant of those around you who may be less fortunate and be as generous as possible. When you have given "enough," give more.

When I would visit her at the skilled nursing facility around dinnertime, my mom told everyone at the table that her daughter would not only pick up the check for everyone's dinner but drive them all home. Her dinner companions smiled, pushed back their chairs, and prepared to walk out before the nurses intervened. How lovely it is to be with someone who feels her primary aim is to take care of everyone else.

There are esoteric philosophies that say there are several exit points built into one's lifetime, and during each of those exit points, one can choose to leave or stay. I knew my mom had already had one near-death experience forty years before, following a botched hysterectomy. She had described it to me much later, saying that she experienced "rising or floating up an incline toward a man—he was like Jesus, but he wasn't Jesus. He held his arms out toward me, and I was happy and at peace." She said she just wanted to keep floating upward, but she turned around, looked down, and saw her husband, who was later diagnosed with Parkinson's. She thought, "I can't leave now. He needs me." So, she came back. Wasn't she ready to go? Maybe I wasn't ready to let her go. Maybe my little Zen master had an additional gift to share with me before she said her final goodbye.

This additional gift turned out to be the gift of time. Those precious months between the first scare and her final passing gave me a chance to tell her repeatedly how much I loved her, how much I admired and respected her, and how much I appreciated all that she had done for me. It was not all seriousness and solemnity, though. That would not be the way of the Zen master. What we did was practice different forms of being in the now. We ate lots of chocolate ice cream and told each other stupid jokes. We giggled ourselves silly after drinking a single glass of champagne. We frequently drove to the beach at sunset (her favorite time of day), and in comfortable silence we watched the play of light on the water. Is there any glory in the world greater than sharing simple pleasures with a person you love?

On a bright September morning, my mother took her last breath. Both her children were with her, each holding a hand, and she made her transition. It happened very peacefully. No fanfare, no drama. It was simply over. I suspect she was able to leave quickly because of her prior near-death experience. She was in familiar territory. There would have been no fear. She would have known exactly what was happening, and I am confident her sisters, my dad, her parents, all those who loved her, were around her, celebrating her coming home.

In the days after my mom's death, I started questioning every decision I had made regarding her care. I was beating myself up over things I should have insisted on: checking her medications, supervising her nursing care, talking more with her physicians—there were so many things I could have done differently. I guess I forgot to utilize the lessons my Zen master had taught me. Then one morning I awoke, and the information I was given was "None of that matters, and everything is okay." It was like a message from my mother. It was a knowingness that settled all the questions and removed all the doubts. Some literature refers to this knowingness as an additional sense. It's not a vision; it's not a voice; it is knowledge that comes instantaneously with unquestionable authority. I knew then that nothing I did would have changed the outcome significantly.

Did I always appreciate my mom when she was still alive? Of course not. We take the things and the people around us for granted. We try not to, but we do. Since her passing, my mother holds a special place in my heart. I know she is with me, and although I don't yet embody the life lessons the way she did, I continue my efforts to 1) appreciate the present, 2) think positively, 3) respect everyone, 4) choose kindness, and 5) extend the limits of my generosity. She will always be my favorite teacher, and especially when there is a spectacular sunset, I greet my little Zen master and thank her.

Frances Baker has always had a passion for investigating the secrets of the universe in science, art, religion, and spirituality. She is a longtime student of various New Age teachers and Eastern philosophers. Her career included administrative work in academic research and medical environments. Now retired and living in Jupiter, Florida, she enjoys reading, attending lectures, and participating in discussion groups.

Erin Remembers Eloise

My mother was thirty-nine years old when she died, twenty days before her fortieth birthday. She always told everyone she would be "forever thirty-nine" so she could hold on to her youth, and she was killed in an automobile accident the first week of my eighth grade year. I was thirteen when she passed away. Mainly it was my friends who witnessed my pain, but my dad also made sure that their moms would look out for me because I needed it. I loved the intentional affection that I received and often chose to spend time with the "moms" while I was at my friends' houses. I swam competitively and loved the release. I also worked with a therapist a year and a half after her death. I was managing pretty well given the circumstances—star athlete, honor student, and socially mature in many ways—but there were times that felt too overwhelming. I intentionally swallowed half a bottle of painkillers to release my body from the pain in the only way my fifteen-year-old brain knew. Luckily for me, I told my father. It was my cry for help. This experience validated that I needed to make proper choices about my health and vitality, and I didn't need to be perfect. I didn't realize it at the time, but losing my closest confidante, my mother, really was a lot for my young soul to hold. No one is above the pain that accompanies loss.

I felt her presence when she first passed away and noticed that particular songs would magically play on the radio like clockwork. "Tears in Heaven," "Over the Rainbow," and "When I See You Again" were the main three songs that kept repeating. I dreamt about her when I was considering different schools for college. She appeared sitting on a wooden gym bleacher and told me to "go higher" on the bleachers, to choose the "gold" rows (schools), and not to settle. This was a great gift because I knew that she was returning to me at a turning point in my life, guiding me through this important shift.

The second chapter of my initial grief was my father's death. It happened seven years after my mother's, when I was twenty-one. At this point my attention turned toward travel, energy healing, medium readings, running, boyfriends, and a deep connection to yoga. Yoga helped me to understand that I could create space for myself and guided me to my authentic self. I became a yoga teacher to help other people thrive in their own bodies and lives and now have a small business teaching kids' yoga. In my thirties, nature, acupuncture, nutrition, psychotherapy, and the family I have created have helped in my healing process.

The grief process is different for everyone; however, I have found that sorrow can quietly find its way into the most special moments. My mother's presence during my childhood gave me a heart full of love. I have also discovered the sting of loss and grief with every baby, every mothering question, and every time I need her loving arms around me. There was so much unknowing, and I wanted to raise my children with her and grow as a mother with her guidance. I finally let myself experience my longing for her after my third child was born. It was excruciating by then. They say that "you can only tell yourself what you can tell your mother." This was true for me because I had been just skimming the surface of my everyday life to just make it through. I began to write her letters again, and initially I could barely write a word. It took weeks to finally write a letter to her filled with sadness, anger, truth, and profound yearning. I feel at peace now. My decisions as a child, woman, and mother have been my own, but how she touches my life continues into my life and my children's.

We have blended my mother into our lives. When we got married, my husband and I displayed both of our parents' wedding day photographs and sprinkled in sweet memory moments throughout the day. I often speak about my mother with my children, and I created elaborate baby books and family picture albums just as she did. Her love and the memories of seeing her resemblance in my children gives me comfort.

When I was younger, I had a reoccurring dream of her. We were both in the woods, and she would always walk away, and I could not find her. I felt abandoned every time, both in my dream and during my everyday life afterward. It helped when I had a consultation with a mystic. I was told that her death was her choice, and my heart softened knowing that she was not a mother leaving her family but a soul making decisions.

I have felt her presence when I dreamt that I was in a room with people who were chaperoning me, and I kept trying to tell them that the room did not have good energy, and they did not listen. I heard my mother tell me, "Shut it down now. Shut down any and all veils you have open." I mentally placed a white light of love and protection around myself and my family. I am spiritual and religious and consciously choose positive people, oracle cards, meditation practices, and prayer to seek and gain insight. I choose connection with God and my soul, and I have learned through medium mentorship to trust what comes through and let go of anything that does not serve the higher good.

The last experience that I had with my mother felt powerful. She had not shown up in a dream for a long time, but I wasn't surprised she helped me positively shift my energy. She had a confident spirit in life, and I knew she had had a connection to God that was strong and trusting. She reminded me of my own power and connection at a vulnerable time. This could have been purely a dream, a metaphysical experience within a dream, or my brain trying to work something out from my life; however, she visited me when I needed her. The power of mothers can show up in so many ways. I asked myself how I am showing up with my children. I was reminded to let go of the mom guilt and trust that my children are getting what they need from me. "Grace" is what I desire, both as a practice and as a gift. Grace, my mother's middle name and my daughter's first name. They have taught me so much about the true nature of living in grace.

Losing a mother is like losing the keys to who you are and where you come from, and it can be lonely to navigate life. If anyone were to come to me after losing their mother, I would put my arms around them. My best advice for someone would be to ask yourself a lot of questions—questions you might otherwise ask your mother. Find the resources that you resonate with for comfort and joy. Rest is also important and underrated. Throughout the years on random days when I felt sad and was unable to function with much zest, I stayed in bed. It was much easier to do this before I had children, but I have learned the quality of time I spend caring for myself as a parent gives me a fuller experience with and for my family. When I listen to my body's needs, my body responds with energy and a feeling of alignment. It is a radical responsibility for yourself. I show up for myself and surround myself with people who feel like sunshine. I have become the mother I hoped to be, only actually better, and I love encouraging other parents to tend to their souls. If I were to have a conversation with my mother about this, I would say, "Thank you for showing me the depth of the word *mother*."

Erin Johnston is married with five children, ages one and a half to ten years old. She is a registered nurse, registered yoga teacher, certified radical remission health coach, and trained grief support group facilitator. Erin homeschools her children, teaching them about the importance of good health and wellness, incorporating movement and mindfulness.

Toni Remembers Patricia

The memories of this day will stay with me forever. It was a month and a half after my eighteenth birthday. It was Memorial Day, May 31, 1993. It was the day my life would be forever changed. It was the day my mother died. I spent the night at a friend's house. She was the one to receive the phone call in the morning. My uncle was trying to reach me, and no one knew where I was except for my mother. He sounded panicked on the phone and told me my mother was in a serious car accident. Since I was nearby, he told me to walk to my grandparents' house right away, where he, my grandfather, and my younger brother were waiting. It was the longest four blocks of my life. My heart felt heavy. I was scared, but my brain only thought of ways we would care for her during her recovery.

It was a long, quiet ride to the hospital. I sat in silence while looking out the window. I saw families setting up barbecue grills and tables, getting ready to enjoy the holiday and the beautiful sunny day ahead. I envied them. I had no idea what lay ahead for me that day. When we stepped out of the car, my grandmother, who arrived at the hospital before us with my aunt, was sitting in the shade under a tree. She was crying. She repeated, over and over,

"She's gone. Patty's gone." My heart sank into my gut. My brain refused to comprehend such simple yet horrifying words.

My mind was in a foggy daze as I entered the hospital. I was confused. Emotionless. I could not comprehend the depth of those words. I robotically followed my family to the entrance of the intensive care unit where my mother was all alone. A nurse rushed toward us. Children were not allowed. She immediately escorted my brother and me to a small waiting room nearby. I was confused. How is it possible that her children were not allowed in? The nurse assured me that she would be back to bring us in. I paced in the small waiting room for what seemed like an eternity, although was likely only minutes. My mother needed me, and I needed to be with her. I needed to hug her. I needed to tell her how much I loved her. I needed her to come back. She can't leave us, I thought. I needed to be strong. I needed to see her. I grabbed my brother, who was clearly in shock, and said, "We are not waiting anymore. Let's go see Mommy."

When we entered the ICU, that same nurse came rushing toward us to escort us back out. I demanded to see my mother. I walked into her room feeling immediately overwhelmed by all that surrounded her: the machines and medical equipment, the white linens piled on the floor next to her bed covered with her blood. I looked at my mom, who lay lifeless. Her eyes were taped shut. She was covered with sheets up to her chest. I was so scared. I wanted her to open her eyes. I didn't know what to do. She was the first person I ever knew to die. My mom. I was scared to touch her. I didn't know what else to do except hug her and tell her that I loved her. As I walked out of the room, I paused to look back at her. Her arm was hanging off the side of the bed. I will always regret that I didn't go back to place her arm on the bed and tuck her in. I was so afraid that I would hurt her or break her if I touched her.

My family cried as we held each other. Walking out of the hospital, still in tears, I remember strangers staring at us. I am certain they saw the pain of loss on our faces and heard it in our cries.

On the drive home, I sat with silent tears. My uncle punched the dashboard in anger. "Why, Patty?" he yelled. I realized that my sister was due home that day. She was away for the weekend with a friend. I envied her at that moment for not knowing and for feeling whole. I dreaded to see her, knowing how much pain my mother's death would cause her. When my sister arrived at my grandparents' house, she didn't make it past the foyer and collapsed when she heard the news. She grabbed me in hysterics, pulling me to the floor with her. Our mother was gone. The one person in the world who loved us with no limits, who knew us better than anyone else could, who nurtured and guided us and supported us in every way imaginable. She was gone forever—our rock, our foundation, our unbreakable, irreplaceable, unconditional bond seemed lost.

The months after my mother's death seemed surreal. I almost looked forward to the first few seconds of each morning when I woke and felt like my old self, whole and complete, until that sickening feeling would overwhelm me again that my mom was gone. Everyone around me went back to their daily routines while I wanted to scream: "Wait, life will never be normal again for me. Life will never be the same! How do you go on after you have lost someone so special?" I was in shock for so long. There were not many tears, except when I cried in the silence of my new bedroom in my grandparents' house. It was then that I was forced to see my reality. My new room, my new home, my new life without my mother. My friends would often tell me how well I was doing, so strong, and how proud my mother would be. So I believed that I was supposed to be strong. No tears. My mom would be proud, even though my heart and soul were aching. When everyone else went on with their lives, I assumed the next step, following their lead. I was supposed to close the door to the past and brave the future. But I wasn't ready. I was still in shock. I wanted my mother to come back. At times, I believed she was still alive somewhere and she would come back for us. I started to move through my life one day at a time. I got a job and life took its course.

I am a firm believer that loved ones can visit us in dreams. As adults, we unintentionally build mental barriers filled with doubt, denial, and fear. When my daughter was two years old, we were driving home from a restaurant on a cold, rainy night when she started talking. I asked her who she was talking to. She replied matter-of-factly, "Grandma Patty!" I wholeheartedly believe that children do not have the barriers that adults acquire over time. When we sleep, those walls come down because we are calm, comfortable, and more open to the energy of messages in dreams. I have experienced dreams that were filled with fear and anger. I have also had dreams that were so painful, I woke to a wet pillow, choking with tears.

I had the most profound dream of my mother two years after she died. This dream gave me comfort and a renewed sense of faith that she is absolutely still with me. In this dream, I was standing at my grandparent's front door, which had been my home now for the past two years. My younger brother was playing football in the street with some friends. My mother was standing in the driveway by a tree watching my brother. I stared in amazement before opening the door to run to her. She was dressed in either light pink or white. I am not sure. Her blonde hair touched her shoulders. She looked so peaceful, happy, and beautiful. She hugged me, and I did not want to let her go. Our embrace felt so real. I felt her love. In that moment everything was okay again. I felt safe. I felt whole. Then I realized I had many questions. I knew she wasn't alive, but her presence was so real. I asked her, "Are you okay? Are you happy? What is it like in heaven? Are you lonely? Do you miss us?" She replied, "It is beautiful. I am okay. Don't worry about me. I just stopped by to watch your brother play for a while. I am still with you all. I visit all the time." I had many more questions, but I felt content with her answers. I wanted her to stay. I was so happy to see her. My mother does come to visit and continues to watch over us. I woke up that morning with a sense of peace that I had not felt in a long time. The dream was so vivid that I truly felt like I had a visit with my mom. I will always remember that dream and several others I have had over the years. I will always wish my mother was alive and physically here with us, but I feel blessed that she visits me in my dreams.

I have learned to accept that I will always miss my mother. Her time here was too short, and I wonder how life would be with her in it. I cherish the many gifts that she gave me—her knowledge, strength, wisdom, her compassion and love, and, most of all, my life. My mother will always be part of my soul, and she lives on through her grandchildren. My husband, my children, and I celebrate her life by keeping her memory alive.

My mother, Patricia E. Sanderson, was thirty-five years old when she died. She was a single mother of three children. She was an extremely hard worker, establishing her own cleaning business to provide for her children. She was an incredibly loving mother who never missed an opportunity to tell us how much she loved us. What a terrific grandmother she would be today. She was a wonderful person with a heart of gold who saw the good in everyone. I will always miss her presence, her laugh, love, integrity, and strength, and the feel of her arms around me. She was killed by a drunk driver.

Toni Freer has been married to an incredible man for twenty-seven years. He is her best friend, an amazing father, and her rock. She has three beautiful children—a daughter and two sons—who are her heart and soul. "They are truly the air I breathe!" The biggest blessing in her life is to be their mother.

Jeanne Remembers Sharon

To understand the power of my relationship with my mother, you must first understand the power and the presence of the woman she was and continues to be in spirit. The words used to describe her included *strong, truthful, honest, spiritual, healer, independent, helper, childlike, endearing,* and *intelligent.* These words just begin to describe a woman whose connection with God was admired, sought after, and appreciated by hundreds. Her love for God began in Catholic schools in Buffalo, New York. As other six- and seven-year-old children scrambled to recess, she stayed inside the chapel at the foot of the statue of Jesus because he was her best friend, and she did not want to "leave him alone." She began life as a faithful Catholic and attended mass every day for decades.

My mom attended college after giving birth to me—her fourth child. This was quite unusual in the early 1970s. She received her teaching degree and began teaching the most challenging children in the city of Buffalo. These were kids on their way to prison sentences for murder, robbery, and drug trafficking. She treated these kids as her own. She expected them to make an effort to improve themselves, setting the bar above where they thought they could go. After she died, I found a worn and yellowed letter from a former student, which Mom had tucked away in her Bible. The student had included a picture of her graduation from high school. She thanked my mom for believing in her abilities and for leading her out of the vicious cycle of oppression set up by her environment. For my mother to hold on to this for thirty-plus years spoke volumes to me. Even though she never received the professional recognition she deserved, she had something even better.

After leaving her marriage to my father, a man with mental illness, she began searching for her own definitions of self, of religion, of marriage, and of society. This was a search she continued until she died. She stopped going to church for many years. During that time, however, she found a spiritual side of herself that led her to her Native American roots, to shamanism, spiritual guides, and her own personal connection to our ancestral Indigenous beliefs.

My mother remarried, and we moved to a small country town in upstate New York. This was a positive experience for all of us. For my mom, this new beginning offered a chance to come back to the Catholic Church without the expectations of those around her. She returned a little wiser, a little more skeptical, but still loving God and believing that love is the answer to all the world's problems. She read Thomas Moore, Henri Nouwen, Thich Nhat Hanh, the Dalai Lama, and others. She knew more Hebrew than my Jewish niece and nephew, and she knew, understood, and respected faith traditions, from Catholicism to Hinduism.

She did not have a blind faith, as her life was dedicated to questioning. She knew that it is only by questioning that you can own your beliefs; otherwise, they belong to someone else. Her questions allowed her to see the truth of what lay at the heart of each religion and in each person. There might be a dark side to people and their faith traditions, but there was also a goodness or "light side." She spent her life trying to help people hold on to this reality, embrace their own goodness, and know they are loved by God. She wanted others to have the peace that comes with knowing that you are loved. At the same time, she wanted them to understand the motivation and the consequences of their own behaviors and beliefs.

Because of her ability to be a conduit for peace, people came to see her for healing. Once she retired from teaching, she was busier than ever seeing people who came for spiritual direction. She used techniques that she had learned from counseling classes along with her own communication style with God to help people feel God's love. Although this sounds very sugary, my mother would not be described as sweet. She challenged you and not always in the gentle way I would have preferred.

She called a spade a spade and challenged people to question themselves. She would not let them use excuses for how their life was going, the same lesson I learned as a young child. Her expectations of others were high, but her expectations for herself were even higher. Given the pain and trauma in her life, she might have easily granted herself a "get out of jail free card," but she never used her mother's abandonment at two weeks old, subsequent sexual abuse, the alcoholism of the grandfather who raised her, or her teen marriage to a man she would later find out was a paranoid schizophrenic as an excuse. She never let these harsh circumstances define her or give her permission to not follow the more difficult path of becoming a good and loving person. Time after time she would remind me that "everyone has a story."

She taught me humility and that I was neither better nor worse than the homeless man who came to Thanksgiving dinner. She taught me about potential, and with her as my role model, it should come as no surprise that I wanted to make a difference in people's lives. I had learned the power and beauty of compassion, and I wanted compassion to be my number one characteristic. It is no wonder that I have chosen to work in a field such as hospice, where people are not judged for life choices or for their spiritual beliefs.

Just as she did not have an easy childhood, I too had a "story" that could have torn us apart. She is the one I credit with giving me strength to endure my own childhood sexual abuse and a father with severe mental illness. She gave me strength in my journey to "come out" as a gay woman. She and I would have many tearful, honest conversations. There was healing, forgiveness, compassion, and love. Our understanding of each other and what made us tick went beyond what most would consider a normal mother-daughter relationship.

When she was diagnosed with stage IV metastatic colon cancer, she was symptom free and wanted only comfort care as needed. Two months later, she entered a local hospital with what appeared to be a blockage. As the physicians assessed the blockage, presenting opposing opinions every day, Christmas crept up on us. Two days before Christmas, my mother and stepfather read one of their favorite books by Brennan Manning. The passage for that day spoke of how we as Americans choose to "prettify" Christmas and focus on the gifts and the tinsel of the holiday season, forgetting the setting of the birth of Jesus, who was born on the floor of a barn surrounded by animals. Even though Mom wasn't very active in her hospital bed, she opened her eyes, looked at my stepfather and I, and said, "That's it! That's our Christmas card! Place a picture of the stable on the front of the card and inside write the words 'You can't change the smell of the stable.'" We knew what she meant, but we weren't sure her friends would understand! My mother spoke the truth, and the truth isn't always pretty. As she knew she was dying, she had no tolerance for platitudes or sugary words. She wanted real connections. She was imploring us to not pretend that suffering was beautiful or try to deny how hard life can be sometimes. You can, however, appreciate the mystery and the beauty of love present amidst the suffering. Hold nothing back, and don't be afraid to be vulnerable in the expression of love in the midst of your own or someone else's pain.

It felt unbearable at times to watch my mother suffer. I couldn't understand why this woman who had spent her whole life devoted to God and to God's people would have to die in such agony. There were times it was clear that she too questioned why this was happening. There are things you learn working in hospice that you can forget when it is your own loved one dying. For me, one of those things was that people die the way that they lived. And in my mother's case, that meant serious internal existential work reviewing her past and her fears of what lay ahead. As her daughter, and knowing how she tried to live her life hand in hand with God, I thought she should be carried home on a white cloud. It was as if I was witnessing the energies of good and evil wage war for the trophy of her soul. It broke my heart to witness her spiritual suffering, almost more than not being able to stop the physical pain. Somewhere inside myself, I knew she and her God would win the battle.

I believe that the events leading up to her death—three weeks in the hospital without her morning prayer routine, without church, without prayer meetings, without feeling up to reading her Bible—led her to a place where she forgot who she was, who God was to her, and the healing she had received as an adult. So, we helped her to remember. Close friends did contemplative prayer around her bed, the aroma of anointing oils was used to bring her back to a peaceful place, and priest friends came and blessed her. These things did bring her peace.

Her pain was relieved with the hospice professionals' help, and I slept on a cot next to Mom for nine days and listened to her breathing, silently talking to her heart, telling her how much I loved her, how I want her to be free, to be at peace and to be happy. I cried for myself and what I was about to lose. There was no more pain. Her children, her husband, her sisters, and best friends were all there with her, and she soaked in the time with them. One night my mother's spirit woke me from a sound sleep. I jumped off the cot and looked at her and realized she was gone. I still couldn't believe it and sat there staring at her. I then saw the little wooden angel that we had kept next to her bed. Mom would hold that angel and in her sweetest voice ask me to tell her the story of the angel. I would tell her about the courage that she had through this whole process and that when she felt she didn't have any courage left, the angel could give it to her. This story appeased her, but you could tell she didn't think that was the full story. In that moment the angel seemed to be speaking directly to my heart. The angel figure had arms raised in a powerful clenched-fist position … as if the angel was signaling victory. I then began to sob as I suddenly realized the real story of that angel. The angel, like my mother, and like Rocky Balboa at the top of those steps in Philadelphia, had done it. She and God were the victors of her soul. My tears were a combination of sadness for my loss, relief, and perhaps bittersweet joy for her reunion with her best friend, Jesus.

There have been many occasions that I have felt my mother's presence since her death but none as remarkable as the day after her wake. I sat in her special prayer room, wanting to feel close to her. Sitting on the table next to my chair was the recorder I had given her two years ago. I had originally wanted her to write about her life, her childhood, and our family so that her story might live forever. A year earlier I had begun transcribing what she had recorded and remember being disappointed, even angry, listening to the first half of the tape. It seemed that she was focusing on the events that were current in her life, and the tone of the recording felt rather depressing. She said, "Nirvana exists only in the moments" and that there is no bliss that lasts longer than a few weeks. I think it was at this point that I had stopped transcribing and gave her the recorder back to "try again." As I sat listening to the entire tape for the first time, I suddenly realized what she was really saying. Nirvana exists only in the moments, and that's why we have to be fully present and aware in each moment so that we may relish them. She ended the recording with her hopes. She hoped her children would know how deeply God loves them, and she hoped that we would know how much she loved each one of us. As I sat there crying, I prayed that I might know her even more deeply in her death. I sat quietly for a moment with tears running down my face and looked across the room at the built-in desk. A voice inside of me called me to go over to the desk and open the second drawer. I hadn't been at that desk for years, but I got right up and opened that drawer. There were four gifts, each one marked for a different child. These were not Christmas gifts. Each was wrapped in black and gold paper. I took the gift with my name on it, sat down, and opened it. There was a familiar old Bible with a note inside:

Dear Jeanne, my dearest daughter who carries my heart, this Bible is for you, my beginnings with Father Lavallee and mission and growth in spirituality. My spirit and life are in these pages for you. You have always been precious and are of God, from God, to God. I love you. Mom

This was the perfect gift. She was bringing me back to God, to faith, to spirituality through my love for her. I had been searching for the path back long before her death, and she had provided it. Days later I sat with the Bible she had given me, searching for a prayer that connected me to Mom. Tucked inside the Bible, I found a piece of paper with a prayer. On the back Mom had written a note: "My daily prayer for years and years with Jack and now for you." Again, I cried as I realized that unbeknownst to me I had selected this very same Native American prayer for the memorial cards at her funeral. It was clear she was still with me and continues to heal my own spiritual pain.

Through Mom's Native American experiences, she was given the name Lil' Feather. After her retirement, she began to explore her artistic abilities and became an accomplished watercolor artist. The name signed on her paintings was Lil' Feather. Perhaps the most constant and symbolic experience that connects my mother to me will continue to be the presence of feathers in my life. Since her death, feathers have become a way for her to let me know she is with me. I always say "hi" to her whenever I am given the gift of a feather. On Mother's Day, my first without her, I was grieving terribly. I felt empty and lonely. I went to work in my yard to occupy myself. As I was weeding, I accidentally put my hand inside a flower. What I pulled out was the softest little feather I had ever seen. I began to cry and was overcome with the joy of knowing she was with me. Not every feather is meant for me, and somehow, I know the difference between *her* feathers and random feathers in my path. When it's for me, I feel that same childlike joy and automatically acknowledge her presence. The feathers always come at the right time, and I pray they always will.

I kept a small urn of my mother's ashes, not understanding why but feeling a need to have some part of her close. Two years after her death, I was fortunate enough to travel to Hawaii. I knew I was to bring "her" to Hawaii and leave some of her ashes in the ocean. I didn't have a formal plan and trusted that the right moment would be shown to me. One beautiful afternoon at the beach I noticed a natural rock formation creating a gentle pool of water between the rocks and the beach. I knew this was where I would leave her because she had a terrible fear of rough water. I swam into the gentle pool and let myself cry. As I was getting my bearing, I found a flat rock to act as a shelf for my container while I opened it and said a prayer. As I set the container on the rock, there, nestled on top of this large lava rock, was a four-to-five-inch white and black speckled stone perfectly shaped like a feather. I knew she was pleased with my effort, and as I released her ashes and stepped back onto the beach, a whale breached the water and slapped its tail in a final gesture of approval. The beauty of that moment still brings a smile and a few goosebumps, while the feather and a small wooden whale sit side by side with the little angel in my prayer room.

Jeanne Chirico is the president and CEO of the Hospice and Palliative Care Association of New York State. She and her wife live on Conesus Lake in Upstate New York.

Stephanie Remembers Doris

It is hard to put down in words what the experience of being Doris DiCerbo's daughter really is. Words typically do not escape me, but this seems a particularly daunting task because there is no way possible to fully express what a blessing it is to be her daughter. My mom and I had some very wonderfully unique ways in which we related and defined the beauty of our own special, distinctive relationship, but it is the poignant moments we shared in her dying months that find their way into our story. Losing my mom propelled me to a place that for a long time was very dark and lonely. After she passed away, I couldn't imagine going on with my own life. The pain that I felt was primal. It rocked me to my core. I began to question with vengeance everything I ever knew to be true and have been on a tireless quest to make sense out of not only her loss but all loss ever since.

Dignified and *graceful* are the words I often use to describe who she was. She was the fairest person I have ever known, and I regularly referred to her as my barometer of reason. She was a Libra and had the very natural ability to consider both sides of every situation before passing any judgment or making a decision. It was not only her ability to be fair-minded that found her well-liked by so many, but she had a gentle strength, was exceptionally genuine and sincere, was exceedingly considerate, and rarely spoke a bad word about anyone.

During the time my mom was so sick, I was keenly aware from the first day of her diagnosis that every moment with her was sacred. For me, the simple things, such as fixing her coffee or driving her to the doctor, transcended all activities. We embarked on a holy journey, and I quickly became her most trusted companion. She transmuted from being my mother to being human. How do I explain the depths of the transformation it was for me, taking care of my dying mother and losing her? How do I articulate this sacred experience when there are not any words in any language to communicate this experience?

During this time, Mother Teresa was being considered for sainthood. She already had two miracles attributed to her intercession and needed a third for the process to continue. I became a woman on a mission—to have my mom be her third! Pride aside, I began to approach friends, family, and strangers alike, pleading with them to intercede with Mother Teresa to cure my mother's cancer. At this point in my spiritual life, I was in a place where I thought that storming heaven was all it would take. So, storm heaven I did. It did not work, and I was angry and had to regroup.

As I write this essay, I am pouring over all the journal entries I made during my mother's illness. The tears stream down my face. The pain overcomes me. It still seems unreal. There is so much I want to say, and I don't know where to begin. I stop to catch my breath, and in this calm moment, it occurs to me to ask my mom's help to move through this pain, to impart to others the joy and hope I was finally able to rediscover and everything in between. And she does help me.

I felt alone when this all started. The day my mom told me the fateful news that she had cancer, I knew on some intrinsic level that everything in my life would change forever. I would never be the same. Hearing this news felt like a force ferociously yanking me from one stage of my life to the next. I felt like my arms were being pulled out of their sockets, my body dismembered. As I sat up in my bed early that morning, listening to her as she provided more details over the phone from the hospital, the little girl I still felt I was suddenly morphed into the grown woman I have now become. A tender "come, pass peacefully and gracefully to the next stage of your life" voice never spoke. Instead, the force screamed in my face like an army sergeant at boot camp. It caught me off guard, startling and frightening me with its booming and commanding voice, shouting at me an earsplitting mandate to make the shift from child to adult. It was not a gentle, loving suggestion, just a piercing order to move from the "little girl" to "big girl" stage of my life.

I was scared and felt so vulnerable. I felt like a Girl Scout thrust into the woods with no time to pack a survival kit. I knew the elements would be harsh and unforgiving. Lucky for me, I guess, I had no idea to what degree, but I would soon find out. It was only three months later that my best friend, my mom, Doris, died. The emptiness left behind felt like an actual space. It was a palpable absence. Years later it still feels just as raw. Although I felt like God was walking with me on this journey, I still possessed a very child-like faith, believing that with enough prayer a cure would come. After all, my Catholic faith taught me "seek and ye shall find, knock and the door will be opened unto you."

After learning my mother had brain cancer, I entered a new psychological and emotional realm that I had never visited before. But that space was filled with lots of sacred moments that masked themselves as ordinary—washing my mom's and dad's clothes late into the evening, getting her to and from doctors' appointments, and helping her bathe and dress. I felt a spiritual presence with me. One evening standing at the washing machine, just being present to the sound and motion of the clothes churning, I began, in truth, to understand that the ordinary all along had really been the extraordinary. The late-night phone calls to my mom when I was in college, the warm summer days at the shore growing up, and even the occasional dissenting moments we shared were all extraordinary. But that moment simply washing clothes, I felt a tangible spiritual presence with me. I was reminded that God was with me. He was right there. It was a pivotal moment as I stood watching the clothes swish, listening to the hum. In prayer, I asked that my heart be open to experience God's love, strength, and support in whatever way that might come. As the old saying goes, "be careful what you wish for."

I was grateful for these moments when my mom and I would experience strange occurrences, like things you would see on the popular TV show *Touched by an Angel*, moments when the same person would appear from nowhere to help us lift Mom out of and back into the car for her last doctor's appointment. Hours had passed from the time we first got to her appointment to the time when we finally left. She was unable to stand on her own. My father and I were not strong enough to help her out of the car into the wheelchair, and she was declining so quickly that none of us realized that the two of us wouldn't be able to help her. We tried to lift her slowly out of the car, and I soon realized that all those trips to the gym were not enough, and our grip underneath her body began to give. At this moment when our strength began to fold, a strong gentleman approached us, and very gently and effortlessly, he lifted my mom up and lovingly placed her in her wheelchair. My dad and I looked at each other incredulously. Where did this man come from?

Getting lost in providing emotional support to my parents at the doctor's office faded any lingering thoughts of what had just happened. But as the time drew near for us to leave and make our way back to the car, my father and I began to worry—me silently, my father aloud. Although I was at times truly terrified being in such uncharted territory, I never spoke a word of my fears because I didn't want to upset them. But I was worried. How were we going to get my mom back into the car? I began to reassure my parents that we would be fine and that I really could manage. As my father pulled the car around and my concern worsened, the same man came over and said, "Let me help you." I nearly fainted! Who was this man? Where had he come from? Hours had passed since we first arrived, and my mom had several appointments that spanned hours from morning to early afternoon. It seemed like a small miracle.

I began to find solace in my newly found spiritual self-righteousness. I was feeling pretty spiritually full of myself. After all, I thought I had witnessed a miracle and was trying to be present to the "sacredness of the ordinary!" Just as I continued to gather steam stroking my spiritual ego (and feeling sure I had it all figured out) keeping vigil at my mom's bedside—she died. As I watched her take her last breath, I felt like God had sucker punched me. Not only did I feel instantly knocked out physically, but I also felt knocked out spiritually and shoved off my spiritual pedestal. I didn't know who I was anymore.

While I could write volumes about what happened between then and now, it is fair to say that I felt like life had dressed me down. I made the switch from being spiritually self-righteous to spiritually indignant. As I slowly began to wipe the dust from my eyes and brush off my badly bleeding spiritual skinned knees, I realized that somehow, eventually, I would have to find my way. During the time that my mom was diagnosed, I was considering leaving my private practice as a therapist and going back to work for an agency. Although I had completed my master's degree in counseling, I was still trying to find where I fit professionally. Obviously, the focus of finding myself shifted after we discovered my mom had cancer, but in the wake of her death, I eventually found myself back where I started. The last four days of my mom's life, our family felt truly blessed to have hospice care for her. They were our angels. I began to wonder if hospice work would be for me. After all, I sure knew something about grief and loss.

Several weeks after she died, I did an internet search for open positions in hospice care, and on the day of her death, a position for a coordinator of a children's grief and loss program had been posted by a local hospice. For the first time after my mom's death, I was aware of my heartbeat again. I shared the job posting with my older brothers and discussed my interest in applying for the job. I printed out the posting to show them, and it was a good thing I did because when I went back to my computer, the posting was gone. Vanished! I refreshed the screen and traced the history, but the posting was nowhere to be found. As I searched for it, something inside me told me that this wasn't strange at all. As disconnected as I felt from my mom, I suddenly knew, knew deep down (and at the time I was questioning everything), that my mom had orchestrated this job for me. After weeks and weeks of feeling like I would never be able to invest myself in anything again, I knew this job was not simply perfect for me but *for* me. At a time when everything in life seemed so uncertain, this I was certain about. "My mom worked this out." The hours were perfect; the location was close to home, and I applied.

The hospice personnel expressed some concern that I had only recently lost my mom, but I convinced them I had identified and rallied a strong, loving support system and that I was a safe bet. They hired me. It is hard to explain how sure I was that my mom was at the center of this. It was through the pain of my own experience and the authentic nature of the primal struggle I continued to sort through that I knew I was being led to work as a children's grief and loss therapist. For almost five years after my mom's death, I had the privilege of working in that capacity. It changed my life. My mom continued to bring me comfort, strength, and peace even in her passing.

As much as my work with hospice was meaningful, I was still very much caught up in my spiritual uncertainty. I decided to seek out spiritual direction and had been doing so for about a year when I had another remarkable and comforting spiritual experience. My spirit had felt ice cold—frozen. My spiritual director asked me at one meeting if I "could recall a time since my mom's death that I felt God's presence." My automatic reaction was to say a big, loud "no." I told her that the only time since my mom's death that I really could feel God's presence was when I was with the hospice patients and their families, and during those privileged moments, I would feel my heart "burn."

I had felt for so long after my mom's death like I couldn't feel her. It is fair to say that it wasn't that she wasn't with me so much as I purposely shut her out. The pain I felt living in a world without her was excruciating, and taking time to reflect on that was not something I wanted to do. My aversion to attending to my pain was similar to the feeling when you have a stomachache and you do everything to avoid vomiting. I would circumvent the psychological pain because it felt like the emotional equivalent of vomiting.

Even though I was a counselor and had explored for many years my own self-discovery process, I felt as if I didn't have the stamina for the exhaustion of emotional regurgitation.

One evening while I was looking for something in my nightstand, I came across a picture of my mom and I on our last vacation together. My sister had given me the picture and framed it for me, but I couldn't bear to see it, so I put it away. It caught me off guard. I began to feel like my mom was trying to push her way into my heart, but I was having none of it. I had slowly been trying to piece myself back together, and seeing this picture just took my breath away. I found myself praying—begging and pleading with God to show me a sign that what I was taught and believed in all my life was true. I screamed at God as loudly as I could in silence. I had put all my faith in him, and I desperately needed to know that I would see my mom again! I needed to know that God is real and what I was hanging my spiritual hat on would hold up. I began to sob as I stared at the picture, confused how someone can be so whole at one point and so broken.

In my confusion, the desire I had to know if God existed intensified. Almost instantly, in that moment of desperation, I found myself reminded of a particular section of the Gospel when Jesus's disciples are deeply grieving after his death. As they walked to the road to Emmaus, Jesus joins them, although I never understood why they did not immediately recognize him since they were his friends. They share their evening meal together, and it is during "the breaking of the bread" that they come to recognize him. As I sat on the floor in the puddle of my tears, I felt as though Jesus was saying to me, "You know I am real in the breaking of the bread." While that was all well and good, what was "the breaking of the bread"? I thought. That experience didn't really bring me much comfort—until the next afternoon when I met with my spiritual adviser.

I told her about my yearning to know if all I was counting on could in fact be counted on. She told me that she felt guided to read me a particular story from the Gospel. She slowly opened her Bible and flipped to the story about the road to Emmaus. I kept silent as she read the passage aloud, not yet willing to share with her that this very story is what came to my mind the night before. Truthfully, I sat there assessing the situation. "Hmm," I found myself thinking. "Okay, one could make an argument that this is a little coincidental." I wasn't entirely convinced that it was in fact far more than a "little coincidental" until she came to the end of the story when the disciples say, "They recognized him in the breaking of the bread." As if that wasn't strange enough, she continued to read the final passage, when the disciples ask themselves how it could be that they didn't immediately recognize Jesus, and they say, "Were not our hearts burning within us?" I began to cry.

I told my spiritual director when she asked that the only time that I felt God's presence was when I had a sensation in my heart of burning when I was with my clients in hospice care. I told her about my experience the night before, and it felt like time was suspended for both of us. God had given me the answer I needed. My mom interceded for me just as when she was alive and pushed her way into my heart even when I resisted her. She found a way to do this when I needed it, and I experienced a peace that I so desperately needed. It was after this extraordinary spirit-filled experience that I realized I was given a gift from my mom and God, and after that, I was finally able to begin healing.

I am equally reminded of how much my mom continues to bless my life. A few months after her death, I was having dinner with some of my best friends who were lucky enough not to know the pain of losing a mother. I was alone in that hurt, and I was throwing myself a colossal pity party. While they were doing their best to comfort me, I told them how I really felt after her death: "like a little girl who had been abandoned in a giant superstore." I felt lost and scared. They did not understand that, and although they tried to comfort me, it wasn't working. Truthfully, I really wasn't interested in feeling better. I just wanted to wallow in feeling forgotten and to be heard and witnessed. But with lots of time, self-exploration, and spiritual direction, the fog of abandonment did lovingly but painstakingly begin to lift.

In my work, I have been fortunate to hear many stories of love and loss, but with all due respect, personally I have found some to be a bit Pollyannaish. Frankly, those narratives annoy me. Please don't mistake my story for one of those. Yes, I have been blessed with guidance and direction from my mom both in her living and in her dying. I know how loved I was and know that she is there for me—just in a much different way, a way that I have come to discover I might not ever fully understand in this lifetime. The pain of her loss has been crippling, and the journey afterward has been frightening, frustrating, exasperating, and exhausting. I don't believe that "the wisdom one gains in loss is worth the price you have to pay to obtain it." However, daughters without mothers is a club to which I now belong because I paid the high price of admission.

I did find that there is hope and love after death. I finally discovered that I am not really lost in some generic, gigantic superstore. The experiences of connection I have had with my mom both in her living and in her dying tell me that my mom continues to hold my hand, love me, and support me, just from a more distant "aisle," and for now, finally… that has become okay for me.

Stephanie Baffone is a licensed, board-certified mental health therapist in private practice in Newark, Delaware. She specializes in grief and loss and working with couples dealing with issues related to infertility. Prior to being in private practice, Stephanie worked as the coordinator of a children's grief and loss program at a local hospice, providing education, support, and guidance to children and their families facing the devastating loss of a loved one and supporting them through the pain and intricacies of the bereavement process. She is a graduate of Villanova University and a member of the American Counseling Association and the National Board of Certified Counselors.

Suzanne Remembers Rene

I never thought much about having children. I was thirty-seven. I had a full-time career as a special education teacher, and I taught therapeutic horseback riding part-time. I owned a horse and rode daily. Both my job and my leisure pursuits were time intensive. I saw the enormous amount of effort that parenting required—with no guarantee of success! I knew I was selfish, and I was not sure I would be a good mother. Although I suspected my husband wanted kids, whenever we saw a child misbehaving in public, he would say, "Remind me never to have kids."

One day in January 1995, my attitude about mothering was forever changed. It began with a phone call from my seventy-four-year-old mother. She sounded very depressed, as she often did, and told me that she had been to see a cancer specialist and that her melanoma had come back. "He wants to take my whole arm," she said. "What do you mean he 'wants to take your arm'?" I asked incredulously. "He said he has to take the arm to stop the cancer from spreading." She was upset but also sounded resigned, and that made me angry. A morbid picture flashed into my mind: my legally blind mother, sitting in a chair in her tiny bedroom, right arm amputated at the shoulder, left arm (rendered useless by a stroke several years earlier) hanging by her side. My once-active mother would be unwilling to move from her room, debilitated by depression after losing first her sight and then her right arm. I called my mother's general practitioner and asked him if the oncologist's proposed "treatment" made sense. He listened and said, "Suzanne, with stage IV melanoma, all you can do is pray."

That night I couldn't eat or sleep. I was about to have my whole life transformed. I started thinking about my mother—how she read to me nightly as early as I can remember, how she gave me her Catholic faith and her love of God. I thought about how she let my sister and I have a cat when I was nine and Sally was six and how she drove me to the barn every day when I was fourteen so that I could work off board on my first horse. I thought about how she supported my love of horses by coming to watch me in shows even though she was afraid to get close to a horse. "They are so big," she would say. I reflected, with appreciation, on the fact that she had never bugged me about not having a boyfriend or asked why I didn't get married. And then, when I finally did get married, she never bugged me about having kids. "I cannot think of anything that is less someone else's business," she would say to me. And I also knew she had made sacrifices too numerous to count.

In the morning, after a few hours of fitful sleep and many prayers, I awoke with this thought, as clear as if someone had spoken it aloud: "No one is going to die this year." I understood this meant that I was not going to lose my mother yet. Although my mother seemed resigned to the doctor's barbaric proposal, I was not. I contacted the American Cancer Society and educated myself about malignant melanoma. I learned, after much reading and many phone calls, that there was a plastic surgeon at Yale New Haven Hospital, which was less than an hour away, who was one of only four physicians in the United States who performed an operation called an isolated limb perfusion on people whose melanoma lesions are confined to a limb. In this highly specialized procedure, chemotherapy is perfused through the limb at a concentration fifteen times greater than what the body could withstand systemically. The operation could last over nine hours and presented a great risk to my mother because she also had congenital heart disease.

In March of 1995, my mother underwent the complicated operation. She not only survived the operation, but she also recovered well and did not have any recurring lesions for several months. She was periodically checked for malignancy in her major organs, but none was evident. In April of 1996, I shared some astounding news with my mother: I was pregnant! It so happened that my sister, Sally, was pregnant with her first baby at the same time. Imagine my joy when my daughter was born, and my mother could hold her in both arms! I shuddered to think of the original "plan."

By early 1998, my mother's congestive heart failure was taking more of a toll on her than the melanoma. Her activities were severely limited, although she was far too proud to admit it to anyone. I was having difficulty getting along with her; she seemed to be undergoing a personality change. She was starting to butt in and tell me how to raise my daughter. That was so unlike her! What I failed to recognize in my ignorance (or possibly my denial) was that my mother was clearly dying.

In March of 1998, I found out that I was pregnant again. It was a more difficult pregnancy than the first—and I had a toddler to take care of. Despite her own failing health, my mother was very concerned about me. One day when both my husband and I were sick with the flu, my mother broke down and cried because she felt "useless" to help us. In November, one week after my second daughter was born, my mother went into the hospital. I brought the baby in to visit her in the intensive care unit. Once again, I watched my mother hold her last grandbaby in both arms and wondered at the miracle of it.

December 19, 1998. It is my mother's seventy-eighth birthday. She is in the intensive care unit of St. Mary's Hospital in Waterbury, Connecticut. I am sitting by her bed, emotionally wrought. She is dying. "Please don't let her die on her birthday," I begged. Yet, perversely, I thought of the symmetry it would offer on her gravestone: December 18, 1920–December 18, 1998. She had been unresponsive for more than twenty-four hours, and now she appeared restless and agitated, like someone having a nightmare. I fingered a pair of plastic rosary beads that a nun had left on the bedrail. I couldn't remember the actual Mysteries that you were supposed to meditate with, but I knew which beads were for the Hail Marys and which ones were for Our Fathers. I prayed the rosary for the first time in almost twenty years. I left the hospital at about ten that evening. I couldn't stay all night; I had a four-week-old infant and a two-year-old toddler at home.

The next morning, I went out on an errand, and when I got home, my husband, Craig, told me that my sister had called from the hospital. I braced myself for the next part, which I was certain would be that my mother had died during the night. Instead, he astonished me by telling me, "Your mother is sitting up, talking. She even knew that Clinton is President." "What?" Sure enough, my mother would live for two more weeks. Although she never left the hospital, it gave us all the time to say goodbye. She lived through Christmas, and on New Year's Day 1999 at 4:45, she died.

I had been the last of her children to see her alive. She was severely compromised and on oxygen. By speaking softly about people and places she loved, I tried to ease her transition out of this life. I use the word *transition* because I felt as if she was moving far away from me even as we shared the same time and space. Her voice was far away, as if she was already in another place. I told her I hoped I would be as good a mother to Katie and Kyla as she had been to me. "You will, Dear. You will," was her reply. I left shortly after that. So did she.

That night I dreamt of bright white light shining down the hallway. It seemed almost cliché to dream such a dream, but I know I heard my mother's voice saying, "Go easy on Craig, Dear." My interpretation of this parting comment was clear. It was as if my biggest fan, the one who loved me the most, was worried that it would be tough on my husband, whose love could never measure up to a mother's love. (What husband's could?)

The day following her death, I was wracked with anxiety. Where was she? Her smell lingered on her clothes in the closet. Her voice and image remained on a home video of my first daughter's birth. I had always believed in Heaven—yet where was she now? I felt like I might go mad. I could not understand the concept of being permanently gone.

It was several weeks later when I stumbled upon the book *Anam Cara: A Book of Celtic Wisdom* by John O'Donohue. Since my mother's death, I had been drawn to all things Irish and Catholic. The book claims to be a "rare synthesis of philosophy, poetry, and spirituality." What I discovered was answers—not absolute, of course, but possible answers—about death that I found comforting, suggesting that the dead are "our nearest neighbors."[76] I also like the imagery the author presented when he suggested that a

---

76. O'Donohue, *Anam Cara*, 214.

burial is a "cesarean section in reverse."[77] His ideas were a soothing balm for my grief.

As I dug deeper into my Catholic roots, I found a treasure, "a pearl of great price" as described in the Gospel of Matthew 13:46. I began to examine my priorities. As I became more assured of her continued existence in the afterlife, I felt my own soul strengthening. I began to live with greater conviction. My mother, it seems, had given me life twice: once at my birth and again at her death. I look forward to being reunited with her in Heaven.

Four months later, my older sister, Kathy, and I cleaned out my mother's belongings. I had dreaded this chore because I thought I would be confronted with painful memories from her whole life, but instead, I was confronted with my whole life and the lives of my brothers and sisters. My mother had no material possessions to speak of. She had given up her books and her car when her eyesight failed. She had no jewelry, no artwork, no extensive wardrobe. The few religious articles we found were evidence that her prayers for us had never ceased. All her drawers were filled with photographs of her children and grandchildren, letters we had written to her, artwork we had made in school. It suddenly occurred to me that we—her children—were her prized possessions. Her legacy to me was the importance of motherhood.

Suzanne Porter is a part-time special education teacher and a former police officer. She is the mother of two daughters. What is the most challenging of her professions? Motherhood, of course.

---

77. O'Donohue, *Anam Cara*, 224.

Laurie Remembers Julie

I am decorated with freckles. Moles, really, but it sounds more charming to say freckles. I never had the chance *not* to have them. My mom and dad were covered. I imagine that Mom had many of hers established by the time she left Lincoln Country Club and headed to college at the St. Lois Girls School. As she aged, she avoided the sun entirely to protect her fair skin. She didn't like to be hot and avoided instances where she might have to exert herself. For our summers at the pool, Mom established a home base under an oversized green umbrella, covering each of us and then herself in a white mess of sunscreen. She never rubbed it all the way in, not that she couldn't. She just didn't care about things like that.

When Mom got sick, she became particularly sensitive to sunlight, which made it difficult to go to outdoor events. The day of our last Fourth of July together, she packed up some drinks, and we went to watch our small-town parade. Mom, Dad, and I set up folding chairs in the shade under a group of thick pine trees at the end of the procession. Face-painted kids rode by on decorated bikes, a historic red firetruck honked its horn, and families full of hope streamed by our line of chairs. Mom had an outfit for every holiday. For this one she wore her holiday colors with a red fleece top, blue stretch jeans, and white undershirt. She covered her balding head with the stylish red cap she bought while visiting friends in California, knowing she would one day need it. Her skin hung around her face. She looked thin and frail, but she also projected warmth and compassion. Friends stopped to give her a hug, have a quick chat, and encourage her to fight. She did not complain that day, or in the challenging months to come.

That night I went to my parents' bedroom to see if they wanted to watch the local fireworks. I heard her cry out and cracked their door enough to see my dad rush to their bathroom. She was in too much pain to go anywhere, and we tried to calm her. Feeling helpless and numb, I drove toward our country fairgrounds and parked in an empty dirt parking lot nearby. I did not call my friends nor join the crowds of people gathered on the street to celebrate the holiday. Instead, I turned the radio on and found a station that was playing festive music. As the colorful explosions filled the sky, it began to rain, and I started to cry.

I lived abroad and had moved to Colorado as a brief stop on my way to the next adventure when my mom was diagnosed. The day she shared this news, Mom left a message on my voicemail saying that we needed to talk. I heard fear in her voice and felt a pit in my stomach. I didn't feel any better when I walked in the front door that evening. Mom tried to fill the conversation with small talk, but things quickly shifted to the test results. My dad sat silently beside her as she laid out the medical details. The air felt heavy. I wanted to hug her, but I could not move. I looked around the room at the comforting and seemingly normal things that surrounded me: picture frames with smiling faces from family vacations and sporting events, the piles of laundry, the recent Thanksgiving decorations in boxes nearby. I felt small. I felt scared. I felt upended. I could not lose her. I was only twenty-six, and I wasn't married, and I didn't have kids, a house, a career, or any of the things I expected to share with my mom. I was not ready. Didn't things like this happen when you were old enough to be a settled adult?

Time did not stop. My mom courageously took on her stage IV breast cancer as the holidays passed and my sister's wedding approached. It was a good distraction but also a surreal event she would not live to see. Her primary diagnosis expanded to include skin cancer and lymph cancer and finally spread to her brain. In the face of it, my mom did not change her diet or begin natural remedies. She didn't seek radical, cutting-edge cures or start attending church. Instead, she walked forward in the way she had for sixty-three years. She trusted her doctors and took comfort in her friends and family. The unpredictability of her timeline made it impossible to know when to take days off, so my dad and I kept working. A neighbor held a celebration of life brunch, and friends wrote special notes to share directly with her. She told the grocery clerk, the bank teller, and anyone she met that she had cancer. She endured a double mastectomy and lost over eighty pounds in ten months. After she began chemotherapy, Mom no longer had to say anything. She shared the news in her very existence.

I thought she was improving because I had to think that. Breast cancer is in every commercial, email, and storyline. I believed that all people win this fight, so why not her? We can beat this. We can do this together. Stay strong! I began taking pictures of our life: my parents making snow angels and playing croquet, her sleeping on the couch, covered in unfolded socks. In one image, Mom is standing at the dishwasher in her stained, plaid, red flannel pajamas. She is forcing a smile, holding a clean plate, a few white hairs from her pale, bald head catching the light of my flash. So vulnerable and strong. When she finally finished radiation, we were all exhausted.

The expected is just the beginning. It is the unexpected that changes our lives. From the outside looking in, it might have been obvious that she was dying. She collapsed when getting the mail on a gorgeous blue-sky day in August. She went to the emergency room, then a rehabilitation center, then hospice… in rapid succession. We did an impromptu wedding ceremony at the hospital, and she smiled from ear to ear. We held the big event weeks later, and she stayed alive long enough to say goodbye to those who attended and drove to the hospital. My sister held two wedding ceremonies, a rehearsal, and a reception, had an emergency appendectomy, and "celebrated" a birthday the day before our mom died. Despite everything, I never saw it coming, and her passing leveled me.

I decided I would move to Denver and get a dog to help my recovery. I would socialize and attempt to work, but everything was clouded by grief. Months later, I was alone in my apartment when I heard a loud, metallic crash in the middle of the night. I assumed it was the smoke detector I had attempted to fix and left hanging from an exposed cord in the ceiling. After pulling the warm covers from my body and moving closer, I saw it was still in place. My bare feet walked the cold kitchen tiles as I silently moved through the dark, looking for clues. The light from the moon illuminated the living room. I walked to the bathroom, and still groggy, I turned on the light. The picture I had hung the first day I moved in, two days prior to her passing, had fallen. The frame was caught in the towel rack above the toilet, lightly leaning against the wall. I walked closer, amazed the glass hadn't shattered and surprised it would fall that night after hanging solid for months. I picked up the frame and read the artist's script: "For a long time she only danced when she thought no one was watching." It was then I realized that my mom was with me.

With a gentle push from a dear friend, I chose to participate in a fundraiser for the Leukemia and Lymphoma Society. Participants raise thousands of dollars, and in return, their training, flights, and San Diego accommodations are paid for. I signed up for a 26.2-mile run, and most people will never run that far in their lives. I drove that distance to work in over an hour in my 1995 Saturn. This seemed impossible. I was not in shape. I couldn't jog comfortably for minutes, let alone six hours.

I went on a short training run after an eleven-hour workday. The weather was daunting, so I added a fleece headband and vest to my too-tight running outfit and hit the road. I looked ridiculous. Almost immediately the wind picked up, and the speckled gray concrete appeared forlorn. Ten minutes in, I stopped focusing on how hard it was and attempted to find peace. Within moments, I fell. I tipped over, but who can really say. I hit the ground hard on my right side, only slightly protected by the hand that reluctantly shot out at the last possible second. The yellow streetlight highlighted my accident. The music was still blaring in my ears as I carefully pushed myself up. I stopped my wrist timer and walked on to avoid the house across the street where teens, sitting on their slumping Victorian porch, bore witness. A block later, I cleaned the blood from my palms and started to cry. Frustrated and embarrassed, I attempted to jog again only to stop at the next intersection. I felt defeated. This was absurd, and I asked myself, "What am I doing?" Just then, the Oscar Mayer Weinermobile passed in front of me. It might have been a hallucination, but I knew this moment was special. It was some kind of sign, even if only a reminder to smile. I wiped my eyes, turned the timer back on, and started running.

I was hoping to lose weight and tone up. I was hoping to become addicted to working out and never look back. I was hoping to feel great and eventually find this whole thing easy. None of those things happened. I never looked good doing it. I was more like an unstable penguin than a gazelle. It never felt easy, and I never found my rhythm, but I kept moving. I saw bunnies that my mother and I had enjoyed during our neighborhood walks. I slept well, and she visited me in my dreams. I started to feel connected again. I diligently trained until my marathon and crossed the finish line with a smile on my face, surrounded by friends.

My mom would have created a homemade poster to display when she greeted me at the airport. She might have accompanied me to California to watch me run and sneak in a vacation in her old stomping grounds. I know she would have been worried but proud. I was healing.

We share our middle name, Anne, our bright blue eyes, our creative spirit, and small noses. She was funny, smart, modest, and wholesome. She loved our friends and laughed with her whole body at their stories; she smiled easily—often with something in her teeth. She embodied a loving and maternal presence that I miss dearly. My mom's life and legacy guided my choices. Mom set the standard by which I live as a mother, a mentor, a friend, an artist, and an enthusiast for life's treasured moments.

Laurie Farr Callahan lived in Niwot and Denver, Colorado, after years of working and traveling throughout Europe, Indonesia, and Australia. She studied architecture and urban planning at the University of Colorado and graduated with a BS in environmental design. She began her career in a green architecture firm, a model building company, and an urban planning role before starting her photography business. Laurie married a wonderful character named Colin and has two daughters... one born the day after the anniversary of her mother's passing (Ellie), and the other has a birthday days before the anniversary of her father's passing (Jules). They have a "foster fail" puppy named Cosmo. She takes pleasure in gardening, art, music, and spending time with friends. She has a desire to experience new things, travel widely, write, learn, and enjoy her days living near familiar and friendly faces.

Michele Remembers Janet

On a stormy night in 1974, my parents were driving home from a shopping trip when they struck the side of a bridge on a country road. The accident was fatal for my mom, but my dad survived. He won't talk about the accident. Dad broke a couple ribs and was hospitalized. I remember visiting him in the hospital with my younger brother Marvin and my paternal grandparents, who had picked us up after driving two hours from their home to ours. I remember being fascinated with the flexible straw in my dad's drink. It was the first one I had ever seen. The few things I remember about that time were seeing a rabbit in the backyard and seeing my dad cry at the wake. My brother and I were sitting on his lap, and we asked if we could touch Mom. He held us up to her casket, and we touched her cheek. At age four, I couldn't yet comprehend what death meant.

I remember waking up the night she died. My brother and I had been put to bed by a babysitter that evening. When I awoke during the night, it wasn't my mom, dad, or the sitter who came to me but my godmother—a close friend of Mom's who lived nearby. I remember thinking that was odd. I now wonder if the reason I awoke was because I intuitively knew something was wrong.

Something was very wrong. I had just lost my mom—the center of my world. It would take many years before I could define myself as anything other than a motherless daughter. I am told that my mom's life revolved around being a mother to my brother and me. Mom was intelligent, tall and thin, and very kind. She had a teaching degree and taught second grade for a couple years after college. She became a stay-at-home mom, though, once I was born. I have very few memories of her, and those I have are foggy. I'm not sure what are actual memories or what's been pieced together from the bits and pieces I've heard from others over the years and then embellished by my imagination. I have nobody with whom to compare stories. Nobody will talk about her with me.

My dad didn't talk about my mom, and I rarely saw anyone who knew her after she died. My dad found new friends, a new wife, and we didn't see my mom's relatives very much. Dad got rid of all of Mom's possessions, and we moved from our home a couple months after her death. When I saw anyone who knew my mom, they avoided talking about her. Yet I longed to know about her. The silence was deafening. It was as if she had never existed—this woman who was so significant to me. The silence felt disrespectful to my mom's existence and my memory of her.

When I was sixteen, I couldn't take the silence any longer. If I couldn't know who my mom was, I wanted to know the specifics of how she died. I didn't want to ask my dad for fear of hurting him. He had already made it clear that he didn't want to talk about Mom, so I figured he would definitely not want to answer questions about the accident. I went to our small-town library and asked if they kept past issues of the local weekly newspaper. I am sure the librarian knew what I was looking for when I asked for the issue from June 1974. She was an old friend of my mother and was also my brother's godmother, now just an acquaintance. (My brother was diagnosed with leukemia after my mom died, and he passed away three years after her death.) I was embarrassed to have someone know what I was looking for, but it was worth the embarrassment to finally have some answers to my questions. I wanted to know if Mom died instantly (I hope so); whether my dad was conscious after the accident, whether he lay there knowing she was dead, and how long he had to wait for help to arrive; who called for help (that was in the days before cell phones); and where exactly the accident happened.

The librarian returned from the basement and said they didn't have newspaper issues from that long ago. She recommended I visit the office of the newspaper publisher, so I did, and they had the issue I was looking for. The cover story was about the car accident, complete with a photo of the car after it had been towed back into town. It still had a sign from the bridge permanently embedded in the hood. The article didn't say what the cause of death was or if she died instantly. It did say on which road the accident happened, that it had been raining, that my mom had died, and that my dad was in the hospital with some broken ribs. I also read that my parents had been returning from a shopping trip. Years later, when I told my maternal grandmother what I had read, she told me that the package from their shopping trip was still in the back seat of the car when she saw it days after Mom's death. That is all I was able to learn about my mom's death.

For many years, I felt no connection to my mom, this woman I so desired to know but could barely remember. While I didn't feel connected to her, she was my connection to spirituality. I talked to her rather than praying to God. I had totally rejected religion because, as I then thought, how could there be a God who would take away my mother and brother at such a young age? When I was in my twenties, psychic phenomena began to intrigue me. It was part of my search for meaning and a connection to my mom, and thus began my spiritual journey. At that time, I was not at all in tune with my own intuition. I believed intuition and psychic abilities were a power held only by a few gifted people—that is, until I was in the hospital giving birth at age thirty.

I had seen a group of nine midwives for my prenatal care while I was pregnant with my first and only child. When I called the midwives to say that my labor had begun, the receptionist told me that Janet would meet me at the hospital. Janet? None of the midwives at the clinic were named Janet, and Janet was my mom's name. I wondered if the receptionist had given me the wrong name, but she explained that because so many midwives were on vacation this busy delivery week between Christmas and New Year's, they had called in a backup midwife to assist me. Instantly, I knew I would be just fine and that this was a sign from my mom that she would be there. Later that evening, as I was experiencing contractions, I looked over at midwife Janet, who was watching me from a rocking chair, and I could feel my mom watching me through her eyes. My mom was there, witnessing the birth of her grandchild! It was the strongest sense of knowing that I had ever experienced.

My interest in psychic phenomena led me to see a psychic medium a few years later. On the way to my reading, I asked my mom for a sign that she was really around me, but I kept changing my mind about what the sign should be. By the time I arrived at the medium's office, I had asked for three specific signs. Just before I opened the door to the medium's shop, I distinctly heard someone say, "Hi, Michele." I immediately replied, "Hi," then looked around for the source of the greeting and saw no one. The voice sounded like it came from a couple inches from my left ear, but nobody was standing there or anywhere in sight. I was confused but entered the shop. I know now that it was my mom. I don't remember how my mom's voice sounds, but the voice I heard that day was familiar and comforting. I remember thinking, "That's the way my name is supposed to sound."

During my reading, every one of the signs I had requested from Mom came up, including funny and cute descriptions of my husband and child. In addition, through the medium, Mom told me that she was present for the birth of my child. Wow—she was validating what I had sensed in the delivery room! My mom greeting me that day was the bonus I hadn't asked for. After the reading, I told the medium what happened just before I entered her shop. She exclaimed, "Well, you asked for a sign. What did you expect?" She obviously had more experience and faith in communicating with the deceased than I had!

Since then, I have connected with my mom through mediums a few more times. She even gave me fashion advice. She told me not to wear black suits. I just happened to be looking for a new suit at that time, so I took her advice and didn't buy a black one. I figured I'm not going to get much advice from her, so I better take the little bit I can get! I also learned that my mom shared my feminist views. She told me through a psychic medium that the civility of a society can be measured by how the women are treated. How true. I liked that we had something in common.

Going to psychics has given me a spiritual connection, not only to my mom and others who have passed but to Spirit as well. My interest in psychics evolved into a spiritual journey. I experienced a number of losses early in life and again this year. While tragic, the losses have made me who I am. They have also led me to a new career as a grief counselor.

I talk to my mom quite often now, knowing that even if I don't sense her presence, she can hear me and that she's watching over me. I have learned that life is temporary, but the soul is forever. The person may have died, but the relationship continues. I believe that while we may never know the reason for any particular loss, there are ways to make meaning from it. And part of the purpose for me losing my mom so early in this lifetime is for me to use my experience to help others get through their losses.

Thank you, Mom, for the great start you gave me in life and for continuing to connect with me. Until we meet again. I love you.

Michele Dettloff is a mother, graphic designer, and grief counselor who lives in St. Paul, Minnesota. She was four years old when her mother, Janet (Kjeer) Dettloff, died in a car accident. Her experiences of loss inspired Michele to become a grief counselor.

Michelle Remembers Maria

The bond between a mother and daughter is unique. Scientifically, hormones initially play a role in the natural bonding that occurs between a mother and her daughter. Daughters are fortunate if they have a mother who loves them unconditionally and fosters a relationship of trust, respect, and encouragement. This special bond is engraved in their hearts and will remain strong even long after one of them has gone to Heaven. The bond between my mom and me began before I was born. When she was nineteen years old and a Cuban immigrant to the United States, she was walking my older brother in his stroller when she developed excruciating abdominal pain. She was taken to the emergency room of the hospital and underwent eight hours of emergency surgery secondary to a ruptured appendix. My dad, who worked three jobs, rushed to the hospital and met with the doctor, who told him, "I have good news and bad news. The good news is that your wife is going to live, and the bad news is that she is several weeks pregnant. She has been exposed to several hours of life-saving surgery and medications. It is likely that she will lose this baby, and if she doesn't, I recommend an abortion." My dad was unsure how my mom would respond to the news but told her anyway. My mom told him that she would not have an abortion and that her baby would be normal. Thanks to my mom's decision, today I can share this difficult time that took place in her life.

My mom was a strong, beautiful woman who lost her battle to metastatic breast cancer in July of 2005. I was grateful to God for the thirty-nine years we were able to spend together. My three beautiful children were able to meet her and spend quality time with her before she passed. My youngest daughter, Celine, was only two years old when my mom passed away. I never thought I would be left with such a deep hole that is so difficult to fill. I spent many days mourning her passing and wishing I could speak with her just one more time. Since my mom knew she was terminal, we had the opportunity to talk about how our bond would live forever. Her only fear was that Celine would not remember her. Shortly after her passing, Celine told us that she would see my mom in the house. She also told us that we could not move from our home because Aba (her name for my mom) would not know where to find us. Celine also told us that my mom visited her at her preschool wearing big white wings. I asked my daughter if my mom spoke to her, and she told me that my mom told her that she would always be in her heart and that she could come to school with her each day.

God sends us signs that our spirit lives on and that our bond will never be broken. Three months after my mom's passing, we traveled to Walla Walla, Washington, where my husband's family is from. During our time there, we visited an old fort museum. As I was climbing the engraved steps up to one of the exhibits, Celine told me that Aba was here with us and pointed behind us. I turned around to look for my mom but did not see her. My husband said, "I don't see anyone." Since I was carrying Celine on my hip, I decided to look down at the next step I was about to step on, and to my amazement, my mothers' complete name, Maria Bertha

Suarez, was engraved on the stepping stone. I could not believe my eyes and asked my husband to look down at the step. He, too, was amazed and turned around and told the kids that Aba was here with us and would enjoy the museum as well. This occurrence brought me such peace knowing that my mom was with us and would continue to be part of our lives.

For the sake of our daughters, we must continue living here on earth until one day we can be in Heaven with our beautiful mothers. Six months after my mom's death, I had a very vivid dream of my mom that brought me so much peace. In my dream, my mom appeared in my kitchen dressed up in a suit and looked very healthy. I was so excited to see her and asked her, "Mom, haven't you heard me? When I am feeling down or the kids are sick, I call out for you." She responded, "Where we are there is peace and joy. I do not hear you calling for me, but I can come down to see you when I miss you." I asked, "Do you know that Celine can see you?" She said, "Yes, she is the only one that can see me." She also told me in the dream that she had seen my grandfather on my dad's side, who had passed away when I was ten years old. I awoke from my dream with a sense of peace and joy knowing that my mom was no longer ill or suffering and she could visit us on earth when she missed us.

Living without your mom is extremely difficult because a large part of who we are comes from our mothers. I have relied heavily on my faith, husband, and children to go on. The time we spend here on this earth is very short, so I always tell our children, "Cherish today, as tomorrow is not promised." I thank God for the videos I took of my mom while she was alive, as these have been the best way that we have all been able to continue to celebrate her short life on earth. I love you, Mom!

Michelle Johnson, DO, is an osteopathic physician and an assistant professor of family medicine and has been the director of simulation and standardized patients at Nova Southeastern University, KPCOM since 2018. She is board certified in family medicine and osteopathic principles and practices. She was recognized as the Faculty Member of the Year by KPCOM in 2023. She received the 2024 Leonard Tow Humanism in Medicine Award. Dr. Johnson and her family reside in Tampa, Florida.

Amy Remembers Judy

My mother loved to read and made countless lists of books that I am still finding as we sort through her belongings, three years after her death. I recently came across her scribbled book titles in the margins of a 2011 cat calendar and was delighted to find a small, blue, spiral flip notebook she kept in her car just for this purpose. I cherish a well-used journal she had that was specifically designed for book readers' lists and "reviews." She left a trail of suggested books tucked into the leather magazine basket near her favorite spot on the couch, and various book titles are written inside her address book and on the backs of envelopes she kept with my greeting cards inside.

When I was twelve, my mom, a former middle school English teacher, went back to work part-time at the library in the town next door. What I loved most about her having that job was that it was like having my own personal librarian. If I just mentioned something more than once (from whales to wolves, Amelia Earhart to Joan of Arc), she brought home a book (or two or five) about that topic.

But when I think of my mom, I don't picture her poring over a book in her reading glasses. I see her in her favorite spot on the couch, watching the birds and chipmunks, Zen-like with her coffee each morning, or on the move, playing tennis or driving herself to the movies, the theater, a hiking trail, or a restaurant to lunch with her friends. She was independent, reflective, active, and social. I learned from my dad that after I left for college, and especially once she retired, she would read for hours on her favorite chair upstairs.

She joined a book club after she retired from the library, and after a few years, instead of reading books, they subscribed to *The New York Times Book Review*. Rather than discussing a full book, they read and discussed the reviews of the latest novels, nonfiction, and biographies to read on their own. I adored this idea, and to this day when I read book, theater, or movie reviews, I think of my mom's group.

For my birthday each year, she gifted me a hard copy of a newly published book that I would never have bought for myself. She gave me a collection of Mary Gordon and Alice Munro stories, an expensive Cleveland Museum of Art exhibit book, and many others, all carefully chosen for me. She also sent me the newest books by people I loved, such as Patti Smith, and those she loved, including Billy Collins, whose work reflects her sense of humor. She continued to be my personal librarian until the year before she died.

After I had my daughter, one month shy of my fortieth birthday, my reading life halted. I stopped reading anything more than a poem or short story in a magazine and blamed this as much on "mommy brain" as I did on the demands of my marketing and event planning job in New Orleans. At the time, I was the captain of the annual Joan of Arc parade, which I had founded two years before motherhood, and any extra energy I had I focused on keeping this new project alive. I was always tired, and reading was not relaxing to me anymore. I envied my husband's ability to read and relax in bed. When our daughter turned three years old, I felt a sense of accomplishment by finishing a full-length book for the first time since she was born—*American Canopy: Trees, Forests, and the Making of a Nation*. I declared to my mother that I had become a nonfiction reader and could only read things that were not going to give me anxiety or annoyance. I wanted clean facts, information, history, and nonemotional subjects—or at least less emotional than the types of stories, novels, and poems I had read in my twenties and thirties about tortured teens, broken marriages, suicides, deaths, and unfulfilled desires. I loved a good World War II novel or reading the works of existentialist French authors. They made my traumas seem less, but they also elevated my grief, fears, and insecurities. Temporarily, I felt that being a mom had melted my intellectual self into mush. What was relaxing to me now was reading picture books to my daughter or watching *Teletubbies* or *Peppa Pig* with her. My husband gave me a subscription to *The New Yorker* during that period because he knew I was struggling to keep a hold on my former self. A cartoon, short story, or theater or book review was ample reading for the few moments I was not worrying, rushing around, or working.

    I talked to my mom on the phone each morning on my way to work after I would drop my daughter off at daycare. She always settled my nerves, and our conversations were full of laughter about something my daughter had said or done, my work anecdotes about strange characters or stressful encounters, or an experience my mom had at a doctor's visit, grocery store, or book club. She knew I was perpetually stressed, and these calls in between school drop-off and work time while she sat on her couch in her robe with her coffee were medicine to me. I cannot imagine how stressed or lonely I would have been those first years of my daughter's life if I didn't have her to talk with and calm me down or make me laugh. It still makes me smile when I remember that she told me these daily talks were also her lifeblood.

In 2016, the eighth year of the Joan of Arc parade, the seventh year of my job, and the fifth year of being a mom, she sent me a list of books to read that she thought would calm me down and help me relax. I reminded her that I only read nonfiction now because I didn't want to read about other people's stories; I had enough drama of my own. "It's an escape," she insisted. "I'll send you a list and you can try." Her list arrived on a card with a painting of a girl reading on its cover. "This reminded me of you!" she wrote. "Here is a list of some books I think you would enjoy. If you have any questions, you can ask me—remember, I was a librarian!"

Her list was numbered one through twenty-eight and written in her perky cursive on three lined sheets of yellow paper. The titles included novels by John Irving, Elizabeth Strout, and Isabel Allende, among others both familiar and unfamiliar to me (after all, I was an English major!). I was so touched—just the idea of the list, her notes within it, and the handwritten recommendations served its immediate purpose. She loved me, she was trying to help me, and I thought she was absolutely amazing for compiling it just for me. I put a photo of the list on Facebook, raved about my mom's bibliophile nature and overall awesomeness, and carried the list in my purse for months, picking up books at used book sales, from shops, and online.

When I finally chose one to read, I was disappointed. It was full of unlikable characters, two of whom happened to be a mom and a daughter. Something awful happened to the daughter almost immediately in the story, and I was aghast at how the mom acted. I hated it. I told my mom it was depressing, and I tried another novel from the list. It annoyed me with its self-important characters and what I thought was a pretentious plot. "I just can't read fiction anymore. I don't understand the voices, or these people..." I wrote to her in a Facebook message. "Well, if they depress you, don't read them!" was her chirpy reply. She was hard to insult, luckily, and didn't take it personally. In hindsight, I hope she knew, the way only mothers always know, that I might return to it someday, when I was ready. (She certainly knew I kept everything, so she could rest assured I'd keep this list!)

As a late-blooming mom working full-time, I had a very different maternal experience than my mom, and I mentioned it from time to time—especially when she didn't understand why I couldn't just sit, relax, and read. She quit working for twelve years after having my brother and I at age thirty and thirty-two, while I had eight weeks maternity leave... and left maternity leave to put on a parade! In these moments of comparison, I was a complete fool, forgetting that my brother had a heart condition that eventually killed him at age eighteen. When I once told her how upset I was about my daughter's countless ear infections and the possibility she would need tubes, she said, "I understand. I was a nervous wreck if your brother even sneezed!" I wrote her countless letters trying to tell her how grateful and amazed I was at her maternal experience, given that mine was nowhere near as complicated and traumatizing. In turn, she sent me precious Mother's Day cards with sweet notes about how proud she was of me. We might have been different in how we handled motherhood and stress—but we were both moms. And as a mom, she was only trying to help me relax.

During Covid, I regained my love of fiction by joining two book clubs. They became lifesavers while going through the nightmarish experience of my mom going to the hospital after collapsing at home, then going to rehab, a nursing home, and eventually home hospice care. I was flying back and forth to Ohio for those horrendous three months. I told her while she was at the rehab center that I had joined a book club and was reading fiction again—and that many of the authors were the ones on her list. She was deep into her dementia by then, and although she recognized me and understood in general, she couldn't have a conversation about the books or the authors. The day I told her I had joined the book club happened to be my fiftieth birthday—and she had no idea. It was beyond heartbreaking to witness this former bibliophile reduced to staring out the window or at a television for hours.

The spring after my mom died, I started a book club called Judy's List. Three of my New Orleans friends joined. I was amused to find that after the third book, two of them admitted they thought my mom's choice in books was a bit depressing! I laughed and told them I understood but that I now found them comforting because her book list served as a window into her psyche. I am sure the characters in the books she recommended understood her suffering, many had worse tragedies, but all of them had one thing in common—they lived to tell the tale of their traumas and share it with others.

Not a week goes by that I am not engaged in a book or two from my mom's list. Reading her recommendations is my best therapy and my most tangible connection to her. It is an escape from my grief, and at the same time, grief is a companion alongside me as I read. I try to understand why she chose these titles, and I understand her a bit more, too, with each book completed. I feel her presence through these books; what a great comfort knowing she read the same words I am reading! And when I read her books, it calms me down more than anything. She would be so happy knowing that I'm finally taking her advice and that I finally understand how to sit, relax, and read.

Amy Kirk Duvoisin lives in New Orleans with her husband and daughter where she works as a marketing and community relations professional and freelance writer. She is the founder of the Joan of Arc Project, an organization dedicated to artistically celebrating Joan of Arc, notably with an annual parade held on Joan's birthday in the French Quarter.

* * *

Part 3 of this book was written to offer some "prescriptions" that you can utilize when you are in need. They were the missing ingredients that I could not find in books on grief. I was desperate for practical solutions that would help reduce my anxiety and bring my body back into balance. I hope that you find these suggestions useful tools that you can incorporate into your life.

Part Three
Grief Wisdom
*Prescriptives for Healing
Mind, Body, and Spirit*

Grief Prescriptions

This section of the book contains grief wisdom culled from personal experience and the voices of other women who have shared their healing recipes with me. All aspects of our mind, body, and spirit are affected when we experience any significant loss, and losing a mother is cataclysmic. These prescriptives reflect the psyche and the physical and spiritual dimensions that are emblematic of the "whole person" because true healing takes place in all these realms. These remedies will not replace the grief process but can offer you support. Restoring your equilibrium takes time, sometimes many years. It is important for you to not only create but accept your pace *in it* and *through it*. Trying to escape this painful process, although appealing, will not be successful because unattended grief does not magically disappear.

The bereavement journey is painful. The word *bereavement* is from the Latin and means "to be robbed." *Bereave* is related to the word *reave*, which means "to rob" or "torn apart."[78] It is the perfect definition because you are robbed and deprived of precious moments that you can never hold again. Sadly, for some

---

78. Etymonline, "bereave (v.)," accessed June 26, 2025, https://www.etymonline.com/word/bereave.

who are grieving, family and friends may bring out the worst of human behavior. I learned that lesson quickly. I heard cliches such as "It is all for the best!"—whose best, I wondered—and "It was her time"—actually, it was cancer's time—and other meaningless platitudes.

Your grief process provides opportunities for both emotional and spiritual growth, and inside of your pain, you can also find insight. You may receive messages from your mother when you least expect them. Trust that these communications are your grief wisdom. I am referring to the wisdom of telepathic impulses, inner promptings to go through a file of letters, drive to a memory-filled landscape, turn on the radio, or other urges. Your mother is part of this magical process. Let her lead you to take initial steps.

How a Fictional Witch Helped Me Heal

It takes great courage to navigate grief, and when I felt bereft and alone, I visualized the image of myself as a strong warrioress who could cope with anything. I also found strength in the unlikeliest of places: on the fictional supernatural TV program *The Good Witch*. The main character, Cassie Nightingale, played by Catherine Bell, reinvents her life in the too-good-to-be-true Hallmark city of Middleton, weaving her web of magic and mystery around those in the community. The show, like most Hallmark programs, is predictable; however, Cassie's abilities to transform herself despite her losses into an embodied woman who trusts and believes in herself spoke to me because I did not embrace either ability. Even the name Middletown as a symbol of betwixt and between makes sense when you are in healing crisis. Cassie is a "good witch" who owns a metaphysical store. She understands and prescribes the correct remedy for those in need using natural foods, essential oils, dream healing, and amulets or other objects. Not only does she utilize her intuitive gifts, but she also encourages others to do the same. She is a terrific example of someone who is in alignment with both her head and her heart. I admired her and wished I could call her for advice. I still have a sign I made hanging in my office that asks, "What would Cassie Nightingale do?"

Cassie Nightingale's character inspired me to create the grief presciptives found in this section of the book. These prescriptives can assist you when you are feeling sad or out of balance or simply find yourself asking, "Now what can I do?" Although the ideas presented may seem deceptively simple, they are effective. You can peruse the different prescriptives to see what remedy appeals to you and trust your intuition. Keeping a record of your thoughts, images, and messages in a journal can be enormously beneficial, giving you the chance to reflect upon these hidden treasures. You may find, as I did, that patterns are revealed over time, waiting for you to discover them. I looked for a remedy, any remedy, that would bring my mother to me, and many years later, I realized that the best prescription was acknowledging and truly accepting that she is always part of me. I hope that you find these suggestions worth embracing.

Grief Rx: *Be Kind to Yourself*

During the grief process, we feel exposed and fragile. We can be harsh and judgmental and obsess over what we "could have done." Often, we scold ourselves needlessly when what we really need is kindness. You may wish to record your thoughts in a journal. I have found that having an ongoing record of your reflections can be quite helpful, especially in the months and years to come. The following exercise may help you bring those kind words into your life.

Exercise Questions

If you find yourself on that repetitive wheel of self-criticism, ask yourself, "What do I really want to hear?" and "What would my mother want me to know right now that would help me?" Including statements of belief in your journal or your thought process can help you turn a difficult day into a day that is much more manageable. You can create affirmations or statements of belief that support you, such as "She is with me all the time," "I will survive these feelings, even though it doesn't feel like I will," "I am ready to transform into my new life with my mom," and "Everything is as it is supposed to be, and I accept that." These statements are part of the alchemical process of grief.

Grief Rx: *Remember Her Love for You*

I was lucky to have Toby as my mother even though we did not always have a smooth relationship. I am and was deeply blessed by her, and I know that she felt the same way. During bereavement, it is so easy to forget how much you meant to your mother. I try to recall supportive words, knowing smiles, and the intimate connection I had with her that was only understood by the two of us. One evening while she was recovering from a particularly complicated and painful surgery, we were lying in bed watching TV, and she unexpectedly reached out and held my hand. I do not remember my mother being so demonstrative before. When I remember the soft grip of her hand, I feel her love and wish I had held her hand longer.

Exercise
Remembering

Can you call to mind a specific moment that has particular significance? It does not have to be a major event; it could be only an instant. When you recall this moment, let yourself feel her energies and accept them as her gift of love to you. Understand the power of your bond—one that only you and she could create.

Grief Rx: *Grief as Your Companion*

There were moments in my grief journey when I literally thought I could not go forward with my life if she was not in it. You probably feel the same. You will survive. Loss teaches us how enormous our capacity for loving another person can be. Because grief is now your companion, it can also be your friend. Grieving is painful and taxes the resilience of the human heart; do not let it hold you hostage.

Exercise
Finding Messages

Grief can be frightening and quite scary, especially if you have never lost a loved one before. If you were to reframe your perception of your grief from "terrorizer" to "companion," what message would it contain? (You can add your answers to your journal.)

Grief Rx: *You Do Not Have to "Let Go"*

One of the biggest fears experienced by women whose mothers have passed is the fear that they must "let go" of her, and that is just wrong. You do not need to let her go. What is required is cultivating your method for letting her in. I heard from many well-meaning people that I needed to release her. I could not let her go, even if I tried. This comment speaks more about their discomfort than mine, and it was obvious that they did not have the same depth of connection with their mothers that I did.

I would like to believe that the people who told me to let go of her were looking out for my best interest and did not want me to be held captive by the pain of loss. What they did not understand is that when grief holds you in its arms, it is not easy to disengage. I know that the bond you have with your mother cannot be destroyed, because your pledge of love travels far beyond the physical earth. Your connection of love with your mother is not bound by physical limitations and has not been severed with physical departure.

Exercise
Letting Her In

I would like you to imagine a part of your life where you wish your mother was participating. It could be a celebration, a birthday, an anniversary, or just an ordinary day. I have found that when I speak with my mother each day, I feel as if she is with me, regardless of what I am experiencing.

Think about how you would like your mother to be in your life. Would you like her to be with you every day? On special occasions? What method would you like to choose for letting her in your life? Through your dreams? Verbal communications? Telepathically "speaking" with her photograph? Using imagery? You can decide what method works best for you.

Grief Rx: *Trust Yourself*

The feelings that grief brings are often terrifying. You may not trust yourself or believe that you can endure this type of pain. Moving through the daily motions of your life surrounded by a thick fog is normal, and this state of mind will not last forever. One treasure in grief is that it offers you the potential for you to trust yourself, even if you never did before. You are *not* your grief journey. You are much more than your sorrow.

Exercise
Trust
· · · · ·

Imagine a time in your life when you felt completely whole—mind, body, and spirit. It may have been a life event that triggered these feelings, such as the birth of a child, a wedding, a job promotion, or when you took a great risk. It doesn't matter what the event was. What matters is that you can recall this experience. Close your eyes and pay attention to how your body feels as you remember. You may choose to remember all the details or not. Ask yourself what you learned about trusting yourself. You may receive a message in words or see a symbol. If you don't receive any message, that is fine. Everyone is different. The point of this meditation is to remind you that you can rely on yourself not only in the best of times but during the worst of times as well.

Grief Rx: *Resolving Grief Issues*

The process of grieving often ignites other areas of heartache in your life and can resurrect painful memories and regrets. Affirm to yourself that you are doing the best you can. One day may be better, followed by the next day of misery, but that does not mean you are not healing. These unresolved issues that scream for your attention commonly occur as you remember the past, and guilt raises its ugly head. Perhaps your mother died and you were not there. She may have chosen to pass away without you in the room because she wanted to spare you the pain. You may feel guilty because your mother died during the pandemic and you were denied the opportunity to be with her.

Remembering arguments will bring up unwanted images, memories, and words that you wished you never said. Self-forgiveness is challenging and is very difficult, especially when you are in emotional pain. Can you forgive yourself for words said and unsaid? Can you forgive yourself for moments that you did not take advantage of? If you are honest with yourself, you truly know that your mother would never want you to torment yourself. We all make mistakes. We are all human. Even the very best of daughters are not perfect! Consult with a trusted professional who can listen and witness your story so you do not carry the burden of guilt alone.

Exercise
Narrative Medicine

One tool that can be very helpful is narrative, a potent form of healing. Write a letter to your mother and express all your truths—good, bad, and ugly. Do not edit yourself. When you are finished—and this may take several tries—write a letter from her point of view. This time in the process, include the words you would like to hear from her. This exercise should not be a form of self-flagellation but an opportunity to restructure aching memories. Share your regrets with her. You have her attention.

Grief Rx: *Finding Support*

Removing people in your life who are not supportive or even toxic is part of your healing process. Some people will be incapable of witnessing grief, and it is not their fault; they don't know what to do or say. Affirm that you will only invite people into your life who support you and are sensitive, kind, and loving. Remove yourself from as much negativity as you can. Do not be afraid to stand up for yourself and let your family and friends know what you need.

Grief support groups can be wonderfully healing; however, some grief groups become competitions with the theme of "who can grieve better?" These do not offer the sustenance that you need. One of the grief support groups I attended was an enormous disappointment to me. I wanted to connect with other women who would understand what I was experiencing. During the meeting, the participants focused only on their pain instead of directing energy in a positive direction so everyone could benefit. Admittedly, grief groups are not one-size-fits-all and differ from each other, so keep looking for one that you feel comfortable attending. Ask yourself when you leave the group: Do I feel empowered or relieved it is over?

Support does not have to be defined as a bereavement group, because connection with other people who share your interests can be stimulating and medicinal and can bring people into your life whom you may never have met. Investigate get-togethers in your community of like-minded people who share your interests and expand your vision of what support can look like.

Exercise
Support
· · · · · · ·

I would like you to make a list of all the people in your life whom you can count on for their support. Ask yourself if you can phone them when necessary. Remove anyone whom you don't feel you can talk to or who has certain caveats for their support. You may find that your list is quite narrow, and that's fine. It is a gift to know whom you can count on when you need help.

Make a list of activities you enjoy that you never had the time to do. Include your heart's desire—attending new classes, going on nature walks, making art, etc. When you are done, look at your list, choose one activity that is actually feasible, and add it to your calendar. Learning a new skill, meeting new people, or simply spending time out in nature can be quite healing.

Grief Rx: *Healing Rituals*

Because grief silently steals energy from the body and psyche, it is important to find healing rituals that are restorative. One of the most soothing rituals I did during my own grief process was walking and listening to the sound of my feet on the pavement. Each night, I would take a long walk and just breathe and try to clear my mind of the significant emotional weight that I was feeling and release my sadness. These walks were quite therapeutic, and I could "hear" my mother's voice in my head speaking with me. I felt reassured, calm, and much more at peace.

I have a collection of her cards, letters, and emails, and when I am missing her, I look through them. Sometimes, I close my eyes, ask for her message, and make my selection. When I open my eyes, I find that the image or text speaks to what I need.

Exercise
Finding Ritual

Discovering a healing ritual is a beautiful thing to do. I found my nightly ritual of walking enormously satisfying and peaceful, but you may choose something else. I want you to think about what rituals you enjoy—taking a bath every night, lighting candles, reading a book, or even cooking a meal. Try to commit to a ritual that you truly love to do. You may choose something that has personal meaning because you shared the experience with your mother. If you find that reading her emails or correspondence is a ritual you would like to enact, then do so. Try to stick to a particular ritual for a few weeks and record in your journal how it felt. When you are ready, you can choose another or continue with the one you selected.

Grief Rx: *Miracles*

The fact that you were chosen by her to be her daughter is a miracle. A shimmer of light during the dark night is a miracle. Learning about your capacity for resilience is a miracle. Laughing again, even for brief moments, is a miracle. Dreaming about her hugging you is a miracle. Having faith in yourself and committing yourself to your healing is a miracle.

Exercise
Commitment Miracle

Everyone has their own idea of what a miracle is. In this exercise, I would like you to entertain the idea that making a commitment to yourself is a miracle, especially in the midst of great pain.

Think about the qualities of your commitment and write them down. Don't think about them at great length; simply write down what your first thoughts are. When you are done, look at your list. You may find that these qualities are missing from your life, and this is excellent information. Write out a paragraph of commitment as a miracle oath that supports your healing, and post it somewhere where you can see it every day as a positive affirmation.

Grief Rx: *Pay Attention to Your Body*

Most people understand that grief is an emotional wound; however, grief symptoms can also present physically. Sleeplessness, anxiety, and gastrointestinal problems are common for many women, so pay attention to your body's messages. Before a physical scar is healed, it is inflamed and agitated and painful, but keep in mind that your body has amazing self-healing abilities. Take the time every day to pay attention to your body's communications.

Exercise
Body Dialogue

Do you notice when you are feeling drained of energy, or do you keep pushing? Have you noticed your sleep patterns? Are you sleeping enough? Too much? Are you exercising every day? What are you doing to support your physical body? Are you feeling any physical pain? Can you identify where that pain is? This visceral knowledge is very important, for once you learn to understand your body's wisdom, you can seek remedies, such as massage, acupuncture, walking, incorporating an exercise program you enjoy, or taking time during your day for extra rest when you need it.

Exercise
Somatic Checks

A valuable tool that you can utilize each day is a somatic check. It does not take a long time to do and can be quite effective. Before you get out of bed in the morning, take a moment to connect with your body and breathe deeply and naturally. See if you can discover the location of your grief today. Grief has its own intelligence. Is it in your head? Your diaphragm? Your throat? Your solar plexus? Visualize your grief and pay attention to what it looks like. What color is it? What shape does it hold? Does it have a sound? Does it have a message to tell you? If so, listen carefully. When you feel that you are ready to release, visualize the energies passing through your body and place them in a container. You can decide how large you want this container to be. Ask Divine Intelligence, God, or Spirit to remove these grief energies for release. Breathe. Repeat the exercise until you feel complete. Grief leaves scars, but like most scars, they remind us of adversity and recovery.

Grief Rx: *Design a Spiritual Altar and Give Honor to Your Mother*

Altars are sacred spaces and that can help you make a connection with your mother. You can choose to create your altar in your home or outside in a healing garden. There is no right or wrong way to create an altar. Follow your heart promptings. Select photographs, books, jewelry, stones, and items of meaning. You can add and remove objects as you feel called to. Your altar is your sacred space to honor and talk with your mother. This can be your medicine. You can purchase ethically sourced sage for smoke cleansing or purchase essential oils that you prefer. The Latin word *salvo* (sage) means "to heal" or "to save."[79] Because grief brings us so much sadness, purifying ourselves in our altar area can remove stagnant energies. Although Native American ceremonial practices have used sage for centuries, if you are not Indigenous, please choose another method for purification as an ethical choice. Jackie Yellow Tail, who was interviewed in Mark St. Pierre and Tilda Long Soldier's *Walking in the Sacred Manner*, shared an explanation of how she prepares for a healing session (below), which I find very enlightening.

> Smudging refers to an almost universal practice. Cedar, sweetgrass, and often sage are added to a burning ember to create a smoke that has spiritually purifying qualities. Healers always smudge themselves, and if they are going to use any ritual equipment, such as pipe, feathers, rattles, drums, or herbs, they pass those through the smudge as well.[80]

---

79. Grivetti, "Sage."
80. St. Pierre and Long Solider, *Walking in the Sacred Manner*, 152–53.

According to Yellow Tail, "If I don't smudge before I start doctoring, then I'll go back and smudge myself afterward. I don't have a set ritual, other than praying for that person right then and there."[81]

I wish I had the opportunity to study with a medicine woman who could teach me all the nuances of using sage as a spiritual medicine, and if you live in a place with Indigenous healers, I urge you to contact them and ask if they would be willing to teach you. There are many books on the use of sage and the various ways to cleanse with smoke, but ultimately, learning from a medicine woman is the best way.

Exercise
Sound Healing

The use of chimes, gongs, and singing bowls can help to raise the vibrations when you are working with your altar. According to a recent study, "sound therapy can significantly alter brain waves changing agitated wave patterns to exceptionally calm wave forms."[82] I especially like using Tibetan Ting-Shas because the sound is not piercing but soft and welcoming. Ask for only the highest and best energies of light to surround you as part of your healing ritual. The blessing of medicine woman Dhyani Ywahoo is particularly poignant to me.

> May you be surrounded ever in the light of wisdom and joy, and may. ... [it] bring many women again to

---

81. St. Pierre and Long Solider, *Walking in the Sacred Manner*, 152.
82. Goldsby and Goldsby, "Eastern Integrative Medicine and Ancient Sound Healing Treatments for Stress," 24–30.

the certainty of their gifts, and may men .... realize the mother within, and may we all realize ourselves in the circle of light.[83]

Grief Rx: *Your Wounding Is a Spiritual Gift*

Although it is hard to imagine that the wounding and pain you feel has anything positive to offer you, it does. The wound you have received during the grief process has a purpose, even though initially this may seem unlikely. Perhaps you realize you never thought you were capable of such love and yearning for another person. Possibly, the shattering of your heart has given you a calmness and true understanding of what love is and can be. You may be more vocal about telling people you love that you care deeply for them. Your impatience with daily irritations may not seem important anymore. You may decide that the current life you are living is not the way you wish to live from now on.

Exercise
Spiritual Wounding

Think about how your grief has given you opportunities to reflect upon your life. Write down what you believe your wounding has taught you. Do you feel more emboldened to take the next steps in your life that previously you may have ignored? Perhaps you feel more at ease in telling people how you truly feel. If you have not discovered how you have changed, that is fine. Pay attention to any emotional changes you may have made. What has your wounding taught you? In time, everyone receives a spiritual gift from this wounding.

---

83. Brooke, *Medicine Women*, 77.

Grief Rx: *Nourish Your Body*

Grief interferes with our normal routine, and often our nutrition suffers. You may find yourself eating all the time or unable to eat at all. Are you stuffing down your emotions using food as the catalyst? Eating healthy foods that are nourishing will support you and help to restore your physical vitality. Because the physical body is overloaded by the stress of grief, eating lightly and choosing healthy foods can help eliminate digestive burdens to a system that is already taxed.

Exercise
Nourishment

Because you need nourishment during your grief journey (and when you are not grieving), it is important to pay attention to your habits. You may also not feel as if you want to eat at all. Make a list of healthy foods (even healthy comfort foods) you enjoy that can provide you with sustenance. Keep this list to consult when you are at the grocery store so you don't load up on sugary treats, which will cause a blood sugar spike. The results will make you feel depleted. Add fresh fruits and vegetables, yogurt, eggs, whole grains, soups, fish, and chicken or even a bowl of your favorite healthy (with no or little sugar) cereal to your healthy eating list.

Grief Rx: *Speak Your Truth*

Chakras make up an ever-changing energetic system located on the surface of our bodies and reflect our emotional, physical, and spiritual landscape. This system is derived from ancient Indian medicine protocols. When our chakras are in balance, we experience optimum health, and when we are in distress, they are affected. The common belief is that there are seven major chakras depending on the book you consult. There are also indirect chakras found in other locations in the body's energetic system. When our chakras are aligned, we enjoy wellness—physically, spiritually, and emotionally. They can also be depleted or out of balance, particularly when we have experienced shock or trauma.

Importance of the Throat Chakra

The throat chakra regulates communication not only with others but with ourselves. The deep feelings that grief arouses can block this chakra, notably when we say yes when we mean no and do not give voice to how we are truly feeling. These thoughts gain momentum and can be dangerous to our health when we choose to self-sabotage.

Exercise
Throat Chakra Questions

Ask yourself if you have experienced any of these symptoms recently. Are you stuffing down your emotions in order "not to feel"? Do you have something to say to someone that you have been avoiding? What are you not giving voice to? If you have not addressed some darker truths that you are feeling because you are ashamed to discuss them, seek professional help.

The throat chakra is also related to the mother archetype and, according to esoteric author Alice A. Bailey, related to the Virgin Mary.[84] Because we often put our mothers on a

---

84. Roseman, "Dance Theory," 14.

pedestal as the "perfect mother," we may mask our true feelings about them after they have passed, ignoring our disillusionment or dissatisfaction. However, articulating these untold frustrations can help usher in deeper healing. I love my mother, but that does not mean that she did not disappoint me, and I am sure I disappointed her. If you have not had the opportunity to settle things with your mother and there is still unfinished business that you need to attend to, ask for the Virgin Mary's assistance or find someone you trust that you can talk to in a safe space. I call on the Virgin Mary often, especially when I feel that I need mothering. That is the primary reason I visit her in churches in my community—to receive her wisdom because she brings me solace.

Being unable to cry or speak clearly and having the feeling of a lump in our throats are all symptomatic of issues of the throat chakra. The stress and trauma of grief will modulate how your throat chakra is functioning. It is also the location of your thyroid, parathyroid, and pharyngeal glands. A blocked throat chakra can also produce feelings of self-loathing and self-deprecation. If you have a lump in your throat that will not go away, don't ignore it, and consult your physician.

Exercise
Throat Chakra Healing

If you are a visual person, you may wish to draw an outline of your head and throat area and visualize or color pink, white, or blue directly on this outline. Practice writing messages to yourself from your throat chakra (just write what comes to mind immediately) to find out where your blockages are.

Making vocal tones, called "toning"; chanting; and engaging in sound healing can also help to free up blocked energy in your throat chakra.

Creativity and the Throat Chakra

The throat chakra is also related to our creative voice. The creative process can offer a tool to express your pain, anger, and depression. The process is not always pretty, but that is not the aim. I am an art therapist, and I can attest to the profound healing process that occurs when we make any type of art, especially when we are unable to verbalize our emotions. Drawing and painting are traditional forms of art therapy, and making art in a protected space can be enormously supportive if we can resist the urge to judge its merits. Any art-making activity that you feel connected with is therapeutic and will improve your mental health because when we are engaged in a creative process of any kind, it is calming to our psyche. It can change the focus of despair into illumination and often uncover truths about our inner world.

Exercise
Mandalas

Mandala-making as a healing modality is especially helpful because it does not require extensive art materials and is not time consuming. Research has shown that working with mandalas brings a sense of peace during times of distress, promotes well-being, and is naturally calming. They are used in many cultures because of their meditative and stress-reducing abilities. In addition, they can be helpful for the reduction of PTSD and trauma as well as relieving depression and anxiety.[85] You can find outlines for mandalas in most bookstores if you do not want to create your own.

My former teacher, Dr. Shaun McNiff, a pioneer in art therapy, has written many books on its efficacy. One of his quotes that I always found inspiring is "Whenever illness is associated with the loss of soul, the arts emerge spontaneously as remedies and soul medicine."[86] I am not suggesting that grief is an illness; however, we often feel as if our souls are lost.

Grief Rx: *Release Your Grief into the Healing Waters*

Water has been used for centuries by Indigenous cultures as a curative, and immersing oneself in water is both physically and psychologically nourishing. If you have ever visited a natural hot spring or reclined in a hot tub of water, you know how wonderful it feels to be submerged. Hydrotherapy can treat both physical and emotional problems and is especially helpful for the relief of anxiety and depression. Adding essential oils can also be effective because many of these essential oils provide emotional stabilization.

Exercise
Hydrotherapy

Some women prefer showers, while others are devoted to taking baths. It doesn't matter what type of hydrotherapy you choose because water is a conduit for healing regardless. Footbaths are not as labor-intensive as full-body baths and

---

85. Henderson, Rosen, and Mascaro, "Empirical Study on the Healing Nature of Mandalas."
86. McNiff, *Art as Medicine*, 1.

give you the chance to literally get off your feet. If you are physically unable to take a full-body bath, they offer the same benefits.

Adding essential oils in the form of bath bombs or simply mixing some into your bath is terrific. I especially enjoy adding eucalyptus soap when I take showers each day and find the scent invigorating. Due to its nature, no one essential oil fits all, and everyone has their own preferences when it comes to selecting aromas that are pleasing to them. You only need a few drops of essential oils in your bath because they are highly concentrated. Some women use grounding scents such as vetiver or pine because of their distinct woodsy smell, but you may prefer lavender or rose oil. Epsom baths are also effective, but for some, they can cause dizziness, especially if you remain in the tub for a lengthy amount of time.

Grief Rx: *Let Mother Earth Bring Her Healing*

During the mourning process, we live in our heads, and we forget that we have a body. We go through the motions of our day on autopilot without connection to our physical form. We may feel suffocated by our emotions because the overlay of grief is restrictive, and we are stuck. Mother Earth can help you feel protected, nurtured, and anchored because she offers you her healing abilities.

Exercise
Meditation with Mother Earth

Close your eyes and intend that you are going to connect with Mother Earth. Imagine a form such as an anchor or another fixed and stable object at the bottom of your feet and send the energies of this image down deep into the earth.

When you feel as if this representation has reached its final destination, secure it in the ground below you. Now reverse that energy circuit and send it traveling up from your feet to your calves, legs, and upper body. You will probably feel a pulsing sensation as your vibration is heightened. Know that you are protected and locked firmly in Mother Earth's embrace.

Grief Rx: *Find an Energy Practitioner*

Our life force is diminished during grief because we are so exhausted; however, we can also reignite that energy with assistance. Working with a skilled energy practitioner is valuable because they can help you to regain your balance by removing the energy that you don't need or may not even belong to you. If you have spent time in a hospital, you may have picked up other people's auric fields and may not realize it, because health care settings are laden with the energetic residue of emotional upheavals experienced by patients, family members, and health care workers. You can recognize a depletion of energy when you feel overwhelmed or as if you are walking through mud. Your body will just feel heavy.

Reiki is a wonderful, noninvasive form of energetic healing that can help you feel more aligned physically as well as emotionally. Emotional freedom techniques (EFT), such as tapping, are very effective. I continue to practice tapping when I am scared, sad, or anxious. Eye movement desensitization and reprocessing (EMDR) is also a psychotherapeutic tool that can help to eradicate disturbing memory patterns. Acupuncture, reflexology, and colorpuncture are helpful because these modalities can remove grief trapped inside your body and return the flow of vitality to your body. Shamanic healings are also immensely therapeutic, especially soul retrieval, as well as massage.

Exercise
Working with Healers

Before you select what type of healing you believe will help you at this time, think about past experiences with healers. Have you worked with energy healers before? Did you find these sessions helpful? I would suggest that before you select the mode you feel most comfortable with you check in with yourself to see what your comfort level is. Do you want to be touched? If so, you may find massage particularly helpful. If you don't want direct touch, Reiki may be the right form of therapy for you right now. If you have used acupuncture in the past and found that helpful to you, then you may want to schedule an appointment with an acupuncturist you trust. Many acupuncturists are very expensive, so you may benefit from community acupuncture, where you will be part of a group receiving treatment; usually these sessions are much less expensive. Colorpuncture is a form of acupuncture using only light on particular points in the body and is noninvasive, so you may want to use this modality. Before you work with any energy practitioner, make sure they are credentialed. Ask family or friends for referrals. It may be a trial-and-error process until you find the right healer for you. You can even set up a phone meeting to discuss your needs before proceeding.

Grief Rx: *Find a Grief Partner*

Initially, when you are in the throes of grief, you may not want to talk with anyone, and that is understandable. Family and friends who circled you in the beginning are probably returning to their own lives, and you may feel alone. Finding someone you trust and feel comfortable talking with is very important. Some women choose to work with spiritual advisers who can offer opportunities to speak about the spiritual components of loss and sometimes can bring to you a new perspective.

Exercise
Grief Partnering

Think about whom in your life you feel that you can trust. Who always offered support and love to you? Reach out to that person and ask them if they would be willing to be your grief partner and tell them what you need. You may want to meet them once a week for lunch, set up a particular time you can call them each week, or just ask them if you can check in with them when you need support or nurturance or when you are seeking someone to listen. Since this is a partnership, you can decide together what would work best, but the knowledge that you have someone whom you can count on can bring you immeasurable peace of mind.

Grief Rx: *Call upon Your Ancestors*

I am fascinated by the word *sankalpa*, a practice in the yogic traditions that I believe is a vow of the heart. It can also mean a heartfelt desire, resolve, or intention.[87] This word spoke to me as a tool for aligning with my mother's spirit and an opportunity to practice my vow of connection. I was told by a dear friend years ago that when I heal myself, I heal my mother as well as my ancestors,

---
87. Tenzer, "The Mysteries of Sankalpa Explained, Again."

a statement that has enormous implications that I wholeheartedly embrace as I continue my self-healing today.

Exercise
Connection with the Ancestors

If you have a meditation or dreamwork practice, extend an invitation to your ancestors to help you regain your balance. One of the most useful ways to make this connection is to choose an ancestor whom you feel connection with. If you have a photograph of this ancestor, you can put it by your bed. Before you go to sleep, ask them if they will accompany you during your dreamtime. Don't be afraid to reach out to them and remind them that you need their wisdom, love, and guidance. They will hear you.

Grief Rx: *Respect the Inward Journey*

It is important to respect and receive the inward journey because it is part of the process. You are not going crazy, although you may feel that way. During the grieving process, you may feel overly sensitive because you have experienced deep emotions—perhaps for the first time in your life. You will probably feel like one moment you can function in the world, and in the next moment, you find yourself sobbing and unable to think. You may be forgetful or angry. You possess the wisdom to know what you need to express, when, and, most importantly, to whom. If you truly feel as if you are "out of control" in your behavior and your heart's knowing tells you that you need help, seek out professional support from someone you trust.

Exercise
Monitoring Your Emotions

Monitoring your emotions without judgment is very helpful if you can resist the urge to make any assumptions about "good" emotions versus "bad" emotions. They are simply emotions.

When you have a check-in with yourself, you can have a better handle on what and how you are feeling each day. Try to imagine your grief journey akin to an enormous wave with high points, low points, and middle points along the way.

One of the monitoring tools I used each day was selecting a number from one through ten that mirrored how I was feeling. One through four meant that I could function well, five through seven was challenging, and eight through ten usually meant that I should take extra care of myself that day. If I choose a number higher than seven, I knew that this was a signal for help and that I needed to meditate, breathe deeply, lie down, or just sleep when I had the luxury to do so. Your number will change daily and often dramatically.

Grief Rx: *Connect with Your Guides*

There are several guides that are important messengers that you can work with, and these guides may be familiar to you. Your Divine Guide may appear as a religious or spiritual symbol during your meditations or dreams, and you will feel comforted by a blanket of emotional peace. The Divine Guide will send you people and often opportunities for healing your wounds. If you have been requesting divine assistance, you can be assured that your pleas have not been ignored.

The Dream Guide
The Dream Guide is an important messenger to help you access and decode your dreams. A dream diary can help you record these messages, and with practice, you will find that remembering your dreams is an illuminating process, even if you have had difficulties in the past. Ask your Dream Guide to help you remember each dream clearly and effortlessly so that upon awakening, you can write down the information you receive. If you are in the throes of making important decisions in your life, invite your Dream Guide to help you make the best choices. Your Dream Guide is accessible, but you must trust that you will receive the information you ask for, and like with any esoteric method, patience is key.

The Guardian
The Guardian is an envoy of protection. You may be feeling unloved, unwanted, and unsure about yourself. The Guardian is a fierce protector to guide you through these unsteady times. If you feel like you just cannot function, bring your Guardian to you through meditation in the morning or before you go to sleep. If you have a dedicated ritual of reflection, include your Guardian.

The Transformer
You are experiencing a major transition, and this is a shake-up. You can expect disruptions from your psyche; however, this upheaval has a purpose. You will learn to navigate your life for the better. Remember that your feelings of sadness will be transformed in time. You can access the Transformer Guide through surrender. Surrender to the depths of destruction, and allow everything that is not needed or unwanted to leave. You will be built up again, a stronger and more courageous person.

Exercise
Connection with Your Guides
・・・・・・・・・・・・・・・・・・・・・・・・・・

This meditation will work whether you choose to connect with your Divine Guide, Dream Guide, Transformer Guide, or Guardian. You may wish to record the meditation and play it back or review the text a few times before you begin. Close your eyes and visualize yourself in a favorite and safe place. Take some deep breaths and surround yourself with healing light. Some women use white light, but it is not necessary to visualize white light. You can use any color you are drawn to include. Ask to meet your Healing Guide or any other guide of your choice, such as a Grief Guide or a Mental Health Guide. Pay attention to any images, words, or even colors that you receive. Listen to any messages that are conveyed to you. Take your time. If you don't receive any information, that is fine. Enjoy the meditation. When you feel complete, open your eyes and write down any inner promptings that you have received. You can also draw any images you saw in your meditation along with any words that you remember. When you are feeling unsteady, you can ask to be protected and guided.

Grief Rx: *Symbols of Grief*

As a trained art therapist, I have discovered that the use of symbols is highly relevant and many times more potent than verbal information. For example, during art therapy sessions, a woman may feel as if verbalizing her grief experiences is much too painful. After my mother passed away, I had to go to the bank to take care of some business in her name. I couldn't explain in words to the teller what my loss was. I wrote on a piece of paper that my mother had passed away and asked her for the materials I needed on this scrap of paper. I just couldn't talk. This was my symbol.

Exercise
Meditation with Your Personal Grief Symbols

Find a comfortable place to relax and simply breathe. Try to clear any immediate thoughts you may be experiencing. It is helpful to imagine a blank movie screen. When you are ready, take a few moments and think about what your personal symbols for your grief process may be. When the vision is clear, draw it in your journal. You may choose to repeat this visualization often and revisit your drawings to track how your symbols change through time and have many permutations reflecting your journey.

Grief Rx: *Sleep as the Ultimate Healing Balm*

A natural symptom of grief is the inability to sleep peacefully through the night. Your body's wisdom tells you that you are physically and mentally exhausted. If you find yourself up at all hours of the night, you may want to read, journal, drink a cup of hot water, stretch, or meditate. You can also work with gemstones; however, before you do any type of stone healing, make sure the stone is energetically clean from all outside influences. If you buy a stone from a store, it probably was touched by many people, so you want to clear that energy.

Exercise
Gemstones for Healing

Before you work with a selected gemstone, you can cleanse its energy in a variety of ways. You can place the stone outside in the sun for a day, submerge it in Himalayan salt, or use a gentle dishwashing detergent. All these methods will eliminate any energy that does not belong to you. All stones have different reactions to water and sunlight. Before you engage in any type of cleansing, make sure the stone can sustain it. Pink stones, including rose quartz, rhodochrosite, and fluorite, can help promote restful sleep, but if you are called to work with another stone, that is fine. Purple fluorite is usually recommended for sleep, but crystal healing is not one-size-fits-all, and I prefer to choose the stones that I am drawn to.

You can place your stone on an area of your body where you feel it is needed or place it next to your bed. Visualize a soft pink light wrapping you with its warmth and grace. You can also hold the stone in your hand. Stones possess their unique vibration, and I believe that when you choose them, there is reciprocity and knowing that they are willing and able to work with you. Repeat this exercise as many times as you like to feel calm, or you can use it to help induce a nap, repeating it until you drift off to sleep. A deep sleep is restorative to both body and psyche and will help you regain your emotional and physical stamina.

Grief Rx: *Find Yourself in Mother Nature*

You may find yourself drawn to the healing that Mother Nature can provide. She can hold you during your grief, especially when, like me, you cannot bear the thought of being around other people.

You may be familiar with the concept of forest bathing—just a new way to suggest that walking in the woods is healing. When we are surrounded by nature, we have a respite from our daily lives and the opportunity to look at beauty, listen to the crunch of the fallen leaves on the ground, and inhale clean and refreshing oxygen. According to research, it takes 120 minutes for people to feel healthy and have a sense of well-being when they are in nature. Nature is a natural antidote for stress, perhaps because people intuitively feel safe in Mother Nature and recognize her healing capabilities. According to Richard Louv, who coined the term *nature deficit disorder*, "nature is not only nice to have, but it's a have-to-have for physical health and cognitive functioning."[88]

Exercise
Discovering Your 120 Minutes

It is not imperative that you find a place to walk for two hours at a time. You may decide to walk in the woods or somewhere else in nature for a half hour each outing, and that is fine. Decide how you would like to "spend" your two hours in nature. Choose where you will go in your community. You may want to take a walk outside (depending on the weather) or visit nature centers, botanical gardens, orchid groves, or sculpture gardens to take in their beauty. It does not matter where you choose to go. What matters is that you allow yourself to visit Mother Nature on your own.

---

88. Robbins, "Ecopsychology."

Grief Rx: *Regain Your Balance*

After the initial shock of loss, you may feel physically shaky and unable to leave the house or, at the opposite extreme, overwork so you don't have to meet the despair of pain and grief. Recognize that you are in a deep process that has changed you and will continue to shape you into who you will be. This is an honorable time. How can you regain your balance? By doing simple activities.

Exercise
Balancing Activities

If you are hiding in your house, unable to answer the phone, take small steps. Choose one hour each day to get out of the house. Go to the supermarket, a museum, a bookstore, or a favorite place you like to lunch, or buy a cup of coffee and sit. There are no rules. Be gentle with yourself. You may find that attending a grief support group is helpful. Yoga and dance classes are very therapeutic, or you may choose to take an art class. Remember that although the grief process feels as if it is all-consuming, it does not have to consume you twenty-four hours a day. Trust that you will regain your balance. You are more than your grief!

Spiritual Prescriptions

Spiritual distress is an important component of grief that is often ignored; however, it is very common to experience. You may feel alienated from previous spiritual or religious practices; be angry at God, Spirit, or the Divine; or question your purpose in life. Through the shattering experiences of loss, the inclination is to turn away from these spiritual or religious beliefs. You may want to cut off any connection you used to believe in. However, God, Spirit, or the Divine will always assist you. All you need to do is ask for what you need and wait patiently for an answer. You may choose to speak with God, Jesus, Mother Mary, Kwan Yin, or White Buffalo Calf Woman. It is up to you to decide whom you want to communicate with.

Saints and Mother Imagery

St. Therese, often referred to as Little Flower, suffered deeply after her mother died. St. Teresa of Ávila also experienced mother loss, and I wonder how their personal experiences of grief and loss informed their religious journeys. I would imagine that both women received comfort and support from the nuns in the convents and from the women who directed the religious enclaves where they both lived. These women probably consulted the head of the convent—Reverend Mother, or Mother Superior—which is appropriate because they provided comfort and guidance, just as the saints' mothers did for them and our mothers did for us.

Teresa of Ávila is one of my favorite women saints, particularly since I found out she used to dance in her room in private. One of her quotes, "every part of the journey is important to the whole," speaks volumes about the grief journey.[89] During the fourteenth century, the mystic Julian of Norwich dared to write, "so also is God truly our Mother."[90] This was a revolutionary philosophy for the time, and any time and regardless of your belief system, I believe that the mother she wrote about—"a mother's service is nearest, readiest, and surest—nearest because it is most natural, readiest because it is the most loving, and surest because it is truest"—is truth for daughters.[91] Her words are inspirational to me.

Spiritual Questioning

Embedded in the spirituality and medicine courses I teach is the use of spiritual assessment tools that medical students can utilize with their patients. In the courses, they are asked to reflect on their spiritual/religious beliefs so they do not project those beliefs unto their patients. Two of the most helpful spiritual assessment tools were created by wonderfully compassionate women who I had the good fortune to know. My former mentor at the Warren Alpert Medical School of Brown University, Dr. Gowri Anandarajah, created the HOPE inventory, and the FICA was created by the director of GWish, Dr. Christina Puchalski.[92] Both had the vision

---

89. St. Teresa of Ávila, *The Way of Perfection*, 127.
90. Doyle, *Meditations with Julian of Norwich*, 103.
91. Doyle, *Meditations with Julian of Norwich*, 105.
92. The FICA tool can be downloaded at https://gwish.smhs.gwu.edu/programs/transforming-practice-health-settings/clinical-fica-tool.

to integrate spirituality in the medical encounter years before it was fashionable. The questions asked in these inventories can help you.

Although it can be verbalized in a multitude of ways, asking yourself, "What sources in my life give me strength, comfort, and peace?" can help you discover new resources in your spiritual community and perhaps resources that you have not considered.[93] Ask yourself the following questions: Who has helped me in my past during a major crisis? What gave me the strength to go on during an upheaval in my life? Remembering your sources of spiritual resilience returns your power to you, where it belongs. Can you integrate any of those strategies now for your benefit?

Spiritual Rxs

The following prescriptions are categorized as spiritual Rxs because after mother loss, the spiritual path is unavoidable whether you have great faith or none, whether you are angry, confused, or not sure of how you feel about the spiritual realm of existence. Everyone has unique perceptions of what the Divine is or what spirituality means for them, and all those definitions are correct, private, and highly sacred. Whether you choose to think of Spirit or Divine Source in a religious, philosophical, or spiritual context does not matter. What matters is that you understand these spiritual prescriptions are living, real, and dynamic and can help you reestablish connection to a higher realm when you need it most.

Spiritual Rx: *Spiritual Rituals*

The spiritual rituals that you create for yourself will sustain you. It does not matter what your faith is or how you decide to fashion

---

93. Anandarajah and Hight, "Spirituality and Medical Practice," 81–88.

those rituals. What matters is that these rituals provide solace and have personal meaning for you. Although I have previously mentioned physical rituals, such as ceremony or even bath-taking, spiritual rituals can offer an even greater sense of peace.

Exercise
Spiritual Comforts

You may find comfort in going to church, synagogue, mosque, or a Zen temple; attending a sweat lodge ceremony; or creating your own spiritual rituals. Spiritual rituals can include journaling, dancing, listening to music, gardening, and meditating as well as praying, because prayer exists in all forms. One of my favorite rituals includes walking around used bookstores because I feel an affinity and comfort there. For me, this experience is spiritual in nature, as I am surrounded by wisdom.

Spiritual Rx: *Write a Spiritual Dialogue*

Writing is a potent tool for self-healing and is transformative. If we pause to listen to what our writing can reveal and allow that voice to address us, we can learn something new about ourselves. By using the following exercise, you can safely invite that conversation.

Exercise
Spiritual Dialogue

Close your eyes. Take a moment and tell God, Spirit, or the Divine everything you are thinking. If you feel abandoned, unloved, angry, and sad, say so. Do not try to say what is polite if it is not true for you. Now breathe. Take a few moments, open your eyes, pick up a pen and paper, and write a letter to yourself in response to what you have shared in Spirit dialogue. Write whatever immediately comes to mind. Do not edit it or spend time thinking. Just write what comes to you. This is called "automatic writing" and requires no previous writing expertise. Automatic writing is a powerful instrument to use during grief because our psychic and spiritual channels are heightened. Trust the information that you receive. You can do this exercise as often as you like.

Spiritual Rx: *Visit a Sacred Space— You Can Meet Your Mother There*

This is an invitation, an opportunity to meet your loved one in a sacred space. Take a moment and think about some of the places that you and your mother enjoyed. It does not matter if it was your backyard, her kitchen, or a restaurant in Paris. All these places are sacred because you found joy and connection with your mother there.

Exercise
Spiritual Connection

Visualize yourself with your mother through meditation. Close your eyes and place yourself in a place that was sacred and joyful for both of you. If you are having trouble choosing one place, you can sit by the ocean... and listen to the waves crashing in front of you offshore. Sit in your sacred place knowing that you are going to meet her. Wait for her; she will come. Look up when you feel her near you. Ask her anything you want to know. She knows you have questions. You can stay here for as long as you wish. Tell her you want to continue your communication with her especially when you are scared, and ask her for any messages that you need to know. You can also invite her to visit you during your dream state. When you feel complete, thank her and write down all you have learned today.

Spiritual Rx: *Everything Is Unright*
You may sense that everything in your life is "unright." Everything in your life has changed after her departure and your belief that things are not as they should be is real. However, this truth is mutable. The "unright" feeling will fluctuate throughout your process of grief and will gain momentum, recede, and gain momentum again. Recognize that this is a process of commitment for you to honor those changes and feelings of uncertainty and certainty. It is part of the path of grief, and you will learn how to move through all of it.

Spiritual Rx: *Do Not Be Afraid—You Have Spiritual Allies*
Although you are afraid and feel like you have sunk so low that there is no emerging from it, you are not alone. Your grief is much bigger than you. Call on your spiritual allies to help. Sometimes it is difficult to believe that we have support from the etheric realm, but we do. The more we practice working with our spiritual allies, the more trust we will have that we are not alone.

Exercise
Spiritual Allies

You can call upon your spiritual allies before you go to sleep or anytime during your daily life. I have worked with my personal spiritual allies in meditation, but I have also called upon them to help when I was entering a stressful and challenging situation. Imagine an enormous healing angel with wings embracing you when you feel scared. Ask your angel to help you, to relieve your grief burden, and to guide you through your day. Even though you cannot see the physical presence of your spiritual allies, they are always available to you. If you ask for help with serious expectations and trust that they will show up in your life, they will.

Spiritual Rx: *Send Spiritual Energies of Love to Your Mother*

Although you may think your mother cannot hear your messages to her, how do you really know? Does it truly matter? You have the ability to send your love to her anytime you wish. Although she is physically absent, the depth of love between you hasn't changed.

Exercise
Spiritual Energies

One of the easiest ways to send spiritual energy to your mother is by envisioning her surrounded by your love. What does your love look like? Is it a color? A feeling? You can visualize her in front of you or use a photograph, whatever you prefer.

Spiritual Rx: *Grieving Is a Mystical Initiation*

I have always believed that the grief process is akin to a mystical initiation. Anyone who has read the literature written by mystics or has had the blessing of a mystical experience knows that their life has changed permanently. You may also experience the paranormal like the mystic, having dreams, visions, or the feeling of divine presence, or you may have unique revelations. Your initiation is just as sacred and has many stages, including disbelief, doubt, trust, longing, and acceptance.

Your grief initiation is unique. It cannot be predicted or explained rationally, but that does not mean it is not valid. Grief initiation is beyond normal analysis and occurs beyond ordinary dimensional thinking. You may hear words spoken, find songs or symbols that seem to appear out of context, or experience unexplainable reassurances that she is with you. Your grief is a sacred journey comparable to the mystic's journey.

Spiritual Rx: *Ask for Spiritual Support*

Trusting that you will receive spiritual support is not always easy during the grieving process. You may feel angry, unsupported, alone, and stuck in a nightmare. All those feelings are true for now, but you can receive spiritual support when you need it. Try to trust that inner knowing.

Exercise
Spiritual Support Affirmation

You may want to repeat to yourself when you are feeling lost and alone, "I receive spiritual support to help me every day on my journey." Or you may wish to create your own words-of-power statement that has a potent meaning for you.

Spiritual Rx: *Take a Spiritual Pilgrimage and Talk to Your Soul*

A pilgrim is traditionally defined as someone who travels to a shrine or holy place as a religious act. Where have you traveled to in the past for spiritual sustenance? There are many ways to go on a spiritual pilgrimage. You can go to a place of meaning, or you can create a psychological spiritual pilgrimage in your home.

Exercise
Honoring Your Healing Journey

Choose a day when you know you will not be disturbed and spend it in silence. Shut off your phone, radio, and television. Take long walks, and read, meditate, or write in a journal. Honor your healing pilgrimage and listen to what your soul wishes to say to you. Pay attention.

Spiritual Rx: *Light a Candle—*
Let the Rays of Light Envelop You with Peace

Light is a powerful force and has been a great healing conduit, especially in ceremony, for centuries.

Exercise
Candle Magic

Visit your favorite candle shop or a local supermarket and purchase a seven-day candle that you are attracted to. What color are you drawn to? This is the correct candle for you right now. When you light your candle, you may wish to bring it into your sacred space in your home or place it on your altar. Light this candle with the intention that the light of the candle is healing you and blanketing you with peace.

Afterword

New Rules for Honoring Grief: A Grief Manifesto was written when I was upset by the clichés I heard from people when I was in the throes of grief, and it is still applicable. Often, what I read or was told made me feel worse. Human nature has the need for explanations and quick fixes, but we don't have the answers, and death does not explain itself. The adage that "everything happens for a reason" may be true and is above my spiritual understanding, but even if you embrace this reasoning, it does not always guarantee solace. I created these rules to educate and elevate the grief journey for you and for others who intersect your path.

For the Bereaved

1. Give yourself permission to grieve. You are entitled.

You do not have to stop yourself from crying or expressing emotion because you do not want to upset anyone. You have a reason to cry. You lost someone you loved. It is not your job to make other people feel comfortable around you.

2. Grieving does not have a deadline.

There is a myth that it takes one year for people to "complete" their grieving; however, grief does not have a cutoff deadline that you need to meet. Take all the time you need and avoid trying to meet other people's expectations. If you find yourself unable to function and deeply depressed, there is no shame in seeking help from a qualified therapist who specializes in bereavement or consulting your health care provider.

3. You have permission to take care of yourself.

It is important to take extra care of yourself right now. This is not selfish. This is prudent. Everyone's needs are different during the grief process, and you may want to explore new methods of healing that you have never considered before, such as meditation classes, yoga, or asking for spiritual help. Create an activity every day that is only for you. Honor yourself and listen to your intuitive voice. It will tell you what you need. Do not desert yourself!

4. Do not apologize for how you feel.

Women tend to apologize much more often than men, and when we do this, we betray ourselves to be "nice." This is a reminder that you are entitled to feel the whole spectrum of emotions, including sadness, lethargy, loss of interest in activities or socializing, anger, and lack of ambition. These feelings will fluctuate through your grief journey.

5. Seek support from people who you know will support you.

Sometimes family and friends will not be able to support, understand, or even listen to your grief narrative. However, you do not have to feel isolated and alone. Reach out to friends, coworkers, or professionals who specialize in the grief process for help. Choose wisely and select someone who has a strong history of love and compassion.

6. Engage in physical exercise.

Although you may not feel as if you have any energy for physical exercise, you may find that once you engage in some form of physical activity you feel much more balanced. Any form of movement will help. Dancing, running, walking, stretching, or any physical activity will allow new and fresh energy to oxygenate your system so you feel refreshed.

7. Interview prospective therapists.

If you choose to work with a therapist, remember that you do not have to work with the first person you speak with. Some therapists are "experts" in the field, while others are not. In my opinion, unless you have walked this path, you are not an expert. Take your time to speak with prospective therapists and counselors to make sure you feel comfortable. How will you know they are the right person? You will know because you will feel safe, respected, and truly cared for. Ask them if they are willing to work with you to create a plan of action that will help regain your power. Jungian therapists, dance therapists, art therapists, and music therapists are also amazing, so don't restrict yourself to traditional models of psychotherapy for your mental health.

8. Do not be bullied into feeling that there is something wrong with your mourning process.

Many times, people will urge you to get out, stop crying, and refrain from talking about the person you have lost or insist that you just "get over it." This is called bullying. If you fell down and wounded yourself and were bleeding, you would immediately get proper and caring attention. Grief is no different, except this time, the wound is internal and not any less painful than a physical wound. Your wounding is emblematic of the love you have for your mother, and like a physical wound, it will heal.

9. This is a blank slate. Create your own grief rule that has resonance with you.

For Friends and Family Who Wish to Help

Often, family and friends truly want to help you after the loss of your mother, but they may not know how. If you find that you are uncomfortable asking for what you need, feel free to share these ideas. Although the idea of giving someone a piece of paper with requests may seem unorthodox, you are participating in a process of grief education, and your family, friends, and coworkers cannot possibly know what you are seeking unless you tell them.

1. Time will not heal all wounds.

Some wounds will not heal in time, although they will not have the same impact as they did at the beginning of the process. Resist the temptation to tell someone who has experienced a loss that "time will heal all wounds." This commonplace adage may be appropriate for some, but for most people, time does not heal. The wounding just transforms with less intensity.

2. You do not know how I feel.

Please do not say that you know how I feel. My loss is mine and unique to me, and you can never know how I feel. You may have navigated your own grief journey and think that I feel exactly as you do or did. My grief journey is sacred and unique, and it would be disingenuous to declare that you know what my internal world looks like.

3. Don't push.

Often, well-meaning people try to push their family members or friends into socializing or talking about their loss or insist they act in a certain manner. Although the core of this pushing is usually to help, it can be quite destructive. Allow the person you care about to dictate to you what they need. They are the experts in their grief process, not you.

4. Be thoughtful. Send a card.

After a person has suffered a loss, it is good manners to send the person a card of condolence, flowers, or any other special offering you can think of. Email cards, although thoughtful, are not the same as handwritten cards or letters.

5. Dress appropriately.

If you are going to attend a funeral or ceremony to honor someone who has passed, make sure you are dressed appropriately. You would be surprised by how many people think it is okay to show up at funerals improperly dressed. You are entering sacred space, and it is important that you show respect to the person who has passed by dressing accordingly.

6. Do not make remarks about how "fresh" the grief wound is.

Often, people who have experienced loss think they are experts on how others should grieve. Do not tell them it has only been however much time (six months, one year, two years, etc.) and that their grief is still fresh, which somehow implies that you are better able to function because your grief process is several years older. Grief is not a competition.

7. Even if you believe that "negative thinking" caused a person's illness and subsequent death, do not speak about this.

Stating that "negative thinking" was the real cause of a person's cancer, heart attack, or other serious illness is not only rude but also a dangerous assertion. I am aware of many, many people, including my mother, whose will to live and courage exhibited during their illness were astonishing. I can't tell you how many people have told me that my mother "caused her cancer." This belief diminishes, dishonors, and victimizes people.

8. Exhibit compassion and just "be" with the person who has experienced loss.

The very best thing you can do to help someone you care about who is experiencing loss is to be present. Although you may feel as if you must "do something," you really do not have to do anything but be present. Ask if you can come over and sit with them and listen if they wish to talk. Give yourself over to your friend or family member and allow them to lead you to where they need to go.

9. It's not about you.

Listening to small talk about the day-to-day life of other people is acceptable and the norm for social conversations; however, during a wake or funeral, when attending Shiva, or at other honoring ceremonies, resist the urge to talk about yourself, your children, your work, etc. It is not about you.

10. If you don't know what to do, ask.

If you don't know how to support your friend or family member, then ask. It is okay to admit that you are not sure what to say or do, and they will appreciate your willingness to be authentic. Grief opens the heart for many. For others, their hearts close, but there are still fundamental needs they, as human beings, have for connection and understanding. Sometimes, simply asking and admitting that you don't know what to do is the kindest and most sincere offering you can make.

11. Make time.

Do not forget that the person who is grieving may be quite vulnerable for a very long time, and checking in with them during the weeks, months, and even years after the passing of a loved one shows how much you care. Compassion, empathy, and listening to someone who is grieving is a gift and can help heal their hearts.

"*Thinking of Those Gone On*"
By Alonzo King

Brightness snatched away
Fast Eclipse that doesn't return the sun
Gone like a magic show trick
disappeared
but
my love is still here
beating
listening in the silence
after each beat
for the echo of
Yes
I love you too
I miss you too
I'm going on with life
you do the same
go on
go on
go on

Acknowledgments

Writing this book has been a challenging yet illuminating journey for me. I am grateful to the courageous women who documented their love stories with their mothers. As I wrote this book, I could feel their supporting presence in the room with me as steadfast companions helping me delve deep into the mysteries of grief.

A deep, heartfelt thank you to Dr. Christina Puchalski, who has been an inspiration to me for many years, and I am appreciative of her sage foreword to this book. My friends Alonzo King and Dr. Bill Frey were kind enough to share their words inside this book, and I am appreciative of their loving friendships. Alonzo's words continue to bring me peace, especially when I cannot find it for myself.

I would like to thank Liz Stewart, Marysa Storm, Kat Neff, Bill Krause, Anna Levine, and all the wonderful people at Llewellyn who helped me bring this book into form. Liz has been a steadfast ally whose words of wisdom (along with the team at Llewellyn) helped me shape a beautiful manuscript. Her support and kindness was notable. Shira Atakpu's beautiful cover brings a gorgeous visual representation of the eternal bond between daughters and their mothers.

I am fortunate to have the love and support of my husband, who stood by me and encouraged me to speak my truth. I will always be grateful to Toby, my mother, whose whisperings speak to me every day. Missing her will be a constant reminder of how much we loved each other, and continue to do so.

Empowerment Resources

The following resources may be helpful for you. Trust your judgment.

Alonzo King LINES Ballet, San Francisco, California
https://linesballet.org

Brilliantly
to help women who have had an experience with cancer
Kristen Carbone, founder
(716) 725-7068
https://www.brilliantly.co

Center for Informed Grief, LLC
Kelly Daugherty, MSW, FT
https://www.centerforinformedgrief.com

Connect & Thrive, Inc. (CAT)
Christine Anastos, founder
https://connect-and-thrive.com/

For Grief
grief support online
https://www.forgrief.com

Get Griefy **Magazine**
https://www.getgriefymagazine.com

Programs with Hope Edelman, Author
https://www.hopeedelman.com

Newport Aromatherapy and Natural Pharmacy
offers phytopharmaceutical products and therapeutic services
Cynthia LaBonte, MS, MH, owner, biochemist and master herbalist
(401) 835-8781
https://www.newportaromatherapy.com

The Sidney Project in Spirituality and Medicine and Compassionate Care™
The Sidney Project in Spirituality and Medicine and Compassionate Care™ was created in 2009 in honor of the author's father after a personal tragedy. This program has been taught for over a decade in twelve hospitals' medical residency education programs in several states. This program offers participants opportunities to engage in a safe forum to help cultivate a consciousness of caring and compassionate medicine with an emphasis on self-care to avoid compassion fatigue. Physician residents reflect on their doctoring challenges and have the chance to candidly discuss their fears, joys, and concerns in a safe environment. Unique among medical education, the program addresses educational program goals for residency training while also teaching strategies to help them navigate the intricacies of medicine.
jroseman@nova.edu

Practitioners

Sierra Bender, Founder, 4BodyFit™ Empowered Method, author, *Goddess to the Core*
https://sierrabender.com

Robin Cathleen Coale, Licensed Psychotherapist and Shamanic Healer
https://sacredshamanichealing.com

Jodi Digiulio, Licensed Mental Health Counselor, Medical Intuitive, Acceptance and Commitment Therapy (ACT) Practitioner Specializing in Holistic Health
Jodidigiulio7@gmail.com

Denise Forlizzi, Everyday Center for Spiritual Living
https://www.everydaycsl.org
forlizzid@gmail.com

Miriam Ismail, PhD, Holistic, Natural Health and Healing, Professional Development and Self-Improvement Coach, Founder, Precious Time, LLC
https://www.precioustime-llc.com
DrMiriamIsmail@gmail.com

Dr. Cheryl Kasdorf, Naturopath
703 S Main St, STE 8
Cottonwood, AZ 86326
(928) 649-9234
https://drcherylkasdorf.com

Pamela Miles
https://reikiinmedicine.org

P. Juliette Owen, BS, LMT
She specializes in lymphatic massage and wellness, detox sessions and women's health.
(502) 681-8281
https://www.studiolymphology.com

Cathy Pagano, MA, Spiritual Counseling
She is a Jungian trained therapist, astrologer, and intuitive.
https://cathypagano.com
info@cathypagano.com

Theresa Prebilsky, Spiritual Director
theresaprebilsky@gmail.com

Rev. Ann Rea, Everyday Center for Spiritual Living
https://www.everydaycsl.org
revannr@gmail.com

Dr. Maya Sarkisyan, Licensed Acupuncturist, National Board Certified Diplomate of Oriental Medicine, Functional Medicine Practitioner
She provides services for emotional balance, including spiritual counseling, neurolinguistic training, and five element acupuncture.
https://www.drmayaclinic.com

Judith Thompson, Naturopath, Dean of Herbal Medicine, American College of Healthcare Sciences
https://drjudithnd.com
drjudithnd@gmail.com

Amelia Vogler
She is a specialist in energy medicine and a spiritual mentor with advanced training in trauma work, past-life work, complex relational patterns, and energy medicine in surgery. She has a deep connection with the earth and weaves the underlying cosmological laws into her work. She is the director of the Vogler Institute and offers multiple trainings for spiritual advancement.
https://www.ameliavogler.com
support@ameliavogler.com

Cherry-Lee Ward, MS Education, Master Practitioner in Energy Medicine and Shamanic Healing, Healing Touch Practitioner
donation-based distance healing group sessions
https://www.cherry-leeward.com
CLWardHT@me.com

Rachel Weller, Healer and Spiritual Consultant, Tarot Consultations
oraclereadings9@gmail.com

Trainings

The Foundation for Shamanic Studies
https://www.shamanism.org

George Washington Institute for Spirituality and Health (GWish)
https://www.gwish.org

Manohar Croke, MA Diplomate Esogetic Colorpuncture, Director, US Esogetic Colorpuncture Institute
https://www.colorpuncture.org

Mental Health First Aid (MHFA) from National Council for Mental Well-Being
https://www.mentalhealthfirstaid.org

Rosemary Bourne, Licensed Acupuncturist, Director, Esogetics Partner
(415) 846-3758
https://www.colorpunctureusa.org

Shamanic Reiki, Debbie Philp, Practitioner and Teacher
https://debbiephilp.com

Society for Shamanic Practice
https://shamanicpractice.org/

Trauma, Grief, and Renewal Certificate Program
The New Earth Institute of Southwestern College
https://www.swc.edu/applying-to-certificate-specialty-programs/trauma-grief-renewal/

Upaya Zen Center
programs on love and death with professional training programs for clinicians in compassionate care of the seriously ill and dying
https://upaya.org

Organizations with Lists of Practitioners

International Expressive Arts Therapy Association (IEATA)
https://www.ieata.org

American Dance Therapy Association (ADTA)
https://www.adta.org

International Association of Reiki Professionals (IARP)
https://iarp.org

Council of Colleges of Acupuncture and Herbal Medicine (CCAHM)
https://www.ccahm.org

American Society of Acupuncturists
https://asacu.org

National Association for Naturopathic Doctors (AANP)
https://aanmc.org/national-associations/

BodySoul Rhythms
https://www.mwfbodysoulrhythms.org/practitioner-directory

SHE RECOVERS Foundation
empowering women to heal themselves, offering workshops and partnerships
https://sherecovers.org

Recommended Reading List

The Soul in Grief: Love, Death, and Transformation by Robert Romanyshyn

This is a wonderful book about the soul's journey in grief, written by someone who knows it intimately, chronicling both the descent and the resurrection of the grief journey.

Bereavement Dreaming and the Individuating Soul by Geri Grubbs

Dr. Grubbs is a Jungian psychologist who documents her grief experiences with the tragic death of her son and how dreams played an enormous role in her healing. She shares her research on dreams and loss, and I appreciated her directions for creating a bereavement dream sanctuary.

Spirited Medicine: *Shamanism in Contemporary Healthcare* edited by Cecile Carson, MD

This book is a compendium of interviews with health care practitioners who straddle the paths of traditional and nontraditional medicine. They offer insights and clinical examples of health using ancient ways of healing into the health care system.

A Time for Listening and Caring: Spirituality and the Care of the Chronically Ill and Dying edited by Christina M. Puchalski, MD

I had the privilege of writing a chapter in this wonderful compendium of essays about death and dying, but also about life, written by health care professionals in the field. The book sheds light on the topic of palliative care and offers creative ideas for its integration into the health care system.

Honoring the Medicine: The Essential Guide to Native American Healing by Kenneth Cohen

This book was written by a traditional Native American healer, and I find myself often opening the pages of the book to reread chapters again and again for insight and to relearn new tools for healing.

Alchemical Healing: A Guide to Spiritual, Physical, and Transformational Medicine by Nicki Scully

This book is considered a classic in energetic healing. The book offers hands-on tools for spiritual growth and techniques you can use to bring your body back into balance.

The Tibetan Book of Living and Dying by Sogyal Rinpoche

This book has a practical compendium on death and dying and living. It offers a relatable text on the famous Tibetan book. I particularly liked the explanations of mindfulness and his interpretation of death and the rewards of the spiritual path.

Bio-Etheric Healing: A Breakthrough in Alternative Therapies by Trudy Lanitis

I have this book in my library of healing books, and although there is a plethora of healing books, this book is concise and offers an excellent education on healing the body using energetic principles.

Essential Reiki: A Complete Guide to an Ancient Healing Art by Diane Stein

This book is much loved because Ms. Stein published the previously secret symbols used in Reiki healing. She explains the ancient lineage of Reiki and offers hands-on protocols for self-healing.

If Joan of Arc Had Cancer: Finding Courage, Faith, and Healing from History's Most Inspirational Woman Warrior by Janet L. Roseman, PhD

I am proud of this book. It was written right after my mother passed away, and I found that studying Joan of Arc was very helpful in my search for resilience.

Bibliography

American Psychiatric Association, ed. "Prolonged Grief Disorder." *The Diagnostic and Statistical Manual of Mental Health Disorders*. 5th ed. American Psychiatric Association, 2022.

Anandarajah, Gowri, and Ellen Hight. "Spirituality and Medical Practice: Using the HOPE Questions as a Practical Tool for Spiritual Assessment." *American Family Physician* 63, no. 1 (2001): 81–89. https://www.aafp.org/pubs/afp/issues/2001/0101/p81.html.

Askitopoulou, Helen. "Sleep and Dreams: From Myth to Medicine in Ancient Greece." *Journal of Anesthesia History* 1, no. 3 (2015): 70–75. https://doi.org/10.1016/j.janh.2015.03.001.

Atomic Physics. United World Films for the J. Arthur Rank Organization, 1948. US National Archives, September 25, 2015. https://www.youtube.com/watch?v=KUvPgArrwE8.

Atsma, Aaron J. "Asklepios." Theoi Project. Accessed March 18, 2025. https://www.theoi.com/Ouranios/Asklepios.html.

Avila, Elena. *Woman Who Glows in the Dark: A Curandera Reveals Traditional Aztec Secrets of Physical and Spiritual Health*. Tarcher, 1999.

Balch, Oliver. "'As with a Poem, Each Patient Is Unique': The Cancer Surgeon Using Poetry to Help Train Doctors." *The Guardian*, February 17, 2024. https://www.theguardian.com/science/2024/feb/17/joao-luis-barreto-guimaraes-cancer-surgeon-poetry-pessoa-prize.

Beischel, Julie. "Spontaneous, Facilitated, Assisted and Requested After-Death Communication Experiences and Their Impact on Grief." *Threshold: Journal of Interdisciplinary Consciousness Studies* 3, no. 1 (2019): 1–32. https://www.tjics.org/index.php/TJICS/article/view/31.

Benz, Ernst, Henry Corbin, René Huyghe, Toshihiko Izutsu, Adolf Portmann, Gershom Scholem, and Dominique Zahan. *Color Symbolism: The Eranos Lectures*. Edited by Klaus Ottmann. Spring Publications, 1977.

Bourke, Angela. "The Irish Traditional Lament and the Grieving Process." *Women's Studies International Forum* 11, no. 4 (1988): 287–91. https://doi.org/10.1016/0277-5395(88)90065-9.

Brooke, Elisabeth. *Medicine Women: A Pictorial History of Women Healers*. Quest Books, 1997.

Brown, Joseph Epes, ed. *The Sacred Pipe: Black Elk's Account of the Seven Rites of the Oglala Sioux*. Penguin Books, 1971.

Bylsma, Lauren, Ad Vingerhoets, and Jonathan Rottenberg. "When Is Crying Cathartic? An International Study." *Journal of Social and Clinical Psychology* 27, no. 10 (2009). https://doi.org/10.1521/jscp.2008.27.10.1165.

Bylsma, Lauren, Asmir Gračanin, and Ad Vingerhoets. "The Neurobiology of Human Crying." *Clinical Automatic Research* 29, no. 1 (2018): 63–73. https://doi.org/10.1007/s10286-018-0526-y.

"Caregiving in the U.S. 2020." National Alliance for Caregiving. Accessed April 18, 2024. www.caregiving.org/research/caregiving-in-the-U.S.

Catherine of Siena. *The Dialogue of Saint Catherine of Siena*. Translated by Algar Thorold. Lighthouse, 2011.

Cowan, Tom. *Shamanism as a Spiritual Practice for Daily Life*. Crossing Press, 1999.

Darwin, Charles. *The Expression of Emotions in Man and Animals*. D. Appleton, 1898. https://www.google.com/books/edition/The_Expression_of_the_Emotions_in_Man_an/ie0tAAAAIAAJ?hl=en&gbpv=1&printsec=frontcover.

"Did Mary lay her hands on all the Apostles in the Upper Room to pour out the Holy Spirit anointing?" StackExchange: Christianity. October 2020. https://christianity.stackexchange.com/questions/73789/did-mary-lay-her-hands-on-all-the-apostles-in-the-upper-room-to-pour-out-the-hol.

Doyle, Brendan. *Meditations with Julian of Norwich*. Bear, 1985.

"The DSM-5 Adds a New Diagnosis: Prolonged Grief." Advisory Board. Updated March 18, 2023. https://www.advisory.com/daily-briefing/2022/03/23/prolonged-grief.

Elsaesser, Evelyn, Chris A. Roe, Callum E. Cooper, and David Lorimer. "The Phenomenology and Impact of Hallucinations Concerning the Deceased." *PJPsych Open* 7, no. 5 (2021): e148. https://doi.org/10.1192/bjo.2021.960.

Fincher, Susanne. *Creating Mandalas: For Insight, Healing, and Self-Expression*. Shambhala, 1991.

Fitzgerald, Judith, and Michael Oren Fitzgerald. *The Spirit of Indian Women*. World Wisdom, 2005.

Frey, William H. *Crying: The Mystery of Tears*. Winston Press, 1985.

Friedan, Betty. *The Feminine Mystique*. W. W. Norton, 2010.

Friedan, Betty. "Women's Rights | Betty Friedan Interview | 1977." Interview by Mary Parkinson. Originally broadcast June 28, 1977. Posted May 11, 2017, by ThamesTV to YouTube. https://www.youtube.com/watch?v=RRICe6iivU8.

Goldsby, Tamara L., and Michael E. Goldsby. "Eastern Integrative Medicine and Ancient Sound Healing Treatments for Stress: Recent Research Advances." *Integrative Medicine* 19, no. 6 (2020): 24–30. https://pubmed.ncbi.nlm.nih.gov/33488307/.

Grigoryeva, Angelina. "When Gender Trumps Everything: The Division of Parent Care Among Siblings." Quoted by Sydney McKinley. "Daughters Provide as Much Elderly Parent Care as They Can, Sons Do as Little as Possible." News release. August 19, 2014. https://www.asanet.org/daughters-provide-much-elderly-parent-care-they-can-sons-do-little-possible/.

Grivetti, Louis E. "Sage." Nutritional Geography. Accessed May 26, 2025. https://nutritionalgeography.faculty.ucdavis.edu/sage/.

Grof, Stanislav. "Psychology of the Future: Lessons from Consciousness Research." *Spirituality Studies* 2, no. 1 (2016): 3–36.

Grof, Stanislav, and Christina Grof, eds. *Spiritual Emergency: When Personal Transformation Becomes a Crisis*. North Atlantic, 1999.

Grubbs, Geri. *Bereavement Dreaming and the Individuating Soul*. Nicholas-Hays, 2004.

Henderson, Patti, David H. Rosen, and Nathan Mascaro. "Empirical Study on the Healing Nature of Mandalas." *Psychology of Aesthetics, Creativity, and the Arts* 1, no. 3 (2007): 148–54. http://dx.doi.org/10.1037/1931-3896.1.3.148.

"Introduction to the Life of St. Teresa." The Carmelite Sisters. Accessed April 1, 2024. https://carmelite-seremban.org/sharing/introduction-to-the-life-of-st-teresa.

Kübler-Ross, Elisabeth. *On Death and Dying.* Macmillan, 1969.

Massey, Gerald. *Ancient Egypt: The Light of the World; A Work of Reclamation and Restitution in Twelve Books.* S. Weiser, 1970. https://archive.org/details/ancientegyptligh0001mass/mode/2up.

Mattioli, G., and F. Scalzone. *Current Hysteria: Disease or Obsolete Original Position?* Franco Angeli, 2002.

McKinley, Sydney. "Daughters Provide as Much Elderly Parent Care as They Can, Sons Do as Little as Possible." American Sociological Association. Updated September 28, 2022. https://www.asanet.org/daughters-provide-much-elderly-parent-care-they-can-sons-do-little-possible/.

McNiff, Shaun. *Art as Medicine: Creating a Therapy of the Imagination.* Shambala, 1992.

McVean, Ada. "It's Time to Let the Five Stages of Grief Die." McGill Office for Science and Society. May 31, 2019. https://www.mcgill.ca/oss/article/health-history/its-time-let-five-stages-grief-die.

Mehl-Madrona, Lewis. *Narrative Medicine: The Use of History and Story in the Healing Process.* Bear, 2007.

"The Memorare." Marquette University. Accessed March 18, 2025. https://www.marquette.edu/faith/prayers-memorare.php.

Muller, Robert T. "When Spiritual Crisis Shows Up in the Mental Health System." *Psychology Today*, February 10, 2022. https://www.psychologytoday.com/us/blog/talking-about-trauma/202202/when-spiritual-crises-show-in-the-mental-health-system.

O'Donohue, John. *Anam Cara: A Book of Celtic Wisdom.* Cliff Street Books, 1997.

O'Hare-Lavin, Mary Ellen. "The Practice of Dream Healing: Bringing Ancient Greek Mysteries into Modern Medicine." *C. G. Jung Society of Atlanta* (2002): 7–9.

Pearson, Patricia. "End of Life Experiences: Advice for Caregivers." *Threshold: Journal of Interdisciplinary Consciousness Studies* 1, no. 1 (2017): 3–6. http://tjics.org/index.php/TJICS/article/view/2.

Prewitt, Taylor. "Take Some Pills for Your Hysteria, Lady: America's Long History of Drugging Women Up." April 28, 2015. https://www.vice.com/en/article/here-lady-take-some-pills-for-your-hysteria-253/.

"Psalm 126:5." BibleGateway. Accessed March 13, 2025. https://www.biblegateway.com/passage/?search=Psalm%20126%3A5-6&version=KJV.

Robbins, Jim. "Ecopsychology: How Immersion in Nature Benefits Your Health." *Yale Environment 360*, January 9, 2020. https://e360.yale.edu/features/ecopsychology-how-immersion-in-nature-benefits-your-health.

Romanyshyn, Robert. "Robert Romanyshyn: The Soul in Grief." Interview by Dolores E. Brien. The Jung Page. https://jungpage.org/learn/articles/technology-and-environment/684-robert-romanysyn-the-soul-in-grief.

Romanyshyn, Robert. *The Soul in Grief: Love, Death, and Transformation.* North Atlantic Books, 1999.

Roseman, Janet. "Alonzo King Creates Amazing Grace in 'Lines.'" *Marin Independent Journal.* October 26, 2000.

Roseman, Janet. "Dance Theory: Symbol and Art of the Virgin Mary." PhD diss., Union Institute, 2002.

Roseman, Janet. *Dance Was Her Religion: The Spiritual Choreography of Isadora Duncan, Ruth St. Denis and Martha Graham.* Hohm Press, 2004.

Roseman, Janet. *If Joan of Arc Had Cancer: Finding Courage, Faith, and Healing from History's Most Inspirational Woman Warrior.* New World Library, 2015.

Schaup, Susanne. *Sophia: Aspects of the Divine Feminine Past and Present.* Nicholas-Hays, 1997.

Seeman, Gary. "The Transformative Power of Dreams." 2005. https://www.yumpu.com/en/document/read/40614361/the-transformative-power-of-dreams-gary-seeman-phd.

Sidebotham, Charlotte. "Viewpoint: Why Do We Cry? Are Tears Purposeless?" *British Journal of General Practice* 70, no. 693 (2020): 179. https://doi.org/10.3399/bjgp20X709049.

St. Pierre, Mark, and Tilda Long Soldier. *Walking in the Sacred Manner: Healers, Dreamers, and Pipe Carriers—Medicine Women of the Plains Indians.* Simon and Schuster, 1995.

Styx, Lo. "Prolonged Grief Disorder: Understanding the Latest DSM-5 Updates." VeryWell. Updated April 7, 2022. https://www.verywellmind.com/breaking-down-the-latest-dsm-5-update-5223956.

Tasca, Cecilia, Mariangela Rapetti, Mauro Giovanni Carta, and Bianca Fadda. "Women and Hysteria in the History of Mental Health." *Clinical Practices and Epidemiology of Mental Health* 8 (2012): 110–119. https://doi.org/10.2174/1745017901208010110.

Tenzer, Laurie. "The Mysteries of Sankalpa Explained, Again." March 5, 2023. https://www.laurietenzeryoga.com/blog/the-mysteries-of-sankalpa-explained-again.

Teresa of Ávila. *The Way of Perfection*. Whitaker House, 2017.

Tevington, Patricia, and Manolo Corichi. "Many Americans Report Interacting with Dead Relatives in Dreams or Other Ways." Pew Research Center. August 23, 2023. https://www.pewresearch.org/short-reads/2023/08/23/many-americans-report-interacting-with-dead-relatives-in-dreams-or-other-ways/.

Treatise on Ascetic and Mystic Theology: For the Use of Young Seminarians and Young Priests. St. Austin's College, 1913.

Tone, Andrea. *The Age of Anxiety: A History of America's Turbulent Affair with Tranquilizers*. Basic Books, 2009.

Tone, Andrea, and Mary Koziol. "(F)ailing Women in Psychiatry: Lessons from a Painful Past." *Canadian Medical Association Journal* 190, no. 20 (2018). https://doi.org/10.1503/cmaj.171277.

Westberg, Granger E. *Good Grief: A Companion for Every Loss.* Fortress Press, 1968.

"Women Carried the Burden of Unpaid Caregiving in 2020." National Partnership for Women & Families. May 2021. https://nationalpartnership.org/wp-content/uploads/2023/02/women-carried-the-burden-of-unpaid-caregiving-in-2020.pdf.

Notes

Notes

Notes

About the Author

Dr. Janet Lynn Roseman is an associate professor in integrative medicine at Dr. Kiran C. Patel College of Osteopathic Medicine, Fort Lauderdale, Florida. She was awarded the David B. Larson Fellowship in Health and Spirituality at the John W. Kluge Center at the Library of Congress and received the first Joseph Moore Presidents Award from Lesley University for her work with oncology patients. She teaches courses in spirituality and medicine, death and dying, and art and medicine and created the Sidney Project in Spirituality and Medicine and Compassionate Care™ to help elevate the practice of medicine for physician residency programs. She offers intuitive healing sessions using color and light therapy and also works with clients as a grief coach. Her program, Sidora Grief Empowerment™, trains health care professionals to learn skills for working with their patients and clients. She lives with her husband and magical cat in Santa Fe, New Mexico. She can be reached at https://drjanetlynnroseman.godaddysites.com/about-us.

To Write to the Author

If you wish to contact the author or would like more information about this book, please write to the author in care of Llewellyn Worldwide Ltd. and we will forward your request. Both the author and the publisher appreciate hearing from you and learning of your enjoyment of this book and how it has helped you. Llewellyn Worldwide Ltd. cannot guarantee that every letter written to the author can be answered, but all will be forwarded. Please write to:

Janet Lynn Roseman, PhD
℅ Llewellyn Worldwide
2143 Wooddale Drive
Woodbury, MN 55125-2989

Please enclose a self-addressed stamped envelope for reply, or $1.00 to cover costs. If outside the U.S.A., enclose an international postal reply coupon.

Many of Llewellyn's authors have websites with additional information and resources. For more information, please visit our website at https://www.llewellyn.com.